THE
GREAT ANGLERS

THE
GREAT ANGLERS

John Bailey

To Armstrong, to Buller, to Clifford . . .
to the whole alphabet of caring anglers

DAVID & CHARLES
NEWTON ABBOT   LONDON

DAVID & CHARLES' FISHING TITLES

The Angling Times Book of Coarse Fishing   Allan Haines and Mac Campbell
Big Fish from Famous Waters   Compiled by Chris Turnbull
Catching Big Tench   Len Arbery
The Complete Book of Float Fishing   Allan Haines
The Countrysportsman's Record Book & Journal   John Humphreys
The Great Salmon Beats   Crawford Little
Ken Whitehead's Pike Fishing   Ken Whitehead
Success with Salmon   Crawford Little
Success with Trout   John Dawson, Martin Cairncross and Chris Ogborne

---

PAGE 2:
Bazley – probably the greatest all-round angler of all time . . .
certainly the Walker of the day

British Library Cataloguing in Publication Data
Bailey, John
    The great anglers.
    1.   Great Britain.   Freshwater angling
    I.   Title
799.110941

ISBN 0-7153-9435-5

Typeset in Garamond Simoncini by ABM Typographics
Unit D, Gothenburg Way, Sutton Fields Industrial Estate, Hull
and printed in Great Britain
by Redwood Press Ltd, Melksham
for David & Charles Publishers plc
Brunel House   Newton Abbot   Devon

CONTENTS

'Escaping to the Stone Age by the morning train from Manchester, the fisherman engages in an activity that allows him to shed the centuries as a dog shakes off water and to recapture not his own youth merely but the youth of the world.' Arthur Ransome

INTRODUCTION

*T*he opportunity to compile a book on the great freshwater anglers of this country both fascinates and awes me. At the same time, I know a history of this leading sport has long been called for and yet I realise just what a task faces me. For the past century, hardly a man has lived who has not fished once in his life. Nearly all have rods in their attics or garages or garden sheds, still used or from their past. Most have wandered in a stream with a net or have stood in a beach pool turning rocks. How many men can pass a river bridge without pausing a while and what heart has not beaten fast at some time with the bob of a float or the flash of a roach or the dimple of a feeding trout? Millions from each and every decade have fished regularly. Thousands have been successful and all of them, therefore, have made some claim to fame. The possibility, the probability, no, the certainty of omission hangs ever over me. Some anglers, either alive or in the grave, are bound to be overlooked and therefore slighted. To many others due credit will not be given. I realise I run the risk of being pursued along the river banks of this world and perhaps of the next also.

Realising the likely pitfalls into which this work could lead me, I have had to weigh my qualifications carefully, always considering that perhaps there are others better fitted for this important, in its own way hallowed, task. Well, firstly I am approaching middle age now and perhaps have just reached a time where I can view events and achievements with some sense of proportion. Twenty, perhaps even ten years ago, I was given over to the usual hero-worships that would have coloured my judgements unfairly. Secondly, I am a history graduate and between 1975 and 1989 I taught modern world history to principally 'A' level candidates. I am not saying for a moment that academic qualifications are essential for this work but perhaps the ability to research the past and an appreciation of evolution are all useful attributes.

More importantly, I have been an angler close on thirty-five years; not a casual angler, but for nearly all this time quite fanatical. I believe it is true to say that fishing has very much guided my life. I have travelled all the United Kingdom and a great many parts of the world and been fortunate to catch good fish; to have access to lovely waters; to meet interesting, talented and even great anglers and, above all, relish every single minute behind a rod or on a bankside.

The fourth qualification that I hope is valid is the fact that from the age of four when I could first read, all I have ever wanted to pick up are angling books. God knows how many volumes, magazines and papers I have read on freshwater fishing in my life but they have probably stopped me reading the novels that I wanted to read and doing the research I should have done as a professional historian. Not, of course, that I regret a word.

Every one of these qualifications has been heavily taxed in completing this book. A year of my life has been dominated by the work. I have haunted libraries. I have read books until my eyes have ached. I have corresponded with literally hundreds of anglers. Telephone bills have rocketed. And I have worried constantly that somebody has been underrated, overrated or omitted. All in all, the task just could not have been completed on my own and the help I have received has been enormous. Facts, stories, viewpoints and above all moral support has poured in and I have never before realised just how apt is the phrase 'brothers of the angle'. Several meetings have lodged in my mind and will be there for ever.

One Sunday, in a heatwave, I met Fred Buller in his home which seemed that day a temple of shade and knowledge. As a young man and as a reader of his classic book *Pike* there could not have been a truer disciple of his. And every minute of that day confirmed the justification of that early hero-worship. It is remarkable to be with a man who is so steeped in a life of thoughtful freshwater fishing. I felt he was rather like a lovely warm book. I felt able to delve inside him, to turn his pages, and to read everything of importance that there can be.

Few men approach the sublimity of Hugh Falkus. As he talks of angling it moves into a sphere where it is hardly a sport. In the hands of Falkus fishing becomes a key to the past, to childhood, to the war, to a tussle between life and death itself. In his memoirs, *The Stolen Years*, Falkus describes how his intense concentration on the rising trout in a foreign land, then in the hands of the SS in 1940 probably saved his life. This is a significant story. Somehow fishing has become life or a way of living at the least. By some magic Hugh Falkus has turned angling into the very stream and spirit of life itself.

These men and others like them are every angler's undisputed 'greats' and I thank the book for leading me to their gates. But how, out of the remaining millions, does a historiographer decide who merits inclusion in a book such as this one? Clear, undisputed yardsticks are almost non-existent. A greatness in any context is a subjective matter and all the conversations and correspondence of a year have not pointed to an absolute definition that will please everybody.

Perhaps this is the place to explain my part-dismissal of the earlier writers – Berners, Walton, Cotton, Venables, Barker and the rest. Their work is more appropriate to academic study than a part of active angling interest. Of course these anglers were an important rung in the sport's formative process but their modern impact is indirect and few modern fishermen would go to even Walton for actual instruction.

Yet, those who ignore Walton completely miss a great deal: *The Compleat Angler* has the securest place in English angling literature. His mix of story and information is a powerful one and has been copied – generally unsuccessfully – ever since. His picture of 'olde' England is as pleasing as B.B.'s, and probably more genuine. The songs of the milkmaids, the aroma of meadows, old inns and lavender sheets contain an optimism that a century of war and disease could not dampen. Hardly surprisingly for a man who knew men like George Herbert and John Donne, the book contains a constant moral message. There is a correct way of behaving and to Walton being an angler meant a great deal more than being a simple sportsman.

The Compleat Angler's interest in natural history is a fascinating combination of accuracy and sorcery. Carp blinded by frogs, and eels emerging from God-knows-

'I have only lived since I have enjoyed your company and discourse and turned angler, not before.' Venator – *The Compleat Angler*

where, find their place alongside the most sensible description of fish-pond management and even primitive salmon tagging. And, at the crux, from what Walton writes on fishing, it is obvious that he would not take long to adjust to the angling of the modern day. His methods of dapping for chub, night fishing, dead-baiting for pike, flavouring pastes and pre-baiting for carp and Cotton's additions on fly fishing are hardly three centuries out of date. Walton and his friends would look curious figures on the bank today but I can think of waters where they would continue to catch good fish in numbers. I do apologise to the long-dead masters: in spirit at least I like to think that they would smile on the following pages.

'Fishing is a real test of character. Your spirits are either on top of a mountain or in the depths of a pit. There are many sufferings . . . the fly in the small of your back, the disintegrated lunch, bulls, wasps' nests, moorhens at the wrong moment, cockchafers in your eye, the cast which doubles back, the matches which you have left at home and, worst of all, water in your wader.'
Plunket Greene

CHAPTER 1
THE ESSENCE OF GREATNESS

*Y*our pathway, however, will be one of thorns; and you will have surmounted your first obstacle if you will refuse to be deterred by fearful and terrifying reports concerning one Mr Smith. There is a Mr Smith in every little town – though sometimes his name is Jones or Brown or even Robinson. He, folks say, is the best fisherman for miles around; and even he can't catch much these days. So if Mr Smith can't get 'em (and he's been on the river since he was a boy) how can you hope to make a decent bag now and again? It's not really worth your trying . . .

You must not be discouraged. Learn to fish a bit better than Mr Smith: a proposition which is not quite so difficult as it sounds.

John C. Moore *Fine Angling for Coarse Fish*

PHOTO:
'Angling is a lifetime study. I remember my father and these words years ago and I often repeat them today.' Captain L. A. Parker – *This Fishing*

*I*n my life as a historian I have been forced over the years to look at what makes good statesmen. Now as an angler I am searching for the essence of a great fisherman. In neither case is discovery easy. Within academic history itself there has been much debate about great men in general; some would have it that certain men are born to do great things, they fashion history and change the way men think, act and live. These men are exceptional. Other authorities claim that great men are rather made so by the circumstances of their period and they simply give shape to developments within society. To give a concrete example, did Bismarck, the architect of German unification, seize the Germanic states and mould them through his own force or were there irresistible social and economic events forcing them towards confederation? (I chose Bismarck carefully. Was he an angler? Certainly he constantly talked about floating on the stream of time and about being the pike in the German fishpond!)

In this way, do we see Charles St John as a man who thrust game angling forward in the Highlands or do we regard him as a personification of a period when transport was easier, more of the upper and middle classes had leisure, tackle was improving and ideas were circulating? So to Walker – the foremost coarse and game angler of this century. Did he take coarse angling, a relatively static sport before World War II, and revolutionise it personally into the vibrant affair it is today? Or, was he fortunate in coming to his prime when tackle was being revolutionised, when nylon lines were being invented, when anglers had transport, time, money and ambition, and when general public secondary education was making all social classes aware of the opportunities open to them?

Perhaps it is fairest to talk of these anglers as great and as opportunist both. Charles St John, for example, capitalised on new transport and the Victorian zeal for sport and adventure but it was his own flair that was to make Scotland immortal. Walker was aware of what nylon, fixed spool reels and rod designs could do and went on to use the vehicle of the brand-new *Angling Times* to spread the word. Walker is the greatest of our fishermen because he had the genius to exploit new technology, a rapidly expanding media and a beneficial social and economic climate. And of course, because he was a brilliant fisherman to boot.

Opportunity without necessarily brilliance often gives the patina of greatness without the actual substance beneath. There are many anglers who have been seen as great because they have exploited a marvellous opportunity when it presented itself to them. Success in angling does depend on good waters, a satisfactory technique and the availability of time. Fish, good ones, even historic ones, will very often follow, but do these make the captors great in a true or an immortal sense? To be at the right place at the right time is to be fortunate, not necessarily skilful or expert. Dedication to the task does not always imply great ability. Many waters go through bonanza periods and a man whose life coincides with one of these periods sometimes cannot help but be successful. A specialist angler, despite a big list of fish to his credit, can sometimes be quite an ordinary or, sad to say, judging by some examples, even a poor fisherman.

Equally in the game world, past and present, this is true. Here money has bought big fish and large reputations. Good rivers, good beats, good gillies and the best times of the year very often make for success – but only in a limited sense – and seldom for greatness. Men who have found themselves favoured by circumstance and capitalised on it to a greater or lesser degree have gone into print and still been at best only adequate anglers. Those who have done well with one species, on one water, with one method, have then gone on to fail lamentably in other fields of the sport. And some anglers have even lied to make themselves seem great. All in all, to sort the fresh run from the stale and the kelt has been one of the hardest tasks my fishing and academic experience has ever encountered.

There are other problems. Does great angling end with the simple, physical act of putting fish on the bank? I cannot believe so. Anglers are not otters, not seine nets, not fish-catching machines alone. This would be to deny the richness of the sport that has become in part an art form. Surely those who draw angling scenes beautifully have contributed enough to be called great. Those who write inspirationally have surely given great joys to those who read and follow them. Those elegant rods and perfect reels that make fishing so lovely for us all have to be designed, and surely the genius of the tacklemakers deserves acknowledgement. And without the river keepers' and conservationists' foresight would we even have the waters to fish in today? Surely their work brings the greatest dividends of all. All these men, even if not anglers in the strictly limited sense of the word, belong integrally to the world of angling and have benefitted it beyond measure and therefore deserve inclusion. In the end, I have had to lay down yardsticks with which some might disagree. A great angler is a man who has made a great contribution to the sport. His achievement, his successes and his lessons must be lasting and important.

I have already stated my good fortune to have met good anglers both in the preparation of this book and in my fishing life and travels. All truly great anglers, it seems to me, are in essence good people. I do not know why but those who have met Richard Walker, Arthur Oglesby, Hugh Falkus, and Rod Hutchinson, for example, will agree with me. These men have no secrets because their greatness is above gimmicks. They harbour no jealousy because they are utterly secure in what they do. Their openness has made it possible to study them at close quarters – not through a microscope, in a removed fashion, but intimately, absorbing oneself into their angling and their thinking. Anglers that I call great do have things in common.

Firstly, great anglers have a oneness with the waters before them. They possess an ability to read and interpret, with unnerving correctness, even waters strange to them. In part this comes out of experience, but there is more to it. They love water; it is their friend, their companion and its secrets are less and less hidden from them until they become almost totally unveiled. A great angler can almost feel like a curling river or a sinister sleeping lake. Water captivates him. He loves its moods and learns to recognise its ever-changing face. He even smells and hears water with a sensitivity lesser anglers lack.

Great anglers share special access to the ways of fish. They have an understanding of how fish behave and why that again defies all logic. Profound experience is a key, of course; as a memorybank grows so the habits of fish seem more comprehensible and fit into patterns previously witnessed. Great anglers have a considerable ability to interpret a fish's behaviour. What they see registers to a degree unknown in the average angler. All aspects of a fish's life and feeding fit together to become the most sophisticated of jigsaw puzzles and only the great angler seems to have all the pieces. Or most of the pieces. Fish will never be predictable to the same extent as a machine.

Experience. Acuteness of understanding. Oneness with waters. All these are tangible skills that lesser anglers can at least recognise and aspire to learn. What is more difficult to believe in, is that in some of the greatest anglers these abilities merge or are even superseded by a gift that can only be described as a sixth sense. There are anglers who again and again in their careers catch sensational fish without quite knowing why. Something in them urges and prompts: go to the shallows; fish hard all the coming night; skip a meal and get quickly to the rods for the time is right! There is no real explaining this. Richard Walker bravely tried to rationalise this sixth sense way back in the 1960s. He described it as the now dormant hunting instinct of our earliest ancestors, when successful capture meant life itself. As a logical explanation, this is as good as any but I feel it falls short in some way today. The one thing to be sure of is that the sixth sense is real. Colin Dyson is the editor of *Coarse Angler* magazine. He is a good, hard-bitten northern angler. His word is one that is respected throughout angling circles and certainly he believes in this sixth sense. Let me quote from a letter that I received recently from him.

My one and only 30 pound pike came out of the blue, in exceptional circumstances, and it means more to me than would a 40 pounder from any unbelievable Welsh water. I have never written the whole truth about that fish but I do not mind telling you now.

I always consider that the Queen caught it for me. She was visiting Sheffield that day and I knew if I left at my normal time I would be stuck in the traffic jams that she had generated so I stayed on at the water, and when the time came that I knew the roads would be clear I still stayed on and the friend who was with me packed up and went, laughing at my reason for staying. 'Something is going to happen,' I said. With every passing minute the conviction increased. It started to go dark and we had fished into the dark quite often at that pit without ever getting a run.

It was a weird feeling. It got so strong I even 'knew' which rod would go and I reeled in the other two. The pit foreman stopped for his usual chat. 'You're here late this time,' he said. 'I thought I would come and see if you were bogged down again because if you are the tractor will be locked up in a while.' I told him I was staying because I was going to catch a big fish. He laughed as well and walked off and as he went I heard this rustling sound. The Optonic bite indicator wasn't sounding but the line was flying out at an unbelievable speed. By the look of the spool it had been running out for a good few seconds too. I lifted the rod high, trying to see the line against the sky and saw a strand of weed flying to the left. That was bad news. There was a huge and dense weed bed to the left.

I just closed the bail arm of the reel, clamped a hand over the spool and marched right, as fast as I dared. I looked over my shoulder as I went. There was a great swirl in the dark patch I knew was the weed. I just kept walking, feeling ever-growing resistance, until it eventually went slacker. The fish had come clear and was now wallowing around the shallows. It was all over in a minute or two, but even after netting the fish I had not a clue whether it was a low double or a 20 pounder. I dumped the net, fish and a fair bit of weed in front of the car and switched the headlights on. I parted the weed and found the middle of a very big pike, and then went looking for the head and the tail! I didn't have to weigh it to know it was a 30 pounder. It seemed the twin to my everlasting mental image of Frank Wright's 32 pound 12 ounce fish from Horsey Mere, twenty years earlier. It turned out to be exactly 2 pounds lighter than that but still a big 30 pound fish. I did not care. 'Thank you, Your Majesty,' I found myself saying. I now call that pike 'Her Majesty' though she has never granted me, or anyone else, another audience! She may be dead, now, though not because of me. The hook holds had been so light the barbs fell out into the net.

Had the circumstances permitted me to play the fish more normally I would have lost it but I think I was meant to catch that pike. I can't explain that feeling though. It went way beyond mere optimism, and while I sometimes know I will catch I have never before felt that certain.

Perhaps it is time to move on from the sublime and allow there are purely physical gifts that the great angler will probably enjoy. Good eyesight is the absolute necessity of the float angler. Matchmen, for example, drop from the top flight when their vision begins to fade. The lack of a level head has lost so many big fish in the past. The great angler, though tense, keeps thinking rationally throughout the hooking, playing and

Colin Dyson (right): just about the most respected voice in angling today. A fund of knowledge and sense

landing of a giant. Problems, disasters even, do not devastate him, he will cope and if a fish breaks free it will not be through human error. Even should this happen there is an acceptance, a realisation that disappointment is all in the game.

It has been said, rightly, that a great fisher will have a good pair of hands. Watch him cast so delicately and control the reel, the float, the fly, or whatever with the deft touch of a maestro. Everything is so elegant, and so simple and so deceptive. And when the salmon, the carp, the pike or the barbel runs, see how he anticipates its moves and works a rod with the guile or the force necessary to subdue it. Tackle has become merely an extension to the man or the woman's bone structure. Control is effortless, effective and unconsciously beautiful.

I have witnessed, even been a part of, some giant battles with fish but there is one that stands out as quite magnificent in my mind. 1989, September, and I was fishing and filming on the Ganges with Paul Boote and director Peter Nicholson. Peter was only a novice fisherman and when he hooked a big mahseer, the great Asian barbel, he obviously had little idea what to do with a fish travelling hard downriver with all the force of a mighty current against its flared pectorals. His reel screeched out well over a hundred and fifty yards of line. He had to follow, stumbling over the boulders, in a desperate pursuit. A quarter of a mile below the taking point, the Ganges makes a left turn and is hidden from sight by a massive rock outcrop. Very, very close to that headland rolled Peter's fish, still taking line. The fish was now two hundred yards from the angler and just a few lunges from freedom when Paul Boote took the rod from Peter.

He clamped the clutch down tight and skipped with incredible speed backwards up the bank a good twelve yards. And then, winding frantically, he ran back towards the fish, stopped, and repeated the manoeuvre ten heart-jerking times. The rod had bent double. The line had strained almost beyond endurance but everything had held. The great gamble had paid off and now the fish, as stupefied as we were, wallowed a hundred yards away. Peter took back the rod and landed his first utterly exhausted mahseer of thirty-three glorious golden-scaled pounds. What we had witnessed was a masterful bit of fishing.

No angler becomes great without loving what he does. Barren times are to be expected and we have to come to terms with them. Nothing worthwhile is achieved without effort. A great angler laughs at the harshest weather; frost, snow, gale and wind are as much a part of water life as the lazy days of the mayfly or the tench pool in June. A great angler is dedicated to a point that bewilders an average man. The time, the effort, the cost, the hardship are nothing to him. True pleasure is a serious business and through it all he sees enchantment and excitement and knows he would be nowhere else. Very often the great anglers have an ability to communicate this passion. Speaking, writing or drawing, the knowledge is so profound, so absolute that it cannot be kept down. It simply overflows and the words and the images flood gloriously through the hall, across the pages or onto the canvas.

OPPOSITE
The late T. K. Wilson playing a grayling on the river Aire near Skipton, Yorkshire (Arthur Oglesby)

Jack Martin – as successful on the bank as in the casting ring – fishes for trout (Arthur Oglesby)

'*Carp*' *by Robin Armstrong* (Robin Armstrong)

Greatness rarely exists in the man who does not have a powerful mind. A great fisherman must have the ability to recognise problems and then possess the logic and the inventiveness to solve them. Sometimes the problem exists in the fish or in the difficulties of the water. Or the problem can be technical. Once again, the example of Richard Walker comes to mind. When, in the 1950s, the existence of big perch was discovered at Arlesey Lake, the difficulty remained of how to cast a bait the seventy or so yards to the deep holes where they lay. All the existing leads tangled the hook length in flight and then offered resistance to a fish taking line. Therefore, Walker designed the Arlesey bomb with an aerodynamic shape which did not foul the line during the cast. A swivel incorporated in the lead also allowed free passage of line to a running perch. Walker took phenomenal catches using the bomb, explained his invention in exact detail through pages of the *Angling Times* and the lead became the standard one for most coarse fishers.

I expect that in this success-orientated world the natural reaction of many is to look for the greatest anglers in the greatest achievers. Perhaps the captors of great fish, the winners of hard fought matches, those who write, paint or make tackle with a dash of genius are those who will cast shadows far into posterity. But I can look back to two men I used to fish with – neither of whom are remotely known – who I still regard as great in their simple ability to enjoy their fishing. Billy and Joe were only average men with a rod, but they could turn their sessions into romps so glorious that there was a greatness about them. Winter nights spent codding on east coast beaches, rods against the stars, tilly lamps against the darkness and a fire to beat the cold. Cans of coffee heated up and drunk in the early hours. Big fish fighting out in the tide and pulled in on the breakers. Wet legs for the gillie, the fire and frost-roasted face of the bubbling captor. 'It's a 10 pounder for sure! We'll cut it into 3 halves when the light comes!'

Carp fishing the hidden mere in June. Camping out on the island. The smell of logs and cooking morning and night. Lazy days in the sun. Short mild nights talking of life and love, laughing while the carp cloop around and occasionally playing a monster. Golden sunrises and afternoons sleeping in the shade whilst the dragonflies hover by the rods.

Winter and dawns of frost, cat-ice in the dead sedge and the pike floats slowly emerging from the mist. Our enjoyment was always total whatever the place, whatever the weather, and everything I, Billy and Joe did and thought and said would be recognised by any brother angler. Great friends, great days and great memories. Anglers do not need records of constant success to be great in their own way. A greatness of sorts lies in us all.

Billy and Joe are examples of what I call the missing men. This is the final problem. Many of the great anglers I cannot possibly know about. They have fished and died with no recorded legacy. Only family and friends have known about them. That is how many have wanted it to be. Their fishing has been very personal and they have had no desire to flaunt their successes and no desire for fame. There are many excellent anglers who are unknown today and were unknown in the past.

OPPOSITE
Chris Turnbull, angler and artist, with a 'lovely' catfish. (Inset) *The carp and the crust: a detail of Chris Turnbull's work*

'Far From The Madding Crowds' Ignoble Strife.' Two successful anglers relax over a pipe and a beer

Take this final example. It happened to me only last week so it is very fresh in my mind. It was evening on a very difficult, very clear tench lake. A couple of my friends sat on the dam with me, fishing hard, talking a little, watching the night close in. To our right, fifty yards along, a solitary fisher sat concealed in rushes on a low chair. We could just make out the tip of his neatly shotted float and but for the occasional sound of a scattering of bait we would hardly have guessed him to be there. He had cast only the once. He moved only to throw out bait. He was as near a heron as a man can be.

For our part, we did no good that night and when the light had all but gone we began to pack our gear away. Then the sound of a reel caught our attention. The stranger on the dam was into a fish. He played it expertly, keeping himself low and rod well up. He knew just the amount of pressure to exert and soon the fish rolled beaten into his net. Never once had he left his stool but had played out the battle in a most composed fashion. The fish was a tench – it was a beauty and it weighed nearly 7lb. We would have been overjoyed to have caught such a fish ourselves. Our caps would have been up in the air and over the fields but this man simply released the fish, smiled slightly with deep satisfaction and left with hardly a word. I do not know his name but he is a great angler. I cannot think how many thousands there must have been like him, unknown and forgotten in this sport of ours.

CHAPTER 2
THE MASTERS AND THEIR SCHOOLS

*S*ir Henry Wotton was also a most dear lover and a frequent practiser of the art of angling; of which he would say 'it was an employment for his idle time, which was not then idly spent . . . a rest to his mind, a cheerer of his spirits, a diverter of sadness, a calmer of unquiet thoughts, a moderator of passions, a procurer of contentedness; and that it begat habits of peace and patience in those that professed and practised it'.

Izaak Walton, *The Compleat Angler*

PHOTO:
An ageing Dick Walker, at peace with his bench and his vice

*T*here are anglers who are too great to pigeonhole. There are men whose influence has spread far beyond individual species, methods or areas. It seems as though these men have been put on earth to develop and benefit angling in many different ways. Their successes can in no way be measured by normal standards. Anglingwise they become universal. Their influence spills into every area of the sport. They have immense experience of all fish, not merely of a single species. They often devise tackle. Invariably they are teachers and they inspire and incite controversy. Their names are linked with conservation and they work for the sport, their fellows, their fish, their waters and the whole image of angling.

Undoubtedly the central figure in angling this century is Richard Walker. In every possible way Walker represents a bridge between the great anglers of the past and the modern masters of the present day. He was born in 1918 and he died in 1985. He was educated at Cambridge and during the war he pioneered the role of radar. He began to write in the 1940s in the *Fishing Gazette* and the *Anglers News* under the pen name Water Rail. It was then that he began to demolish the old shibboleths of angling lore using his logic, his precision and his powers of observation. He brought to angling a whole new approach that could be criticised as scientific but is better seen as clear-sighted and innovative:

> *You are entering a field of angling which has very great possibilities which have remained unexplored for many, many years. Just consider these points – how many anglers fish for carp at the right time of day? (Early morning and night). In the right part of the lake? (The shallows, except in rough or cold weather). With the right tackle? (Correct rod and line, proper hook, no float or lead). With the right bait, of the right size, on the surface or bottom – never changing? With soft soled shoes and from behind cover?*
>
> *Is it any wonder then that carp have a reputation of uncatchability, and that there are great carp in many waters that can be caught by anyone who goes about the job in the right way?*

It was only fitting that in 1952 Dick Walker should catch the country's most famous fish. Her name was Clarissa. She was a common carp and she weighed 44lb. Her size in that era was extraordinary and her capture exploded all the old myths that carp were uncatchable and that a man's life was not long enough for their pursuit.

1953 was an important year for Walker and for angling. He joined the fledgling *Angling Times* and wrote continuously for it over the next three decades. His words reached literally millions during that time and the *Angling Times* was a perfect platform for his clear-sighted views to spread to the new millions of anglers after World War II. Also in 1953 he published *Still Water Angling*. It is impossible to overstate the importance of this book which has gone into many issues. Its originality is staggering. Indeed, in many areas Walker's words of nearly forty years ago have not been bettered. Throughout the fifties, sixties, seventies and well into the 1980s Walker dominated angling. He continued to write books. He wrote in all areas of the angling press and caught big fish of all species. He designed rods, leads, ground baits and all manner of

Walker the inventive genius with the Heron bite alarm he developed to alert a generation of carp fishers

methods and terminal rigs. He continued to be controversial and exciting. He inspired legions of disciples who like him wore floppy bush hats as they fished. In his later days he moved into stillwater fly fishing and began to revolutionise it in virtually the same way as he had demolished coarse fishing in the 1950s.

Such is the stature of Dick Walker that on the 4 June 1988 The Carp Society held a memorial conference for him at Dunstable. The conference was organised partly as a commemoration of fifty years of carp fishing but very much in honour of the memory of the late Richard Walker. A memoir was also published and distributed at the conference as a permanent record of the man and his works. Extracts from it must be included to illustrate just how central Walker's role in angling has been.

> *Time has canonised Izaak Walton; if history has a sense of justice, time will surely elevate Dick Walker above all others as the greatest man to emerge from the angling ranks – if it has not already done so.*

Tim Paisley is absolutely correct. Richard Walker is the most important of anglers. He is rightly a legend.

> *Walker spoke with almost unrivalled authority on coarse and trout fishing tackle and was a rod designer of acknowledged renown, especially in the field of carp and trout angling. A tireless tackle innovator, many of his prototypes are now commonplace items of all coarse anglers' terminal rigs. As a trout fly designer and tier with few equals, his patterns, especially those so detailed in their dressing by his own hand, have been the downfall of many specimen fish.*

Jack Thorndyke illustrates quite correctly that Walker was a tacklemaker of genius.

> Walker's Pitch *took me straight to the heart of Walker's world, a world of exciting, monster-haunted waters, where logic, common sense, innovation and imagination made angling dreams come true. I read* Still Water Angling *and its sequence of four classic fishing stories that inspired so many anglers to turn their attention to carp.* No need to Lie *is a collection of wonderful tales. And though it is in some ways just one long success story, Dick somehow managed to be consistently modest, making it perfectly plain that he was as human and fallible as the next man.* Drop Me a Line *(with Maurice Ingham) shows a genuine sense of excitement and though the letters were never meant for publication, they contain some truly superb vibrant writing. We shall always be able to benefit from his wonderful, thought-provoking books. We must be eternally grateful.*

Chris Yates is correct. Walker was the writer of a clutch of classic books that will live on for century upon century.

> *Perhaps his most valuable editorial asset was that beneath his kindliness he was always slightly abrasive. Controversy is no bad thing in a columnist. Part of the job of a regular writer of Dick Walker's genuinely innovative character is to stir things up. Walker certainly did that.*

Colin Wilcock illustrates just why Walker was the primary angling journalist of the twentieth century, contributing to all magazines, both game and coarse, and a weekly column for the *Angling Times* for thirty incredible years.

Walker set out to convince anglers that big fish could be caught by deliberately setting out to do so. In pre-specialist days, the capture of big fish was something that happened by chance and was maybe expected once or twice in an angler's lifetime. Dick taught us that luck played very little part in the matter.

Jim Gibbinson, himself a great angler, emphasises that Walker was the original big-fish specialist. 'He was the captor of a record carp, an unclaimed record trout, huge perch, chub, dace, roach, barbel and rudd, and indeed every other species that swims. He was the inspiration behind the specialist angling movement of today.'

Maurice Ingham, Dick Walker, Ken Taylor and I sat around the camp fire under the big ash tree. A big pot bubbled furiously on the edge of the embers and crayfish, freshly gathered from the Ouse, turned bright red in salt water as it boiled. We had literally hundreds of them, having caught all we needed for both bait and food during the afternoon. As the contents of the pot diminished, fresh stocks were added to the salt water and we talked our way into the darkness. It was not our normal procedure to fish through the night for chub, but tonight we were going to try. The crayfish feast was just a typical part of one of our weekends on the Upper Ouse. These were social gatherings spiced incidentally with odd catches of big chub, perch and roach. They were never really meant to be serious attempts to catch big fish. That we had our share was probably down to the fact that we were not in the business of trying hard to prove anything. We enjoyed what we did.

Towards midnight, we sat in line and talked of great carp fishing of the 1960s. We sipped from hot flasks, nibbled at sandwiches, and tried different baits to avoid the ever eager crayfish. I can remember few nights as dark as the one in question and, because I saw little hope of success, I dozed in the warm night air on the soft grassy bank.

I was awakened by Dick's quiet voice in my ear. 'You got any lobs left, Fred?' ''Course I have,' I said. 'Then chuck us a couple over,' said Dick. 'I'll try one free lined.' I reached into my roomy tackle bag and groped around for the bait box. I could not find it but I DID make contact with a fully grown hedgehog which Dick had introduced previously before zipping up the bag completely! I happen to have a very soft spot for hedgehogs but in the early hours of a very dark morning such an introduction is off putting to say the very least. If I am honest, I was scared witless!

Fred J. Taylor describes perfectly why Walker was a friend. His humour, his humanity, his generosity all led him to become the centre of a group of dedicated, progressive anglers. Taylor called them 'the jolly crew' and they assembled by reason of Walker's warmth, his brilliance and his forceful personality.

Reading this marvellous memoir makes me personally feel stupid. Between 1978 and 1982 Dick and I corresponded regularly, as he did with so many other fortunates, and the ending of each letter was the repeated offer of a bed, a meal and a talk whenever I might be in his district. Many times I hovered by the phone and yet never did I make the call, book the date and meet the greatest angling hero. Since 1985 I have regretted that failure constantly, sickly, with utter bewilderment. All the excuse I can ever offer is that

I had met other 'great figures' and been disillusioned and that I did not want the image of Dick to be in any way tarnished. How stupid, how pathetic this marvellous memoir shows that precious fear to have been. Through my cynicism or timidity, or laziness, I spurned the chance to meet one of the greatest anglers ever.

I have however heard Walker speak. Very often my old piking friend Bill Giles of Norwich talked of a 1960s trip that he, Reg Sandys, Pete Thomas, Fred Buller and Richard Walker had taken to Loch Lomond in Scotland. They had camped and met at dinner times for food, wine and talk in a central caravan. Night after night Bill had, he said, placed a recorder on the table and taped the evening's debate. One winter Bill and I piked together consistently and cold day after cold day I pressed Bill for the tapes. Then, on 25 December 1988, I received them, all wrapped up, as a Christmas gift.

I began to play the tapes in the car at dusk as I drove home. At first I found them hard to follow until I realised Dick's habit of talking in so many different dialects that it seemed a whole cluster of anglers was present. There are many exciting pieces. Dick always dominated and Fred Buller was a constant foil and the one most obviously holding his ground, countering argument with argument. The tapes showed just why Walker was the centre of such a strong intellectual group of anglers that included men like Taylor, Buller, Thomas, Ingham, Giles and Stone.

Generosity comes out of the tapes as he talks about helping people learn to trout cast. There is humour too as he explains how his old grandad always used to give taking pike ten minutes by his fob watch before striking. There is a great awareness of the need for conservation in angling and the promotion of new fisheries for the ever-growing number of anglers. He is also, constantly, controversial. On every issue he provokes debate and flares Buller into constant retaliation. Every view that Walker held was originally argued. It is no wonder that friend after friend of Walker's miss him. Walker has left a gap that it will be impossible for angling to fill.

Walker himself was also very appreciative of these people who surrounded him. If he were the master then his school was always a vibrant one. There is nobody in the sport of angling who has not heard the name of Buller. Equally Fred J. Taylor has gone on to make his name synonymous with angling journalism. Walker appreciated Taylor deeply and in 1965 in *Creel* magazine he wrote a lovely homily to the man. It shows more than ever the gifts of this most famous of Walker's pupils. It was entitled 'My Friend Fred'.

Like me, Fred was born in 1918 and we share the same roots, in the country of which Leighton Buzzard is the spiritual centre and Luton the despised industrial interloper. We share the same background of a little youthful poaching, ferreting, shooting and lots of fishing, friendly farmers, green grass, trees, hills no higher than Ivinghoe beacon and a kick in the rear when we transgressed, instead of juvenile courts and psychiatrists. We can spot a fake countryman a mile off and the world seems to be full of them.

It is this intimate identification of himself with the countryside and its wildlife that makes Fred such a fine angler; but unlike many countrymen, Fred never developed distrust of, or contempt for, science and logic. He always had that precious asset, an open mind. Not for Fred the usual country pundit scorn of 'book learnin'', and the often-repeated belief that 'you can learn more in an hour at the waterside than from all the books ever written!'

Walker's own Friar Tuck, still fishing and still happy (Kevin Clifford)

Fred took care to learn all he could from the waterside and from the books, until the time came for him to write books of his own – and how well he wrote them! One passage from Favourite Swims *sums up his angling philosophy very well. He tells how he and his brothers, Ken and Joe, had each caught 15 tench, every one over 4 pounds, and then he says, '. . . the rivalry had gone now and it would have been wrong to try and catch any more tench. This was the proper ending to our day, and we removed our baits from the water before the magic of it could be spoilt.'*

'Happier those that go out to please themselves, and not to astonish others,' wrote R. S. Surtees. Fred never sets out to beat anyone, either in fishing matches or in attempts to catch the biggest fish. Measured by conventional yardsticks, Fred's angling feats do not feature in angling history. He has never won a big match or caught a record or near record specimen; yet he has caught enormous numbers of fish that can fairly be classed as big. And he has thoroughly enjoyed every minute of it despite his classic comment on one icy day, when with sleet pelting down and not a fish feeding, he said, 'Oh, I shall be glad when I have had enough of this!'

It would be impossible to sum up what makes Fred so successful. He casts accurately, whether he is fishing float, fly, spinner or ledger. He has tremendous ability in watercraft and, despite his weight, he can be as light on his feet as a mousing cat when occasion demands it.

Of the many contributions Fred has made to the success of those who read his books and articles, perhaps the most important are the lift method and the use of the dead herring in pike fishing. Neither is original. References to the lift method, or shot ledger as it used to be called, can be found in angling literature half a century old, as can accounts of catching pike on dead herrings. What Fred did was to turn these forgotten methods into ones that could be and are being used with confidence and success by thousands. Fred has this knack of communication. Whenever I remark on the value of knowing water temperature, I am accused of being scientific, but Fred could write about Einstein's theory of relativity without incurring a similar charge.

What else do you want to know about Fred? Everyone knows what he looks like, and many have likened him to a jovial friar – Friar Tuck of the Robin Hood legend. In fact the resemblance goes beyond appearance. Fred has enormous physical strength and he understands and appreciates good food and drink, having spent part of his career as a chef. His girth is deceptive – he can move fast when it is necessary and he belongs to a judo club where he is flung about by attractive young ladies and by Fred Buller. He has a first-class singing voice which it is difficult to persuade him to use. Perhaps Fred's personality was best summed up by Pete Thomas when he said, 'I'd rather have a blank day with Fred than catch a hundredweight of fish in some people's company!'

Walker's teachings had a profound effect on a new and up-and-coming generation. Very many great anglers have grown out of the Walker mould. Men like Jim Gibbinson, Peter Stone and Kevin Clifford are all great anglers spawned from the Walker school of thought. In many ways, however, Bob Church should be seen as the truest disciple of Walker who was indeed his hero. Church for years proved himself to be the archetypal specialist angler but then in the 1960s he was able to change direction and move onto the reservoirs where he pioneered techniques and lures for rainbow trout. Moreover, like Walker, Church was always generous with his secrets and strings of books, magazine and newspaper articles have helped thousands of anglers towards their dreams. Finally, like Walker, Church has become involved in tackle; Walker's Mark IV rod gave the angling world its standard big-fish weapon. Along with Peter Drennan, Bob Church has designed and made the tackle that an increasingly sophisticated market has needed.

In his early years, Church was a member of the Northants Specimen Group. Then it was a legend, in part for the wildness of its stagnights. Invitations were issued nationwide and to receive one was the highest accolade. Guests were top names and included Walker himself, Billy Lane the match champion and Bill Keale the great specialist angler. Entertainments were wild. Once a fight broke out between Peter Mead and Bill Keale with fire extinguishers. On another occasion a circus showman nailed Fred Wagstaff to a wheel and threw daggers at him, only just missing his most vital private parts. More vital was the brilliance of the members of the Northants Specimen Group. To fish with the likes of Fred Wagstaffe, Ray Clay, Jim Gibbinson and Cyril Inwood must have been a remarkable experience, even more extraordinary when one considers the links that the Northants boys formed with the Herts Chiltern Group. Bob here had access to the minds of Jack Hilton, Bill Quinlan, Bob Buteux, Tony Williams and Peter Frost. These were all giants and Church today is quick to acknowledge the ricochets of glory that reflected in his direction from them.

Arguably, the most charismatic of all was Fred Wagstaffe, the dedicated eccentric who gave up work to fish and who electrified the *Angling Times* with his series 'Footloose' accompanied by Bob Reynolds. These adventures were read by thousands on whom they made an indelible impression. Big-fish hunting became linked with adventure, romance and travel. Wagstaff boated the whole length of the Thames, writing and fishing as he went. He raided Ireland and landed great brown trout and pike from Lough Mask. He explored Scotland where there are still legends of his escapades of a quarter of a century back. Wagstaffe was largely responsible for Church's introduction to the Broadland piking scene and the trip they had on Horsey with Ray Clay became sensational news. Clay himself was quite a man to share a boat with. In the earliest days of serious carp fishing, Clay decided to begin his career at the hardest water in the country, Billing Aquadrome. On his first session, all equipped with the new Sportex glass blanks, Clay took a 42lb common carp, a fish second only to Walker's record at that time.

With such friends, it is hardly surprising that Church's successes were ever-spiralling. Pike, eels, tench . . . whatever big fish swam, Church would be after them. However, in love with coarse fishing as he was, Church began to move under other influences. At the turn of the 1960s, Midland reservoir trout fishing was in its inception and Church was captivated. Once again he was fortunate in his associates and his teachers were Cyril Inwood, who was so excellent at fishing nymph in the upper layers of the water, and Dick Strive, who was mastering the use of the lure, deep fished on sinking lines. With them, Church was in at the near beginning, learning on the split-cane rods and silk lines of the day. Eyebrook first, Pitsford from 1963 and then in 1966, the golden year, Grafham Water opened. Stocked fish had grown from 10in to 3, 4 or even 5lb in only eighteen months. Church was there, steeped in coarse experience and now game fishing expertise at exactly the right moment. The eyes, literally, of the angling world were on Grafham and on him in sharp focus. He was young, inventive, able and charismatic and to those with vision, like Bob Feetham at *Angling Times*, personified a new, glamorous branch of game fishing. From 1966 trout fishing ceased to be strictly the preserve of the rich, and was flung open to the normal man. Bob Church, through his enormously successful columns in *Angling Times* and *Trout Fishing* magazine was there to guide him in his first faltering steps from canal to reservoir, from float to fly. Soon he appeared on television and working with Terry Thomas helped to make over twenty half-hour programmes in the 1970s.

In the UK, Bob was the first to use Chenil Maribou flies. He created Church Fry, the Appetiser, Goldie, the Spring Favourite and the June Fly. He was the first to use lead core lines as shooting heads to work flies really deep. He designed the square boat drogues that are easily pulled in, collapsible and a dream to transport. Equally important was Church's early involvement in trout match fishing. It became only natural for trouting clubs to evolve and matches to begin. The famous Benson and Hedges event has become Church's stamping ground and he has been a constant member of the English national fly fishing team. It could not have been easy to turn fly fishing, for so long the epitome of easy English county grace, into a competitive sport, but again Church's gift as a public relations man helped accomplish even this. Today

Bob Church applied his mind to reservoir trouting with phenomenal success

his company sponsors one of the great competitions of the calendar – the Bob Church Classic. The match is a symbol in some ways of Bob's success as his family based company goes from strength to strength with an annual turnover of millions. His first wife divorced him for his love of angling. Her last words to him were, and he remembers them well, 'Nothing of any good will come out of all this fishing. Forget it – that's my advice.'

Church's ability and bubbling enthusiasm are plain to see. His generosity is just as real. One April we were part of a salmon party on the Dee. In atrocious conditions a rather portly, rather tipsy man grabbed Bob's rod to 'give it a try'. The spigots weren't taped ready for this. The timing of the cast was appalling. The wind hit all wrong and 18ft of carbon collapsed into a million matchsticks. Bob struggled with words. 'Don't worry about it,' he called down, fighting back the tears. 'It could have happened to me just as easily.' And that was all that was said about the whole affair for the rest of the week.

We do right to canonise Richard Walker but it is essential to understand that he did not appear from an angling vacuum. Great men before him had been at work and had in good measure prepared the ground for the mid-twentieth-century lift-off in angling tackle and tactics. Walker himself appreciated this. He constantly acknowledged his debt to the past and difficult as it is to imagine a god like Walker having heroes, Walker obviously idolised Hugh Tempest Sheringham. He never tired of quoting him, most obviously over carp fishing. He had a favourite paragraph of Sheringham's which appeared to caption a photograph in *Still Water Angling* and read

'Having laid out your rods you are at liberty to smoke, meditate, read and even, I think, to sleep if all goes well. Nothing will happen to disturb you. You and the rods and the floats gradually grow into the landscape and become part of it. It is like life in the eye of the lotus.'

Hugh Tempest Sheringham was the Walker of his age. Born in 1876, he died in 1930 and like Walker was one of the few anglers ever to have an obituary in *The Times*. He was angling editor of *The Field* magazine from 1903 and he edited the *Where to Fish* guide in 1921–8. He sat on the Fresh Water Committee in 1917–19 and wrote *An Open Creel* in 1910. More essentially, in 1912 he published *Coarse Fishing*, a book that had a real impact on his age, a great effect on Walker himself, and should be read even today.

A great deal of Walker's philosophy was contained in *Coarse Fishing*. We see Walker's love of all fish reflected in the preamble: 'Salmon fishing is good; trout fishing is good; but to the complete angler neither is intrinsically better than the pursuit of roach, or tench, or perch, or pike.' Like Walker, Sheringham loved fish, felt himself to be a hunter and part of the natural order of things. And like Walker he could argue with passion, humour and logic.

Yes, you are right; I do feel affection for that little fish, and, indeed, for all little fish. They are cheery companionable creatures and I cannot explain the instinct which makes me want to catch them. It certainly seems illogical and the humanitarians can make out a case which is specious on the face of it. But when you think seriously, you see they are only playing on the surface of things. Sport is an intrinsic part of the world scheme. The spider quite obviously takes an interest in the pursuit of a fly; the dog finds most of his life's pleasure in hunting rabbits and even the rabbit feels a thrill at the sight of a defenceless lettuce. It is no good telling me that a lettuce does not feel. The principle of life is in a lettuce just as much as in you or me. And your humanitarian will eat lettuces without a pang, also nuts and apples and perhaps even eggs. On his own showing he is therefore a brute fellow.

As an angler Sheringham was, within his times, as good as Walker. He had the widest knowledge of British waters, all fish species and methods of angling. He was not as successful as Walker and that can probably be put down to three things. Firstly, he probably had to work harder. Walker was well off and the director of a successful family company. He certainly could take more time on the waterside than was ever possible for Sheringham. Secondly, probably, there were bigger fish to be caught in the 1950s and 1960s than Sheringham ever had access to. Remember that then most fish, coarse and game, were taken for the table and it needed a wily fish indeed to survive year in, year out, to the type of age to make him a real specimen. Thus, for Sheringham, a 15lb pike, a 5lb bream, a 3lb chub and a 1lb roach were genuine targets.

Thirdly, Sheringham did not enjoy the technology of Walker's world. His float rods were often 14ft, made of whole cane and greenheart and weighing 1lb 4oz. Lines were of silk, soaked in linseed and in lengths of 50yd. A monumental cast off a brass Nottingham reel with a 1.5oz weight might just reach 40yd. Travel was miserably difficult also. Trains were inflexible and limited gear could be taken. Frequently, Sheringham had to leave a boiling swim in order to pack up and catch the last train back to the city. Peter Thomas' car might have broken down on the way to Redmire in 1952 on that fateful trip to catch Clarissa, but it was mended in time to deposit Walker for the record carp's breakfast.

Comparisons, though, are odious. Both were forefront anglers and supreme teachers. Both showed humanity and when Radcliffe wrote of Sheringham that 'I have never heard him belittle or say ought ill of anyone' this generosity could have applied equally to both.

Sheringham, like Walker, was the centre of much angling ferment. His links extended to naturalists like Frank Buckland and to anglers, major figures of their time, like John Bickerdyke, Francis Francis and William Senior. Sheringham also knew, corresponded with and published the works of the masters of the River Trent school.

Like attracts like and great anglers have the habit of forming friendships with other fishermen of passion. So it was with a group of men from the mid-nineteenth century who continued an angling relationship well into the 1930s. Let us call them the Trent school – a loose term but a fair one, as most were Nottinghamshire based and the Trent was their natural home and learning ground.

My grandfather, Martin Hempel, was one of them. He fished avidly the last two decades of the nineteenth century before the Trent lost much of its life to pollution and heavy barge traffic. He died before I knew him but my grandmother, sensing she had an infant fisherman in her lap, used to tell me of the heydays of their courting and fishing together. How she made that river come alive for me! She would look out over the canal beside which we lived and dismiss it totally. The Trent was broad and fast-flowing whilst the canal was narrow, shallow and stagnant. The river's bed was all gravels and lush streamer weed compared with the silt and pond weed of the canal. On the Trent there were deep, splendid pools so far removed from the festering lock pound we could see if we stretched our necks.

I remember well how I learned my first French from her. Trent, she always said, comes from the French 'trente' – relating to the thirty streams that feed into it and the thirty species of fish that swam in it, at least in my grandfather's day. The canal held sticklebacks, gudgeon, and, it was rumoured, roach. Thirty species! I looked at her with a child's disbelief. We found my bible, *The Observer's Book of Fishes*. We went through the pages, counting as we went. Barbel, yes, grandad had those, and bream, silver bream, bleak, roach, rudd, chub, dace, tench, gudgeon, pike and perch. He caught minnows, sticklebacks, bullheads, stone loach, lampreys and ruffe for bait. He took eels on long lines and gave them as food to the poor Jewish population of Nottingham's depressed textile quarter. Professionals on the river caught the strange burbot and there were, she said, constant tales of carp seen, hooked and lost. At twenty-one species we both seemed stuck until she remembered a grayling grandfather had once taken and a trout, possibly even sea trout, for there had been occasional salmon caught in grandfather's young days. Of course, certain sea fish would have run the Trent as well; flounder obviously and mullet and smelt and once, quite definitely, the sturgeon of the Baltic seas.

On the left, the grandfather I never knew . . .

We still worried about that missing thirtieth species. Do bass wander so far and surely there is a sea lamprey? And shad must have run at times to spawn. We had made the thirty quite safely, and considering how delightful I found the canal, it was easy for me to dream of the Trent wonderland of grandfather's days.

The Trent obviously was inspirational. It was simply too large, too rich and too dynamic not to attract anglers and inspire brilliance. So, in 1857 William Bailey published *The Angler's Instructor*. The book has been criticised as dogmatic and pompous but Bailey obviously loved the river deeply and was a greatly successful chub and bream angler. Moreover, Bailey met, fished with and taught handsomely the greatest of them all – J. W. Martin, or as he is better known, the Trent Otter. Martin was a barbel man supreme, but in the way of a true pioneer, his ability could not be

'All the great tackle-dealers were good fishermen. I think of J. W. Martin, the Trent Otter, and of poor Walbran who drowned while grayling fishing.' Ransome

We may, of course, add Jim Bazley to the list and, today, John Wilson, Dave Plummer and Geoffrey Bucknall, amongst others

contained. Martin proved himself on all types of rivers and in 1905 he wrote, 'For nearly 50 years, I have been a fisherman in many of the rivers, lakes and broads of England and have had exceptional opportunities of studying the styles and methods adopted by the most noted local men on 25 different rivers.'

In this alone Martin was exceptional; though he was born poor, finished school at eleven, and worked on canals and farms as a labourer, he had the drive to explore and to write with huge natural talent. He eventually became a tackledealer in a shop in Seymour Street near Euston station. This became a central point in the capital for anglers as the twentieth century began and as transport and leisure time opened up new

OPPOSITE
Eric Horsfall Turner netting a nice trout from the Foston Trout Stream, Yorkshire (Arthur Oglesby)

possibilities. In every branch of coarse fishing Martin, in person or in his books, was there to guide them. Martin was a lovely man. He built a group of friends who remained steadfastly loyal to each other. His writings are full of stories of their Sunday fishing sessions, of nocturnal jaunts and of nailbiting poaching, hidden, fit to burst with laughter, under bushes and bridges. What is also clear is that a great deal of angling lore and knowledge was passed on to the members of Martin's circle.

Just as Martin learned from Bailey, so did Henry Coxon develop from Martin. Coxon was born in the mid-nineteenth century and died in 1927. He met Bailey and fished with Martin and those old Trent regulars such as Sunman and Charlie Hudson. Coxon is immortalised by his reel creation – the Aerial – that took over from the Nottingham centre pin which needed some force of thumb to begin its revolution. The Aerial, by contrast, is a wondrous tool. The breath of a butterfly will make one spin and continue spinning as if by magic. Even old Aerials never lose their sureness and provided they are treated well will fish on and on through a man's lifetime and his son's after him. Coxon dreamed a long time of such a weapon and worked with a whole series of prototypes. It was the development of two new materials in the 1890s, ebonite and aluminium, that provided the solution. He collaborated with toolmakers and tacklemakers and the Aerial was completed in time for him to enter the float casting competition at the Wimbledon tournament in 1896. The Aerial and Coxon won easily and the triumph was taken from the parade ground to the waterside where Aerials remain supreme as centre pins even to this day.

Coxon was true Nottingham. He was a laceworker and hence his interest in and knowledge of machinery. He was eventually scorer for Nottingham County Cricket Club. Here he met the cricketing great – W. G. Grace – and introduced him to barbelling in the Trent. Angling also owes *A Modern Treatise on Practical Coarse Fishing* to Coxon. Published in 1896 it aids and abets the books by Bailey and Martin and adds valuable passages on Trent salmon that ran the river then in the spring and the summer. Coxon's testimony stands to show just what the Midlands has lost even though the river is stronger today than for generations. Certainly, by World War I, the Trent was suffering badly. Coxon found it necessary to travel to find the fish he had been used to; in the 1920s he and his Nottingham partner F. W. K. Wallis began their now famous pilgrimages to the Hampshire Avon. From Bailey to Martin to Coxon and now to Wallis the line of master fishermen continues.

Sometime in the 1920s a hundred or so barbel were taken from the River Thames to Christchurch where they were released. Some eventually found their way into the Stour through the joint estuary at Christchurch. From Christchurch others moved upriver and found a habitat perfect for them. The Royalty fishery was made for barbel. Its clear water runs over immense gravel beds where weed grows, providing

OPPOSITE
Jim Gibbinson with a fine pike. Teacher, author, angler, thinker and traveller . . . true heir to Walker and his own hero, Bickerdyke (Jim Gibbinson)

Fred J. Taylor: one of angling's elder statesmen, still catching tench from his old stamping ground, Wootton Lakes (F. J. Taylor)

tremendous amounts of natural food. Here, on the Royalty fishery, these Thames barbel grew and multiplied. During the early years of fishing a very limited number of anglers were permitted on any one day and the whole length of the fishery was underexploited.

It was now during the 1930s that F. W. K. Wallis made his appearance and was the most successful fisherman of the day. He had learnt from Coxon and he could skilfully apply Trent talents to the very productive waters of the Royalty. His results were tremendous. For example, in September 1933 he landed ten double-figure fish which included monsters of 14lb 4oz and 13lb 8oz, two of 11lb 8oz, three of 11lb and three of 10lb. In 1937 he went on to land a barbel of 14lb 6oz which equalled the British record. In all, during those heady days of the thirties he landed eight barbel of over 13lb including scores of fish into double figures. All the Trent training had come of age in a barbel record that can never be bettered in this country.

By the 1950s, I had been inspired sufficiently by my grandmother to want to fish the Trent myself. I joined a local club that ran matches there and early on a Sunday morning in 1959 I was on a coach chugging southwards. At first sight, I saw why the Trent had inspired anglers; it was as wide, it seemed to me then, as the eye could see and drove along like a train. My canal tackle was swept aside and I resorted to fishing a pathetic slack under a bush. I also realised why Coxon and Wallis had been driven off the river. Detergent foam swept down the water in creamy icebergs inches deep; a barge passed me by and such was its wash I nearly drowned as I scrambled for dry land. Apart from gudgeon and a few roach, it seemed the Trent had passed away into history.

Twenty-five years on, however, I was again back on the river, this time under the wing of the present Trent master, Archie Braddock. That day I found the Nottingham school does live on and that the river itself has been reborn. After a tremendous day during which Archie taught me a little of his Trent techniques, the river came alive with fish. It was a long August sunset, the water was unruffled and all the way down I watched fish rising that would have gladdened Bailey's or Martin's or my grandfather's hearts. There were bream and chub everywhere, barbel rolling along with carp and into the roach and dace shoals rolled pike and perch. Now, this was the river of my grandmother's tales and even if the thirty species do not roam in the Trent yet, I could not believe that night that they would be long in restoring themselves.

Archie Braddock is from the same mould as Martin, a man who experiments, enquires and thinks things out in a positive fashion. On the Trent, he has baited massively with meat in the way Bailey did with worm and positively brainwashed the barbel into his food supply. He developed the use of sea fish as chub baits in the early 1970s. He designed his own large swim feeders from sections of vacuum cleaner pipes. He experimented widely in flavouring pastes, maggots and ground baits for all Trent coarse fish. Recently, he has perfected a style of upstream feeder fishing which will revolutionise river ledgering. And, again like Martin, Archie travels and takes with him the confidence of a Trent background. In January 1966 he caught a 20lb carp – a most unusual catch then – but on floating crust it was amazing. In the same period he devised the anchored crust rig. He has a true affinity with pike and has devised pop-up dead bait rigs and fishes flavoured baits now in the upper water layers.

This chapter on the masters comes back to Walker in the person of Hugh Falkus. His links with Walker were established through Fred Buller and the three of them in many ways represent the three intellectual giants of angling in the later twentieth century. The achievements of Falkus are immense. As an angler few today can match his record of salmon and sea trout. His casting skills are legendary and he teaches them probably better than any man alive. As a maker of natural history films, he enjoyed great fame for such work as *Shark Island*, *Self Portrait of a Happy Man*, *Salmo the Leaper* and *Highland Story*. For *Signals For Survival* he carried off the prestigious film award, the Prix D'Italia. He is a campaigner and a conservationist in the top rank and the EEC actually gave him money to lime his beloved Cumbria Esk against the worst effects of acid rain. As a countryside author, he is well within the standards set by Williamson and Ransome with *The Stolen Years* and *Nature Detective*. As an angling writer, both *Salmon* and especially *Sea Trout* have become classics and probably the best angling tale ever written is from his pen – *The Sea Trout*, which appeared in an anthology assembled by Maurice Wiggin in 1961.

It was in his role as teacher that I met Hugh Falkus for the first time. It was mid-summer and very warm when I found Falkus' valley. The Lake District I always thought of as a hectic, teeming place, but not here beneath mountains, clad in forest and under the clear blue sky. I walked a stretch of his river and though I found it much shrunken in

'Of all fish, the sea trout fights the best in proportion to its size. There is no fish with which one has to be so much on one's guard against being surprised, either by sudden rushes or by jumps in the air.' Dusk creeps up Falkus' sea trout river

that drought period I soon saw its potential. In a very deep pool, seven sea trout were lying. As far as I could see, three were good fish, three were big fish and one was enormous. And this was my first sight of his river! I passed his cottage; it was old, romantic and remote. It was clinging to the south face of the hillside and I carried on past it down the lane to a farmhouse where amidst duck flights I met him, teaching his pupils, Mr Mavin and Mr Stephen, to cast.

For half the afternoon, I watched them. Once I was a teacher myself and I can appreciate a good one when he stands before me. Falkus has all the skills. Firstly, he casts so brilliantly well all you want to do is to copy him. He was like Sergeant Troy from Thomas Hardy's *Far From the Madding Crowd* when he is practising his swordplay around Bathsheba Everdene. The 16ft rod was a blur when he cast, bending, cutting and dancing through the air. Forty yards of line were aerialised, arcing, floating and arrowing over the water. He stood there like Moses with his staff, commanding the water, framed in spray and sunlight. The poise, the grace, the timing and the carefully controlled power were the inspiration every teacher has ever sought to give.

Not that Falkus revelled in it for simple display. No. He taught Mavin and Stephen through his every move, demonstrating and explaining his grip on the rod, the position of his feet, the angles, the loops and the timings that were all necessary. He made complete and utter sense of that so frequently misunderstood physical action, the Spey cast. The pupils took up their rods and Falkus was at their side. At times he encouraged warmly and as their confidence swelled so their ability grew. At times he criticised sternly, but constructively. 'No, no Mr Mavin. The loop! Don't forget the loop.' Or, 'Mr Stephen, you will never Spey cast unless your shoulders are still. You're jumping like a marionnette.' And with that, he stood behind the caster, his huge hands planted firmly on the now immobilised shoulders. Hour upon hour Falkus maintained a controlled impatience that made both Mavin and Stephen sweat and try and never dare to do anything but their best for him.

They took a break and in the fishing shed we talked. Falkus told us all a story which showed that fishing and teaching have always been central to his life. In the lead-up to World War II he was teaching fighter pilots to prepare for the Battle of Britain. In the midst of all that he had arranged for a Saturday on a salmon river. 'Forget that,' his commander told him. 'Smith must be flying solo by the end of the day... No... Falkus he must! No arguments about it.' 'Smith,' Falkus said five minutes later, 'you'll take me up, do everything perfectly, quite perfectly you understand, and I'll be fishing by lunch.'

Smith was the most talented of pupils. Everything was perfect and they landed half a mile from the control tower. 'Rather than carry everything all that way, Smith, take me up again and drop me closer,' Falkus demanded. His mind began to work. What fly? Which pools? 'Smith!' he awoke with a jolt, 'Shut down a bit. Your air speed is too fast.' No reply. Smith had frozen at the controls and the fighter was nose-diving to the ground. Falkus took Smith's hands, wrenched them back and shallowed the angle of impact. And then they crashed. In their seats, Falkus and Smith tobogganed away from

OPPOSITE:
The Master in his Schoolroom – Falkus in full, glorious flow

the wreckage. Falkus felt himself over and stretched. He stood up and walked over to Smith who was intact but like a ghost. 'Smith,' he hollered. 'Smith, you bastard, you've just bloody ruined my afternoon's fishing!'

Nor does the art of teaching belong to Hugh alone in the Falkus family. *The Stolen Years* is a testimony to the power of his father over him. 'Father' is ever-present in all the stories in a wonderful teacher-pupil relationship. It was from him that Hugh learned to love marsh and creek, hill and stream, hunting and fishing. The lessons were taught unerringly and picked up with fervour. They had to be. In the last story Falkus rescues his father, who is cast adrift, by making use of his knowledge of currents and tides. Had not the father taught the son then the wild world would have taken him; his love and generosity were repaid in bounteous kind. Indeed, the breath of death is ever-present in the world and the fishing of Falkus.

Casting continued into the afternoon. 'Mr Mavin! What cast on God's earth is that?' Mr Mavin stopped thrashing the water and looked up hurt rather than aggrieved. 'Look here, sir, watch me again. See! See the angle of the rod, the loop. Don't forget that loop – the very essence of the roll cast.' Within minutes, Mr Mavin's loop was voluptuous and his lines were singing out. Falkus returned to our bench. He sees casting ability as a curve with the generality along its middle. A very few stand at the high point and are naturally brilliant. The sad one has to prop up the whole structure. 'He thought it was his rod, you see, although there wasn't the least thing wrong with it. I told him "Well sir, I'd practise with that rod a while longer if I were you and then, only then, if you do not get any better, trade it in. Yes, trade it in for a bloody hand line!" '

It was evening now and the rods were waggled, inspected, compared and stacked away for the night. Alas, whiskey was taken indoors as the midges came out to be troublesome. We discussed conservation a while.

If I thought there was any way the salmon could become an endangered species then I would protest. I would protest outside Thatcher's house. I'd be there day and night for months if necessary, out there on the street until something was done. Mr Mavin. You are a businessman. If someone said their business was failing you wouldn't simply pump in money. No, you'd demand an accurate analysis. Well, it is simply the same with a salmon river. Count the redds. Assess the predators. Check on the polluters. It's not the nets that are the only problem. Providing a few mature fish get through they can stock a river if it's up to receiving them. Give nature a chance and she will function well enough.

Truly a time with Hugh Falkus teaches any man about casting, about nature and, in a strange way, about how angling can take over life itself.

CHAPTER 3
THE GREAT FLY FISHERS

I find in the Fly Fishers' Club and other centres of efficiency that there is a certain distinction attaching to the man who has never tickled a trout. That he should have arrived at a fair comprehension of the dry fly without this previous training in subtlety is a somewhat notable thing. But he would never do for a chairman at the annual dinner. He would have nothing, or almost nothing, of which to repent him with tears in his voice.

H. T. Sheringham *Trout Fishing Memories and Morals (1920)*

PHOTO:
'A trout! That is more sharp-sighted than any hawk you have named, and more watchful than your high-mettled merlin is bold.' Walton

*T*rout are most remarkable fish. They feed on the top, on the bottom and in mid-water. They feed at dawn and at dusk and during the day. They can be caught in spring frosts, in summer heat and autumn chill. Trout sometimes seem to fight forever. They are beautiful and good to eat, if that be your wish. They live in mountain torrents, in lowland streams, in pits, lakes and reservoirs. They can be small and foolishly obliging. They can be elegantly discerning. They can be vast in size and almost eternally aloof. They can present challenge to any man.

The salmon is the finest of fish, so silver, huge and brave. With the back of nature and the hand of man turned almost inevitably against him, still the salmon runs and battles against obstacles in the great struggle for his race. Salmon have inspired every angler's imagination, tested every piece of tackle and tired the rod arms of those fortunate enough to hook into one. Rightly it is said to be a privilege to fish for salmon today. To catch a fresh run fish is above privilege. It is a blessing many are never fortunate enough to receive.

The sea trout are the guiding stars in the fishing firmament for those who hunt them. Their spirit, their fight and their beauty make them mesmeric. There it is the drama of fishing for them at their favourite taking times – after dusk, into the dead of night and on towards dawn. To be on the lonely, darkening river is something in itself, but to hook a fish that feels as if it would jump to the moon is ecstasy come to earth.

The grayling arouses, incredibly, distaste in a few and, understandably, the deepest love in others. Those who see them as the poor man's trout, as the invader of the trout's domain, must now be outnumbered by those who appreciate their pluck and their willingness to give sport whatever the weather.

The artificial fly has held an appeal for anglers since time immemorial, in fact ever since it was found to attract fish. Excitement with the fly started slowly, smouldered gently, began to crackle at the end of the eighteenth century, and broke into full flame by the middle years of the next. For over a hundred years it has raged with hot intensity. Fly patterns number thousands and fly dressers tens of thousands. There are anglers who have never used any bait whatsoever, just the artificial creations of fur, feather and tinsel whipped to a bare hook. The study of natural flies, the dressing of artificial flies and the fishing of them has become a science and a religion. Intellect and passion are both involved in a brand of the sport that has produced its saints and its sinners. Truly there is no 'better' way of fishing than with the fly. Fly fishing demands a neatness, artistry and understanding of the complete life of the water like no other branch of angling. Well, almost. There is the worm . . .

In 1935, Witherby's published a book entitled *Clear Water Trout Fishing with Worm* by Sydney Spencer. A great deal of truth is contained there. Mr Spencer states rightly, 'Clear water worm fishing is a branch of the art which teaches as no other can the way of the trout.' The worm fisher, Spencer says, takes fish from their lies and knows therefore, intimately, where and how the fish live. The worm fisher is like a surgeon cutting the heart out of the river. He makes no mistakes and everything is precision. The worm fisherman is the stalker, the osprey-eyed master of concealment. He reads the river

'It's a great moment when, for the first time of the season, one stands by the side of a salmon river in early spring. The heart is full with the prospect of a whole season's sport and one begins to cast, trembling with excitement and eagerness.' Lord Grey

more happily than his palm. His cast is perfection. He keeps constant contact with his worm. He knows, in short, the spirit of the summer river in the uplands as well or better than any fly fisherman can ever do, and must never be despised.

When the bell rang on the chapter 'The Masters and Their Schools', Falkus was in the lectern and perhaps simplicity would be served by picking up on him and sea trout now. For many years, since 1975 certainly, the name of Falkus and sea trout have been synonymous. The revised edition in that year of the 1962 production *Sea Trout a Guide to Success* was revolutionary in its depth, beauty and illustrations. The book became a bible for the thinking sea trout angler and it rocketed the species forward in the way that early works by Maxwell (1898), Stuart (1917), Bridgett (1929), Crossley (1939), Bluett (1848), Clapham (1950), Balfour-Kinnear (1958), and Holliday (1960) for instance, had never done. Not even the McClaren's 1963 book, still rightly revered, did for sea trout what Falkus did.

No one before had got to such grips with night fishing. Throughout, the vision of him grows, a brooding presence in the day, simply waiting for the sun to dip over the Irish Sea and throw rosy light over the Cumbrian hills; a relentless hunter using the night shadow and his incalculable experience to bring about the end of his prey; a man who only relaxes when dawn begins to soften the east and when light suffocates the deadening pools of the Eden. The book also reveals the man who understood every whim of this ghosting fish. What, why, when, where and how a fly would be taken is all discussed. Falkus loves his river, his world and his fish; how strongly, this is made plain

Falkus – colossus of the Eden

at the end of the greatest fishing story ever, *The Sea Trout*, when Falkus has just landed his greatest ever fish. The dawn light finds him at his cottage, alone but for his dogs and the yard of silver, his fish:

I thought of my sea trout in the dark sway of the sea, swimming his hours away under the stars and stayed where I was, feeling no particular pleasure, just a vague regret, and an intangible sense of defeat, with the great fish lying there on the table, staring at me with his dead eyes and seeing nothing.

Falkus is a typical, if famous, sea trout angler; a man who lives by the river, knows its every pebble and can be there on it the instant the conditions scream 'Fish now!'. There are many replicas of him, perhaps less talented or more private, who have fished their lives through for sea trout with Falkus-like intensity. The south-west of England has sea trout men who can turn the Tamar, the Dart and all those sparkling rivers upside-down summer long, and Wales, my God, how many Welsh maestros are there? Here there are men to whom sea trout is god; men who live beside the Teifi, the Towy, the Rheidol, the Conway and many, many other rivers. These are men who are out whatever the night the sea trout might run. They fish on hard-pressed Association waters where success demands the highest skill. There are many thousands of these men, anglers who have taken sea trout throughout their lives, perhaps without ever having heard of Falkus.

One of their number was an Englishman, a Midlander named Cyril Inwood. He proved himself in the 1960s to be master of the Conway and on his frequent holidays to Wales caught fish in the tens of pounds. Inwood was a natural sportsman at home with gun, rod and ferrets. Sea trout fishing suited a man of his calibre perfectly and he understood the night waterside world like few other Englishmen. True Welsh is Cecil Thomas, a man well over seventy years of age and vice-chairman of the Llandysul Angling Association. He first encountered the beloved 'sewin' on the river Teifi in the 1920s and in over sixty years has rarely taken less than a hundred fly-caught fish each season. He still fishes. He will always do so, in the dark pools, threading his lines through the grabbing branches and guiding his fly down to where the big fish lie. Cecil is just one Welsh sewin man and he represents thousands of others.

It is this background of excellence that has produced Wales' most famous sea trout son, Moc Morgan. Conservationist and longtime contributor to *Trout and Salmon*, Morgan published in 1989 the book that is the worthy successor to Falkus. *Successful Sea Trout Angling* was co-written with Graeme Harris and is Falkus expanded, covering possibly a greater geographical area.

A great deal of the genius in fly fishing has occurred amongst chalk stream men and there are good reasons for this. The chalk stream is a special environment in many ways. The river will rise from springs on chalk downland. This porous rock acts as a supply but only gives out the precious water slowly. The rivers are therefore strangely constant in temperature, spectacularly clear and do not dwindle like northerly spate rivers in droughts. Chalk streams are therefore reliable in flow depth and temperature and provide excellent habitats for aquatic life. The water is also rich in minerals, is slightly alkaline and produces lush weed growth which in turn harbours fly and fish. All these factors come together to create the perfect trout environment wherein a man can see exactly what his fly, his fish and its food are all doing.

Chalk streams have also – certainly for a couple of hundred years – been expensive places to fish. They are relatively few in number, tend to be in the more densely populated south and for generations demand has exceeded supply. This has resulted in a richer, better educated group of men fishing the chalk streams. And, being wealthy, they have not faced the need to fish, like so many others, for the pot. These men were curious; more eager to watch and understand their quarry, to test their flies and their theories, than simply to catch fish. Discussion arose and chalk stream angling became a science. Its literature expanded rapidly and knowledge spread. This was fortunate for the very advantages of a chalk stream are its disadvantages. Extreme clarity means the trout can see the angler and his tackle as clearly as the man can see the fish. Extreme richness of water means the trout has a great larder of choice before him and is all the less likely to snap at a poor imitation or a fly clumsily presented. Learning was therefore vital before any substantial developments could be made. Even Skues, probably the greatest of chalk stream men, only caught two trout in the 1874 season. Lord Grey's delightful memories of fishing the Itchin at Winchester also show how hard chalk stream trout can be and how great is the need for skill and understanding.

The early and abiding high priest of the chalk stream, the man to elevate fly fishing from sport to religion is indisputably recognised as Frederick Halford. Halford was born into a wealthy family who settled in London. He was above all a passionate angler – not simply a fly man – and he fished the Thames and the Serpentine gladly with worm and bait. Around 1868 a conversion took place on the then clear Thames tributary, the Wandle. There Halford first used the comparatively new dry fly, fished upstream. In 1851, George Pulman had written in the *Vade Mecum of Fly Fishing for Trout* that . . . 'if the wet and heavy fly be exchanged for a dry and light one, and passed in artistic style over the feeding fish, it will, partly from the simple circumstances of its buoyancy, be taken, in nine cases out of ten, as greedily as a living insect itself.' Anglers at that time had listened to this and Halford was entranced. His future course was determined. By the late 1870s, he had been accepted by the Houghton Club and in early middle age he had retired from business to concentrate his energies on dry fly dressings and techniques.

From 1879, he collaborated with the tall, gaunt G. S. Marryat, and between them they analysed the fly life of the Test Valley.

I have heard men lightly joke about these worthies going about the meadows with a bug net . . . it meant collecting hundreds of tiny insects, selecting the fittest, preparing, preserving and mounting them. It meant the endless autopsy of fish. To stand by while Halford and Marryat with their scissors, forceps and whatnot laid out the contents of a trout's stomach was most fascinating.
William Senior

'I fail continually. I leave flies in the fish's mouth; I am weeded and broken. Some evenings I go home dead beat, tired out, depressed and ready to declare that I will give up dry fly fishing altogether.' F. M. Halford

Between 1886 and 1913 – he died in 1914 on the return journey from Turin – Halford published six books which preach the doctrine of the dry fly, the 'high art' as he called it, that was so efficient and so exciting to practise.

Halford was certainly fortunate in enjoying technical developments. Greenheart and six-section split cane had replaced the heavier ash, hazel, whole bamboo and blackthorn rods. Dressed silk lines were now available. They were tapered, heavy enough to cast into a wind, could be made to float and were less tangle-prone in a breeze. Eyed hooks were now available to the fly tier and Halford took advantage of all these developments. In a short space of time, Halford transformed the primitive flies used from Cotton's day into the modern form. He utilised quill bodies that repelled water and stiffer, more pronounced hackles that helped the fly to float better. Double split wings aided the fly in an upright journey.

In 1834, Ronalds had published *The Fly Fisher's Entomology* – the first true classification of the trout's insect larder – and upon this foundation Marryat and

OPPOSITE:
'If Halford had never written a line after 1889, his title to a supreme place in the anglers' Valhalla would still rest secure.' G. E. M. Skues

The angler of the nineteenth century prepared for the river

Halford were able to work. *Floating Flies and How to Dress Them* (1886) and *Dry Fly Entomology* (1897) both classified chalk stream fly life as never before. Halford was painstaking in his approach and his notekeeping was methodical and accurate. Halford was also the first to suggest that study of the fly and the accurate dressing of it is a basic essential of true sport. 'A trout may more easily be landed on worm or minnow, but it is the manner of the capture that is everything to the sportsman.'

Henceforth, Halford concentrated on vital aspects of fishing the dry fly – the fly would be fished upstream, to an individual fish, in an attempt to deceive it into believing it was entirely natural. None of this was entirely new; Chetham in the early seventeenth century had advocated casting to specific fish, in 1662 Venables had discussed upstream casting and in the 1850s both Stewart and Pulman investigated both ideas. It was Halford, however, who combined all the aspects of the art and brought them to a modern form. Better tackle, flies, and presentation were all interwoven and explained with logic and skill, in a way that all could understand and would wish to follow.

In 1889 Halford wrote *Dry Fly Fishing in Theory and Practice* which remains as his most influential book and was in fact reprinted as a centenary edition with an introduction by the modern dry fly master, Dermot Wilson. The work is *the* thorough explanation of the art of dry fly fishing and has been the target of reverence and derision in the decades that followed. Much of the controversy was due to the most prolific and exciting of Halford's own disciples.

G. E. M. Skues was the unlikely rebel of the chalk streams. He was born in 1858 and he died in 1949. He began a coarse fisherman, like many other great fly anglers. At fourteen years of age he went to Winchester School. Skues and his River Itchin began to merge therefore in early adolescence. In March 1874, Skues tried first to catch a trout from the Itchin. He had to wait four months and only landed two in that entire season.

In 1878 he became an articled clerk but continued to fish. In 1883 Cox, one of the owners of *The Field*, gave him permission to fish the Abbots Barton stretch of the Itchin. Now Skues had better tackle than as a schoolchild and found himself on a first-class beat. He was in his mid-twenties and a fanatical fisherman, possessing carte blanche to fish the stretch whenever he wanted. That permission lasted until 1917 and then he became a member of the syndicate formed until 1938. He was at first primarily a dry fly man, especially after reading Halford's book in 1887.

Then in 1888, the capture of a single trout crammed with nymphs was the beginning of his move to immortality. He began to write a few articles but was still little known and in 1889 Halford's classic *Dry Fly Fishing in Theory and Practice* held him totally under its sway. The two men met and Skues became a firm follower of the master. In 1893 Skues became a member of the Fly Fishers' Club and by 1895 was experimenting with upstream wet flies when trout were not showing on the surface. A further four years went by and in 1899 he wrote a letter to *The Field* advocating this simply as commonsense.

OPPOSITE:
Skues – often a lonely man and a confirmed bachelor. Ignored by sections of his favourite club – the Fly Fishers' – stubborn as a mule but loved by many with a rich humour

As the seasons rolled by he moved to using wet flies with short hackles and no wings, similar to the emerging nymphs that he saw. In 1910, he published *The Minor Tactics of the Chalk Stream*, a book that was still really devoted to a discussion of wet flies. Between 1910 and 1920 more articles appeared and more experiments took place. In 1921 his own classic book, *The Way of the Trout with the Fly*, was published and coincided with the use of the marrow spoon, the baby plate and artery forceps, all vital tools in the tying of the accurate nymph. By 1921 Skues was describing nymphs with separate bodies, thorax and wing cases. Over the next eighteen years he moved on to perfect the modern nymph with a translucent look to it, and matching the size of the natural. Skues was responsible for twenty-odd patterns, notably the Blue-Winged Olive, the Blue-Winged Pale Watery Dun and the Little Red Sedge. His observations of the naturals were extraordinarily acute, especially considering that he had only one good eye and had an operation on the weak one at the age of nine.

Skues and Abbots Barton were made for each other. The river here was deep, generally calm water with a pleasant current and strong surface film. This presented a formidable barrier to the struggling nymph which often became food for the waiting trout. The sub-surface struggling nymph therefore became the key to Skues' angling philosophy. Skues had access to 1¾ miles of both banks of the main river and 4 miles of the carriers. William Senior thought this stretch the most difficult piece of water and Skues knew that his triumphs were hard won. Prolific fly hatches made the trout there very selective and the slow current allowed them time to study and decide what fly or nymph to take. It was a piece of river that Skues knew intimately for over fifty years and this absolute knowledge allowed the acutest of observations. Skues loved Abbots Barton and his Will makes that clear: 'I desire that my body shall be cremated and the ashes scattered by the River Itchin on the Abbots Barton fishery, preferably in the tussocky paddock on the east bank of the main river adjoining the clump of trees near the Winchester gas works.' Appropriately, his wish was carried out.

It was a tragedy for Skues that his philosophy of the nymph should provoke such fierce reaction. In 1938 Skues left his water on the Itchin when objections were made to his upstream nymphing method, and he took a rod on the River Nadder. The controversy continued in the press and a debate on nymph versus dry fly was held at the Fly Fishers' Club. In 1939 *Nymph Fishing for Chalk Stream Trout* emerged as the definitive defence of Skues' methods. Skues continued to fish the Nadder and the Wylye after his retirement from the law in 1940 and only in 1945 did he lay down his rod, when too infirm to walk the river banks.

Sad it is that the debate so muddied the clear waters of the chalk streams. At first it was fashionable to debunk Skues, then in the postwar years men laughed at Halford. The truth is that both were complementary and neither was dogmatic personally. It was neither man's fault that a strange madness appeared on the fly fishing scene during these years. Halford certainly was as tolerant a fisherman as one can get. As late as 1891 he wrote, 'The bottom fishers are as true sportsman as the true purist in fly fishing.' He had respect for the wet fly fishing '. . . which required considerable natural aptitude and prolonged study of the subject.' Halford did not see dry fly as a question of superiority. He did, however, believe dry fly-only water should be preserved as such and he only objected to the nymph in that it pricked fish and made them difficult under certain

'The dry fly bubble has burst. Skues has burst it and the *Salmon & Trout* magazine, in a recent number, has put the lid on this dry fly nonsense.' A. Nelson Bromley – *A Fly Fisherman's Reflections 1860-1930*

A display of the tackle and letters of Skues at the Salisbury Angling Exhibition

conditions. What remains a further tragedy is that Halford is seen as both prickly and stolid by later anglers. Rubbish. His pen name Detached Badger surely shows humour and he was deeply revered by his many friends. 'He was just a specimen of a real man you can respect, admire and trust; and, should you know him well enough, you may add your love without being foolish,' said Senior.

What Halford did do and what Skues was to follow, was to go back to the old art of exact imitation. Halford 'dug deep' as William Senior put it. He raised adult flies from eggs to nymphs, to duns, and finally to spinners. He differentiated between males and females and became friendly with Mosely, the head of the Entomological Department of the British Museum. Skues in fact was right in his early years to idolise and follow Halford and it was Halford's precise approach to detail and acute observation that became the hallmark of Skues' own success.

H. T. Sheringham felt obliged to comment on the debate in the 1920s and began by quoting the story of the message sent downstream by G. S. Marryat to Francis Francis who had enquired what fly was responsible for the former's success. Sheringham reports that Marryat's answer seemed to enshrine a considerable truth. 'Marryat, we are told, said that the responsible agent was the "Driver" whereupon Francis asked what that might be. So a second message came down to him. "Tell him, it's not the fly but the Driver." (A fly in those days was also a horse drawn cab as well as a trout-catching implement).' Sheringham had more to say on controversies. He discusses up- and downstream fishing. He talks about worming and the use of a light or heavy rod. For salmon he talks about fly and prawn fishing and he concludes by saying

. . . people get led on by the sheer lust of battle . . . Often betrayed into saying something which is in excess of their real opinion . . . The result is that they are then under the regrettable necessity of sticking to it . . . And so end up in a thoroughly false position . . . And committed to a confession of faith which by no means coincides with their inner belief.

Of course the challenge of the nymph remained. Skues had concentrated on nymphing in the surface film or fractionally beneath. There were realms still to explore and in 1906 Frank Sawyer was born for this task. From boyhood, the river was his fascination; the 'living water' offered pike for him to snare, trout to poach and all the mysteries that he sought from early years to unravel. Sawyer was destined to be a waterkeeper and as early as 1928 he took control of the Services Dry Fly Fishing Association water on the Avon upstream of Bulford. His work as a keeper could easily justify his inclusion in the later chapter, 'The Guardians of the Stream'; he improved the river's efficiency by breaking up the gravels to find upward pushes of oxygenating water and a greater percentage of eggs hatched as a result; he pioneered the chalking of rivers to produce more shrimps, snails and crayfish and this also purified the river bed by lowering the souring effect of sedimentation. The influx of calcium broke down impurities, he discovered and could recreate the chalk streams he loved and desired to see flow again.

Brilliant a keeper as he was, he deserves his place here as a chalk stream master-fisherman. The 6 miles of river at Bulford he got to know as Halford did the Houghton Club water and as Skues did the Abbots Barton stretch. Skues was wise enough to recognise Sawyer's ability when they met, and to recommend his ideas to the angling press. Sawyer had the ability to watch the water with the eye of one who really sees and understands it. Skues realised that when Sawyer examined a nymph under a microscope the years of watching and thinking were approaching the final solution. Sawyer had always trodden his own path, and he disagreed with Skues, for example, over the movement of hatching nymphs. Sawyer saw them struggle to hatch and thrust their thorax through to the air. Nothing to Sawyer was inert as it was to Skues, least of all a hatching nymph. It was not that Skues was displaced by Sawyer but the great man himself saw that progress must continue.

Sawyer began to develop his ideas in the *Fishing Gazette*. In 1952 he wrote *The Keeper of the Stream* and in 1958 *Nymphs and the Trout*. The Netheravon Style was

OPPOSITE:
'From the time I was old enough to toddle along its banks, I have been crazy about the river, and to it and to the valley in which it runs, I owe much of the happiness I have had in my life.' Frank Sawyer

truly put before the world. Not only did Sawyer, like Skues, watch nymphs in the upper layers, but he observed them deep in the water, scurrying here and there, alert, waiting for the right conditions to rise to the daylight. Now trout deep lying were not safe. Sawyer got to them with the deeply fished nymph, using a heavier hook and the accentuated thorax of copper wire, rather than tying silk. Sawyer, of course, fished upstream using his natural gifts of eagle eyesight, oak-beam forearms and in-built knowledge of a trout's lies. He was able to see the white mouth of a trout working yards off, was able to time the strike to perfection, but also he developed the induced take, using the lift of the rod, line and fly to simulate the action of the natural, active nymph. Sawyer did not fish in isolation; he worked constantly with others and this latter idea was taken further yet by one of his own followers, Oliver Kite. Howard Marshall was also a Sawyer man and so to an extent were all men of the chalk streams by the mid-twentieth century. By his death in 1980, Sawyer had achieved all he had ever wanted to accomplish as a boy. He was a master of the chalk stream and never again seen as the intruder.

The chalk stream today is not greatly altered from the times of Marryat, Francis, Halford, Sheringham and Skues. True there are indications that the fly hatch on many rivers is not what these men knew and even that the surface films have subtly altered, but money has to a great extent kept the streams recognisable today, even if there is no guarantee of security tomorrow.

The valleys that shelter these rivers are paradisical where again wealth has kept serious intrusion out of the fairytale. Every trout man wants to fish a chalk stream and perhaps 5 per cent do – for it is a perfect schoolroom, laboratory, call it what you will. Every move of the trout can be analysed and every conceivable part of its fly diet is scrutinised from the egg to the spinner. Expert anglers have come and learned and written and the body of knowledge has grown massively in a hundred and fifty years. And, because so much is known, it is ever more difficult for a modern chalk stream angler to make his mark in history, certainly as deep and as permanent a mark as Dermot Wilson has made.

In 1970, Dermot Wilson produced a book called, with characteristic simplicity, *Fishing the Dry Fly* and what he did there was to strip this form of fishing of the nonsense accumulated around it and make it comprehensible to every angler. The book explains effortlessly everything about tackle and its use, the trout and its food, and how to put a hook between a pair of lips. There is no dogma. Nothing legal is decried. Everything is made clear without condescension and with abundant humour. Dermot Wilson is the ultimate debunker:

> *. . . dry fly fishing, on the chalk streams especially, has often been described as an art, and sometimes as a cult. People in fishing books always seem to be 'initiated into the mysteries of the dry fly', so that all sorts of secrets and probably painful rites come to mind and they may get the idea that acceptance into the brotherhood of the elite can come to them at the end of a very long process. If they take up dry fly fishing, they may think they will have to pass through long years of apprenticeship during which they slowly approach Nirvana until at last, old and grey, they become high priests too late to do anything except sit on the bank, talking about the Latin names of rare riverside insects – what a lot of nonsense! Dry fly*

fishing takes less time to learn than most other sports. There is only one secret in dry fly fishing, which is to make an artificial fly float over a trout in such a way that it looks appetising enough for him to swallow.

Of course, *Fishing the Dry Fly* has a deal to offer but it is this sense of fun that marks it out. Fishing has become something to be enjoyed and shared and Dermot Wilson makes it plain that pleasure is there for everyone. Feeling he was a generous man, I sent a letter requesting a short meeting with him. By return, I received an invitation to be his guest on the Wiltshire Avon. The letter was a long one and full of dates, times and directions, containing advice on tackle and on sandwiches. It ended with all the fun of the book itself: 'I'll be in a Fiat car. You may also recognise me by the fact that I am extremely ugly and a bit stunted!' Dermot is in fact not ugly at all but admittedly lean with the look of a pixie to him, and a pixie's ability to burst into loud and long laughter at the slightest provocation.

That day he had a tall trilby hat that for some reason he wore only in his car and rarely on the bank. Dermot obviously likes pulling people's legs, especially his own. Within minutes a sneaky wind had caused a bird's nest in his line – 'That's what you call the Dermot Wilson knot . . . an unholy tangle'. We spent hours on a river seat, enjoying the sun, trying to decide whether the rises were trout or grayling and occasionally even casting to find out. Half an hour was spent for a pretty fish under our bank. Though a rod in my hands has the grace of a broomhandle, Dermot was kindness itself and did what he could to help a bungler catch the fish on a dry fly. We tried just about everything from a small upright to a 'daddy' and finally a mayfly. Then on went a Sawyer nymph and even a killer bug and on the failure of those we went off to find something easier. Day long, Dermot hardly fished. His pleasure was to help and give advice and encouragement. He guided Joy to catch her largest trout. A perfect teacher, he was. Tolerant and patient, suggesting and applauding and thoroughly enjoying the whole experience. That fish represented 1lb 10oz of pure contentment to us all.

So far, Dermot was a lovely man who obviously knew and enjoyed his river but as the sun set, the breeze dropped and the fly began to lift off in a frenzy, he became a man transformed. Like the hatching nymph itself, now the great angler emerged into the evening air. The rod that had been so docile in my hands was electrified in his. In fact, it was hard to see where the man stopped and the material began, they seemed so bonded together. He travelled the river quickly and delicately, hunting each rise, casting twice to each and moving on to the next. For half an hour he was intense and passionately involved. He talked quietly all the time; some of his words I caught – 'Duns, spinners, olives', 'Try a sedge soon', and so on until the rise reached a crescendo and he insisted that I try a last time.

Darkness now, and the magic faded with the final rings of the last rising trout. Dermot drew our day to a close in the fishing hut, with a beer by lanternlight. The keeper joined us and we all laughed loud over a Ted Hughes poem in Dermot's tackle bag – far too rude to be published here or anywhere. Finally the four of us packed up Dermot's enormous array of bags and rods and carried them across the bridges into the wood and to his car. Our goodbyes were said. Dermot got into his vehicle, pulled on his trilby and his tail-lights disappeared away up the track. I think that Joy, the keeper and I

all felt that little bit poorer, as if a spark had gone momentarily out of our lives. Greatness is made up of more than fishing ability.

From the middle of the twentieth century population increases, the demands of industry and government planning all created a new angling dimension. Vast reservoirs were built to supply the enlarging world with water and were stocked with trout. The hugeness and richness of these waters soon meant the fish were as wary as any wild ones and took a great deal of catching. It was also true that established fly fishing techniques were not fitted to the task of catching reservoir fish on a regular basis. Beginnings had been made earlier, of course, on older reservoirs such as Blagdon, but the 1950s and 1960s were largely pioneering days and many anglers felt intimidated and demoralised at the sight of the inland seas before them. A great deal of help was needed.

In 1952 T. C. Ivens published *Still Water Fly Fishing*. It was in exactly the same era as Richard Walker's *Still Water Angling* and both anglers recognised the demise of the river systems in a small overcrowded island. Both men realised the ever-increasing importance of the expanding reservoir and gravel pit complexes that were the one good byproduct of industrialised Britain. Of course they were correct. Stillwater angling for trout and coarse fish is the area of fastest growth in modern angling.

Of course, neither man sprang from a vacuum. Just as Walker leaned heavily on Sheringham from the past and on Ingham, Taylor and Thomas in his present, so did Ivens draw from the traditional work of fly fishing. He wrote in the preface of the 1952 book that 'Skues' writing of nymphing has contributed something of importance to my technique.' Skues however could only have limited influence on waters like Grafham and his perfect little Leonard rod, for example, did not offer much when transported from the gentle features of Abbots Barton. Ivens realised new weapons were necessary, especially for bank fishing these miniature oceans. Even at Blagdon pre-war, most fishing was done from boats, loch-style, and Ivens had to design virtually from scratch. The Ivens Ferrulite, the Ivens Superflyte, the Ivens Original, the Lake and the Ravensthorpe were all pioneering rods in a field of very fast growth. The new rods needed to be married to new lines and Ivens developed shooting and floating heads and recommended reels capable of holding a 100yd of backing – vital on those heady opening days of Grafham fishing. Ivens alerted anglers to the fact of the weakening nylon leader, picked up on American Al McClane's work on the tapered leader and evolved the double tapered leader for Britain's still waters.

Largely thanks to Ivens, the stillwater angler now had the basic tackle, but the technique to use it remained hidden. Ivens again borrowed from America the concept of 'left hand line acceleration' in casting. Ivens' casts travelled fast and far and were captured in his book in a sequence of nineteen photographs.

If Ivens had read Skues on the question of flies he drew even more heavily from Skues' own disciple, Sawyer. He continued the Sawyer rationalisation of flies, looking all the time for simplification and streamlining. He stated that the ideal stillwater fly '... shall sink readily, its hackle fibres shall be soft and sparse and its wings very narrow and

OPPOSITE:
Probably the best dry fly man in England, and certainly the nicest . . . Dermot Wilson

tied to lie low over the body.' Ivens was responsible for the tying of the deadly Black and Peacock Spider, for example, and early lures like the Jersey Herd and the Polar Bear, but more than on pattern design did he lay emphasis on how to fish these flies. He expressed a constant regret at the clumsy and unthinking way that many bank anglers fished their flies and pleaded throughout his career for greater artistry. Ivens and his colleagues, like Walker in the coarse world, were helped by the revolution in tacklemaking. New rod, line and leader materials gave them the tools for the new craft and step by step they exploited every technological advance. This was the motto of the Ivens school; adaptability and awareness of opportunity. If Tom Ivens were the head of this institution and if Bob Church emerged as the head prefect, then Dick Shrive must be regarded at least as second master.

The late Dick Shrive

Shrive died in 1987. He was a quiet, modest man, and though extremely inventive was only drawn out to make his ideas public by the pressure Ivens and Church put on him. Along with Ivens, he developed the shooting head but his greatest advances were in boat technique. The portable rudder revolutionised sunk line fishing and is the only efficient way to approach deep water fishing on the large reservoirs. Having sown the seed, the Northampton style of drifting inevitably followed and Shrive invented next the lee board. For this effective drifting technique, a thwart board is clamped to the gunwale and extended below the water in front of the bow angler. The boat will as a result cut across the wind. When the far bank is reached, the lee board is changed to the other side and this brings the boat back again. In the days of the oar, the drift could be so extended ten times as long.

Such control of the boat allowed Shrive to pioneer his deep water, sunk line tactics. When everyone else was fishing on the surface, Shrive was able to get his flies down deep, where he used lures to capture the specimen fish and avoid the stocked fish of the upper layers. For this, Shrive tied the Missionary lure – a New Zealand pattern originally, but modified to resemble roach, rudd or bream fry. The tying-in whole and flat of the silver mallard wing feather was Shrive's innovation and attracted fierce takes, on the drop especially. Shrive learned his trade at Ravensthorpe, Hollowell, Eyebrook and later at Pitsford and Chew. When Grafham, Draycote and Rutland opened, he had such a fund of experience on which to draw that his catches were outstanding.

Today the best reservoir fly fishermen are probably the most competent fly anglers this country has ever seen. The work that Ivens, Shrive and Church have done over thirty years has been picked up quickly and developed to such an extent that outsiders

OPPOSITE:
Peter Stone holds a lovely rainbow, proof that he can even triumph on small trout waters –
an area where men like Alan Pearson and Peter Cockwill excel

The late Cyril Inwood – happy ferreting, sea trouting or here, seen tench fishing

are flabbergasted by it. My own local club entered the Benson and Hedges qualifying match on Grafham; all the members were considered very good locally, but they were beaten out of sight on the Midland circuit. The men who fish the likes of Rutland Water had developed skills way beyond those of the casual visitor. Quite simply the new generation, spearheaded perhaps by Chris Ogborne, could catch in a variety of ways once never dreamed possible.

Trout, of course, live far from the soft underbelly of the South and the Midlands and there are many anglers whose trout fishing has taken place entirely in the rough streams and spate rivers of northern England, the South West, Wales and Scotland. The whirligig movement of the water forbids the studied observance characteristic of Skues or Halford, but any angler there must be equally in tune with the water before him, knowing its moods and currents and exactly where the trout will lie. The great fastwater men possess an instinctive oneness with the water. Major Kenneth Dawson recognised it in his book *Salmon and Trout in Moorland Streams*: 'Now my theory is that the very successful anglers are those who habitually send out their magnetic impulses on the right wavelength to be received by the fish, whereas the not so successful are the ones whose sets are not tuned in right.'

That is how things are on the fast little rivers where it is all creeping, crawling, back-handed casting and short lines. The classic style of the chalk stream is out of place. An angler must be utterly in sympathy with the stream bounding before him.

The Ceiriog is about the most perfect trout stream I have ever fished and you can meet with all and every type of water, from the dead long-still pool to the sparkling ripple that finishes in a miniature whirlpool under some hanging roots of an ancient tree. Other places, the best of all, are almost covered from bank to bank with overhanging branches, where it takes a real expert to get the fly on the water at all. Here indeed the old saying 'Patience and perseverance conquereth all things' holds true, as sometimes one has to bend and squirm and almost crawl up the centre of the river to get a cast in at a required point. But the game is well worth the candle, as I have found the Ceiriog trout, size for size, fight harder than any trout I have caught elsewhere, and a one pound fish on fine gut will give one as much or more fun as a four-pounder from some easy water.'

Fishing Fantasy, by J. Hughes-Parry.

Welsh, Devenish and Scottish wizards have always existed on fast waters but, traditionally, the stronghold of rough stream fishing has centred upon Yorkshire. Mike Mee, secretary of the Grayling Society in Yorkshire, has researched many of the men who have lived for the Dales, for their trout and especially for their grayling. He has sent this summary of their history.

Dear John,
. . . Since the graceful gliding grayling made its way up the Humber and into those rivers that flow into it some ten thousand years ago, the fish was presented with a wonderful diversity of habitats from the Chalk streams of the East of our County to the spate rivers of the Pennines.

I suppose that the Industrial Revolution destroyed the southernmost of our river systems; there is a preponderance of industry on the Aire, Calder, Dearn, Don and Rother but the Swale, Nidd, Ure, and Wharfe are still beautiful clean rivers, particularly in their upper reaches, and the Ure must, for its historical connections as well as superb grayling stocks, be regarded as one of our country's leading rivers.

Historically Yorkshire must rank amongst the foremost of Grayling Counties. With a few exceptions from those who take their uninformed bigotism from the 'Purist School' popularised in the South of England, Grayling are well regarded and specifically fished for throughout the Autumn and Winter. I should add that the Prince of Purism, Halford, was a keen Grayling fisherman. He fished in Yorkshire in 1890 on the Wharfe, Costa, and Driffield Beck.

We were of course the 'inventors' of modern Fly fishing. William Lauson [Lawson] was the first to describe the 'cast of the fly' and to mention the casting of a line of more than twice the length of the rod. Walton was only some twenty-three years old at this time and, later, Cotton, in his additions to The Compleat Angler *in 1676, claimed that the best rods were made in Yorkshire.*

However, to more 'recent' times and my countrymen's exploits with observations, pen, fur and feather.

The Ure is the setting for much of this early work, beginning with Michael Theakston and A list of Natural Flies *(1853). Theakston did his own thing and produced a splendid little book. I have the copy revised by Walbran in 1888. This second edition, called* British Angling Flies, *gives Theakston's own listing of the insects, which were beautifully sketched by his daughter. His Duns were the sedges, his Browns the stoneflys and the ephemeroptera were Drakes. Theakston was a native of Ripon which straddles the Ure. This is where Walbran spent his childhood, fishing the Skell which flows into the Ure at Ripon. I do not know of Theakston's influence on the young Walbran, but one might fancy that a fisherman and naturalist of Theakston's standing must have been known to him.*

John Jackson of Tanfield Mill, some six miles upstream of Ripon, published The Practical Fly Fisher *more particularly for 'Umber' or Grayling in 1854. The layout is similar to Alfred Ronald's* The Flyfisher's Entomology *of 1836. The book has the natural insect and the dressed fly shown on the same page.*

Jackson liked his flies tied to horsehair, and this medium was still popular right through to the early part of this century. A good hair, he said, would stand a 1lb weight. They certainly fished fine.

The hair was chosen from the stallion, ideally white, and carefully checked for a round profile throughout its length. Pieces with flats were ignored as having weak spots. Stallion hair was selected not because it was stronger but because mares pee on their tails and cause staining. (I don't know if this causes a chemical change in the hair's makeup or mechanical strength, and I don't feel like performing the necessary research.)

There is a nice story of Jock, a white pony from the Sandringham stables, who was brought to Wharfedale for King George V to ride when he visited the Duke of Devonshire's estate at Bolton Abbey on the Wharfe. This pony, praised in verse by Betjeman, was prized by our local flydressers as a source of fine hair, possibly for its Royal connections. Perhaps its superior diet and care provided perfect hair . . .

Francis Walbran . . . was . . . to me . . . one of the most influential of our Grayling Fishermen. His ambition was to be an allround angler. A tackle dealer in New Station

Street, Leeds . . . his fame with both flyrod and float was legendary. He fished with and seemed to know everyone: Francis Francis . . . R. B. Marston editor of the Fishing Gazette, *Halford, Marryat, Major Antony Carlisle, William Senior, Bradshaw, and Pritt . . .*

The Northern Angler, a weekly magazine, commenced publication on September 3rd 1892, price 1 penny. Walbran was one of the first major contributors. His article 'Grayling and How to Catch Them' was published in 24 weekly instalments to 11th February 1893 . . . These were then collected and published in his book Grayling and How to Catch Them *in 1895. In 1889 he published his British Angler Series on Salmon Trout and Grayling, price 1/6d [7½p]. He was Halcyon of the* Leeds Mercury *and Wharfedale of* The Field. *In 1888 he was living in Wharfedale. His cottage is still there by the roadside and looks over the fields towards the Wharfe. These lengths of the river are however and were strictly preserved; his fishing on this river was further upstream. He introduced the most famous of fancy Grayling flies, the Red Tag, to Yorkshire in 1878 (from Shropshire) and was converted to the Dry Fly for Grayling by William Senior who was on a visit to Tanfield 10 October 1886.*

The grayling or umber . . . a fish to inspire passion in a northern angler

Walbran would fish for Grayling while his fishing companion fished for and caught Salmon on the Ure in the Autumn – this certainty puts his commitment to the graceful lady beyond mine.

One of his most famous recorded expeditions was to the Test at Stockbridge to fish the Houghton Water with Halford in November 1892. His capture of a Grayling of 3lb 9oz on a worm with the finest of gut was acknowledged by Halford, who netted out the fish for him, as a considerable feat. Halford on the same day took a 3lb grayling on a Gold Ribbed Hare's Ear, a fly he was later to discard from his repertoire . . .

Walbran was a great advocate of taking . . . half a pint of brandy in case of an untimely ducking. This he urged on his most temperate of readers. Sadly it was to do him no good in

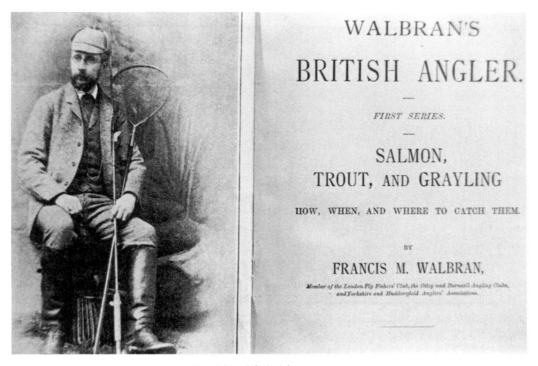

An old and faded frontispiece

February 1909 when a sudden flood came down the Ure and swept him from his feet. He lost his spectacles (he was very short sighted and almost blind without them) and was drowned. His grave in Tanfield Churchyard has a most splendid headtomb with carved rods, net, creel and fish.

In 1871 a railway line was built and access to West Tanfield and Masham was suddenly possible for the fishermen of Leeds and Bradford. Those who had made considerable fortunes in the Textile Industry, and had leisure time, had much easier access. On 9 June 1875 by way of Leeds and Ripon the first train arrived at Masham. I bet it was packed to the roof with anglers . . .

Pritt, who fished in this area and was angling correspondent to the Yorkshire Post, *produced his first book* Yorkshire Trout Flies *in 1885, the second edition appeared as* North Country Flies *in 1886. It is possible that these patterns were a collection of those tied in the Wharfe and Ure valleys by local tiers. The Keeper at Burnsal Angling Club on the Wharfe where Pritt and Walbran were members certainly supplemented his income with tying and Brumfitt from Otley had a similar list in the 1870s. However I do not wish to make my comments sound critical, for Pritt collected and publicised our lightly dressed spiders to a wider public and his* North Country Flies *became the bible and standard to tie to . . .*

Pritt produced his Book of the Grayling *in 1888, which appeared in two forms, a smaller and a large paper edition. This latter edition sold for £1 at publication – not exactly destined for a wider audience. The pictures in this book are special; his Grayling was sketched on the bank of the Ure at Clifton Castle above Masham.*

John Roberts keeps alive the passion of the north for grayling. He is seen here weighing a lovely fish, watched by 'Robbie' from Norfolk (Roy Shaw)

Into the twentieth century, Edmunds, Carter Platt and John Roberts have maintained the Yorkshire association with grayling. Perhaps, though, Reg Righyni, son of a French cavalry officer and later to become a Bradford woolbroker, was to become the most efficient grayling roughwater man of them all. Like many a great fly man, he began as a coarse fisher, twice winning the Yorkshire Ouse championships. The ability to read rivers and control tackle are the essentials of roughwater fishing with either fly or bait. Terry Thomas once saw Righyni hook a grayling at a measured 100yd. Righyni kept a tally of the rivers that had given him grayling, and when he died in 1987 that list totalled nearly a hundred. It took Righyni many years to catch a 2lb grayling – a fish to be truly proud of, taken on the fly or on a bait, trotted delicately from a centre pin. His 1968 book *Grayling* was a work written by a man totally in control of his material.

The Grayling Society today reflects the love of roughwater fishing that Yorkshiremen have felt through the generations. Ron Broughton founded the society with Righyni and a small band of enthusiasts, who set up the first committee. He remains the chairman and recently edited *Grayling, the Fourth Game Fish*, the first international book on the species.

Halford liked grayling and Skues hated them. Skues' attitude has tended to prevail in the South and even Sheringham wrote in *An Angler's Hours* of his happiness to net grayling '. . . and the only thing that keeps my unconquerable hope alive is the possibility of being able to stamp on the grayling a yard long when he has been netted onto the bank.' Thank God for the sense of the Yorkshire brotherhood and the love and knowledge they have invested, as much in grayling as in trout and other species. Amongst Yorkshire fly men there has been an openminded acceptance of all fish and fishers that has been a bright light in a world frequently riddled with dogma. T. K. Wilson was an example of one who could appreciate all Yorkshire had to offer from its trout and grayling, through its barbel, roach and pike down to the dace and even, I suspect, the gudgeon and the bullheads. They were fish and he respected them all. Mirroring this Yorkshire school, perhaps, C. F. Walker wrote in his *Riverside Reflections*:

> *Let us, then, live and let live, remembering that, whether we fish for trout with a dry fly, for salmon with a golden sprat, or for minnows with a bent pin, we are all fellow members of an ancient brotherhood, which until quite recent times was untroubled by schisms and petty jealousies. And instead of tilting against each other, let us unite in combat against those who, by polluting, poaching, or extracting water from our streams, threaten our sport with extinction.*

The list of successful salmon fishers over the years is a long one; the number of books written about salmon is equally overwhelming. A local landowner has a salmon fishing library that holds just about every volume ever written. It is immense, filling a wall of a room. And these, of course, are only the books. Salmon fishing has always attracted sportsmen for it represents an ultimate glamour. Big, fresh run, hard-fighting salmon caught in wonderful surroundings are hard to resist. Certainly, the list of successful salmon anglers over the past two centuries is never-ending and includes Kelson, Scrope, Hughes Parry, Balfour-Kinnear, Waddington, Ashley Cooper, Hugh Falkus, Neil

The Lady of the Stream: Ann Voss Bark fishes the Lyd (A. Voss Bark)

Tricia King, a successful lady coarse angler (Dr Bruno Broughton)

Satisfactory conclusion . . . or sad end?

Graesser, Crawford Little and many more from each generation. Arthur Oglesby, though, has probably been the most recent of the genuine greats and has a history of successes stretching over twenty-five years.

An expert caster with a deep understanding of fish since the minnow traps of boyhood, and nourishing an obvious love of what he does, Arthur could hardly have been expected not to take his opportunities both here and abroad. His books have been the bibles of most newcomers to the salmon scene for over a decade; I respect my copies for their intelligence and clarity. His latest book, *Reeling In*, is a fishing autobiography which must be read to form any picture of the game fishing scene since World War II. It should be said also that Arthur Oglesby has made one positive contribution to game fishing: with Roy Shaw, again of Yorkshire, he ranks as angling's best photographer, certainly in the game world. (A third Yorkshireman, Jim Tyree, pushes them close in the world of coarse fish and trout.) Arthur's photographs have graced books and journals for nigh on thirty years and he has found what is a telling balance between instruction and inspiration. There are, however, two salmon anglers of earlier times and of a type unusual in their brand of angling. They are men who have concentrated their fishing on one river, even one beat of the river, until they have come to know the water with complete intimacy. It is then that true progressions can be made.

OPPOSITE
Arthur Oglesby trotting for grayling on the River Air near Skipton, Yorkshire (Grace Oglesby)

Arthur Oglesby, that 'prince among salmon fishermen', has always had a soft spot for Jaguars as well as fish. Here he is seen between his car and his friend, that really admirable Norfolk sportsman, Jim Deterding (Roy Shaw)

So it was with A. H. E. Wood of Glassel, who seventy years ago, as J. W. Hills said, turned the salmon world 'topsy turvey'. Wood fished almost exclusively the prolific Cairnton beat on the Aberdeenshire Dee and reintroduced there the concept of the greased or floating line. Both Laming and Grant had moved away from the constant use of a sunken line before him, but it was Wood who pushed the technique the furthest in detail and furthest under the public nose. Wood's beliefs, summarised, were that the the fly must fish close to the surface when the air was warmer than the water, that the fly must cross the fish slowly and at the correct broadside angle, that the line must float, be mended and be thoroughly controlled as the fly was fished and that the hooking procedure should be left to the power of the current as much as possible. Wood simplified both the number and the dressing of fly patterns until he was quite happy to fish with just three types of differing sizes, and all sparsely dressed. He tried to see the fish and the take and he himself likened the game to super nymphing with lighter rods, line and a far greater delicacy than known before in the salmon world.

Wood was rich, privileged, dogmatic, enjoyed a prolific beat, fished from expertly managed banks and many of his beliefs have been challenged. His square and even upstream casts, the broadside approach of the fly, the importance of air temperature, the use of his 'current-alone' striking technique, and the frequent mending of the line have all been questioned and modified over the years. So be it but, to an extent, so what? Wood brought life and feel back into a sport long dominated by dead and lifeless tackle. He reinstated observation in a way that Halford had done on the Test. Philip Green in *New Angles on Salmon Fishing* sums up Wood's career perfectly:

> *So what is now left to me, and to the majority of floating line fishermen today, of the grease line method as practised and described by Mr Wood? Low water flies certainly; his method of hooking partially; but principally the floating line. What a blessing it is! Every time I use it I give silent thanks to God for the life of the man who gave it us.*

A second giant devoted his life equally to one river, the Wye, but unlike Wood looked for no publicity. Robert Pashley began angling on the Wye in the 1890s, fished it then for half a century, and in 1936 took 678 salmon averaging 16lb, but could never be persuaded to commit his ideas to paper. His knowledge of the Wye was so profound, and he kept such a silence, that visitors came to watch him through fieldglasses, hiding

'A magnificent body, a magnificent mind, and a will and imagination ready for any call upon it . . . one of those remarkable men who excel at everything which they take up.' J. W. Hills
A. H. E. Wood was also a generous teacher – seen here instructing a lady on his stretch of the Dee

behind the trees on the steep slopes below Goodrich Castle on the far bank from him. Should Pashley see observers on the bank then his instruction was for the gillie to drop a pool to avoid them.

What is known is that this 'Napoleon of the Wye' fished the prawn with deadly precision. He believed the salmon developed a liking for the prawn in the sea but evolved a great respect for its serrated spear, which was liable to penetrate the soft lining of its mouth. The salmon therefore needed a special form of attack which could account for the occasions when the prawn was recovered in a much-chewed state without the angler being aware that his bait had been taken. Pashley was under the impression that salmon swam alongside the prawn and crushed its head and body without touching this painful spear. As a result he always took half a dozen spinning prawns and half a dozen non-spinning prawns.

If the spinning prawn returned in a mess he would replace it with a non-spinning one. Then, very often, this would be taken at the same spot. His belief was that the original salmon was more willing to take a dead-looking prawn as it floated past than one that could inflict severe injury on its mouth. Once the prawn was taken, Pashley watched the slight curve in the line where it entered the water and when this curve straightened out he struck immediately, without waiting for any pull to materialise.

Pashley began fishing the Wye in the 1890s when H. C. Hatton of Hereford was carrying out his experiments with the light minnow. Pashley himself gave up using heavy metal minnows and adopted Hatton's blue and silver and brown and gold ones,

Two of the travelling, writing greats of the game world . . . Ritz (on the left) meets Hemingway

and others painted especially to his own requirements. He came to have very definite views on the minnow and demanded a harmony of shape, size, weight and colour. He stipulated specially strengthened hooks and fins large enough to spin the bait at a fair speed, but not so big that they blanked off the hook. Somehow, too, he devised a strike to draw the hook into the salmon's mouth and at the same time pull away the body of the minnow.

It was, however, Pashley's way with the fly that was most impressive. His tackle and his methods were the result of experience built up over decades of successful fishing and were put together with cold logic. Once hooked, a salmon hardly ever got away from him for he held it tight and made it do all the work close to the boat. His tackle, however, was only a little stronger than that used by chalk stream anglers and consisted of an 11ft Hardy cane Perfection rod which was eventually changed for a steel rod of about the same length. He used a simple trout line and leaders of 5–7lb breaking strain. Pashley suffered badly from arthritis and this he turned to his benefit. His bad hip made fishing from a punt essential, and the punt was always poled by his gillie Jack Whittingham. Between them, the two men had a vast and intimate knowledge of the pools, and Whittingham could move Pashley into exactly the right position and very close to his fish. This meant that Pashley had complete control over his tackle and was constantly fishing on a short line.

Pashley died in the mid-1950s, an aged reminder of a class to whom sport was almost sanctified. His presence dominated the Wye – he was chairman of the Wye Board – and he received constant invitations to fish throughout the river. Often he would decline, reminding the riparian owner that his beat was not then in prime condition. A man who averaged three hundred salmon a season had to be fastidious!

For a third giant salmon fisherman we move back to Yorkshire and back to Reg Righyni. 'Reg Righyni is a man who cannot accept anything just as he finds it . . . he must probe relentlessly, enquire, examine, inquest with a lancet of logic.' So wrote Bernard Venables in an introduction to *Salmon Taking Times*, written by Reg Righyni in 1965. This is the best of books and is a debate and a challenge. It shows a desire to search into the ill-understood corners of the salmon fishing world. Righyni wanted to test out that supposed sixth sense possessed by some salmon fishermen and look into why and when salmon do in fact take. What Righyni produced was an unusually keen look at the water and a searching examination of river life.

One of the two principal themes of the book is a look at the salmon's need for oxygen. This is isolated as the only external factor at work on salmon in a British river. Righyni looks at the availability and the accessibility of oxygen to the salmon, and reasons that a specific level of availability of oxygen for the fish produces a 'surge' of energy. The fish reaches a climax of mental and physical activity when oxygen availability is at its peak and it is then that the fly stands its greatest chance of being taken. Righyni goes on in the book to anticipate taking times by looking at weather and water factors and ends by forecasting the possible taking times on normal rivers.

The second theme of the book is a deep reading of the water itself. Righyni was a man who could control the float better than any other man in Yorkshire, and the one most capable of investigating the laws of water and the way salmon must obey them. A better description of the behaviour of water has never been written. Righyni understood water as a living three-dimensional entity. His feel for it was born of observation, love and intuition. Describing the body of a salmon river, he becomes a bankside scientist ready to isolate and analyse the very last oxygen bubble. The last quarter of the book is given over to commentaries by Bernard Venables and, especially, Terry Thomas. This is how it should be for the book is pure debate, but it was a brave thing to do. There were few men who knew more or who were surer about what they knew than Terry Thomas, and Thomas frequently provides a counter to Righyni's ideas. At one point in the commentary, the author even responds to the commentator! Righyni, Thomas himself, Buller and Walker . . . what giants of angling intellect the mid-twentieth century produced.

It would be impossible to let this chapter on the great fly fishers end without having a look at the men who tied the fly dressings in the first place. For this book Jack Heddon of The Fly Fisher's Guild was asked to supply a list of the essential figures in fly tying history. The list of fly tiers both of the past and of today is simply too long and too involved to contemplate a thorough exploration. Heddon writes:

Apart from some new designs in fly dressing, there has been nothing radical in the way of developments since Skues and his imitative nymphs. Patterns yes, Wulffs, Muddlers and Tom Ivens' rehash of some very old dressings . . . but nothing radical. Today we have a very high standard of amateur fly dressers. The great professional rooms maintained by Hardy brothers, Allcocks, Ogden Smith, Farlowe and the rest have gone. It was sweated labour but there were many fine professional dressers. Fishing has changed and since about 1950, still waters have taken over from rivers. Probably 85 per cent of modern fly fishers only fish still waters for stew-bred rainbows. One result is that the highest ambition of most amateur dressers is to produce the biggest dog-knobbler ever seen!

Heddon goes on to make a list of the major landmarks in the history of fly dressing. He mentions the *Treatyse of Fysshynge wyth an Angle* written in 1496. This provided the first printed list of fly dressings, and of the twelve flies at least eleven are identifiable today. Heddon moves on to *The Art of Angling* published in the mid-seventeenth century by Thomas Barker. This listed the first new dressings since the fifteenth-century work. Barker was also the first to write of a hackle wound around the hook. Charles Cotton comes third for his part in *The Compleat Angler* and the first comprehensive list of fly dressings. In the mid-eighteenth century Richard Bowlker wrote *The Art of Angling* which is the foundation of modern fly dressing. In 1936 Alfred Ronalds published *The Fly Fisher's Entomology*. Ronalds was the first angler entomologist and published the first real attempt to match 'the hatch'. As Heddon says, this was a very important landmark. Sixth in this list comes H. S. Hall for his articles in the *Fishing Gazette* in the 1880s and a chapter in the Badminton Library series of *Fishing For Salmon and Trout* in 1885. His was the first published list of dressings of flies designed for dry fly fishing. It was he that also developed the up-eyed hook for floating flies and provided that vital stage in the dry fly development. Seventh comes *Floating Flies and How to Dress Them* by Halford in 1886. This book came as a result of close collaboration with Marryat and Hall, and provided the first set of dressings with coloured illustrations of artificials for dry fly fishing. Halford, as Heddon says, found

'The fly tier will think nothing of clipping his wife's fur coat or shaving the family cat to acquire the materials of his trade. Austin of Tiverton clipped urine-stained fur from the private parts of a ram to get the right body colour for the Tups!' Conrad Voss Bark.

The Fly Fisher, painted and engraved by W. Smith

Most treasured possessions – a collection of the great man's tackle

dry fly fishing in its early stages, worked out improvements in all departments and published results for all to follow. The last in this list of major landmarks is *The Way of the Trout* by Skues and his book *Nymph Fishing for Chalk Stream Trout*. The evolution of imitative nymphs Heddon sees as a signpost to the future.

Heddon mentions other 'major minor' figures! Mascall from the 1590s was the first to suggest special designs and materials to make flies float. From the early years of the nineteenth century he mentions Roger Woolley, who was a sound professional and much of his work still lives on. He mentions W. J. Lunn, the famous riverkeeper, and Mary Ogden Smith who with her husband was the founder of Ogden Smith as leading tackledealers. Jack Heddon mentions three modern dressers. One of his favourites was Jim Niece who died in 1987 and was one of the most individual modern professionals. Lots of his work is still preserved by collectors. To Heddon, Thomas Clegg, now retired, was probably the most professional of the modern professionals. He praised the work of Peter Deane, a man just retired, but one of the leaders of the modern fly dressers who sent most of his work to America.

This list is, of course, to some extent limiting. It must be. Virtually every fly fisherman has his vice and his collection of materials and loves to while away the winter hours making what he feels are the exact patterns best suited to his own local waters. Tying flies for trout and salmon has become an art and a pastime in itself, and has been recognised as such by some of the greatest fly tiers of all. Many men have known that to take a fish on the fly is to some extent an indulgence. David Jacques, for example, has said 'Fishing is not just a method of taking fish – it is not.' Halford too echoed this and found his investigations into fly life just as exciting as those into the life of the trout itself: '. . . we are stimulated into an intellectual exercise of the highest degree.' Others have even had the sense to poke a little fun at this world of the fly tier and C. F. Walker has written '. . . let us drop the pretence for a moment, and admit that we fly dressers collect fur and feather chiefly because it is very good fun.'

The fly must also be cast. A coarse fisherman can cast a bait from a fixed spool reel within minutes of starting to learn but to cast a fly delicately and a long distance is much more difficult. In fact the fly fisher's cast is part art and part athletic skill. It demands practice, technique and concentration to effect properly. Today there are excellent casters, men like Falkus and Oglesby, but the latter at least would recognise Captain T. L. Edwards as the all-time master.

The versatility of the Yorkshire School is overwhelming. Eric Horsfall Turner (fourth from left) is pictured with a catch of huge tunny

Edwards was born in 1885 and began fly fishing at the age of three. He landed his first salmon at the age of eleven and was a natural sportsman. He played football and cricket for Devon and also ran and swam for the county. For a while he worked in the motor trade but in the 1920s watched that casting tournament at Crystal Palace. He was little impressed by what he saw and practised hard for a year. Next time round, all the events at Crystal Palace were won by Edwards and he joined Hardy's. He sold his motor business and set up the London School of Casting. Tommy Edwards was not just a caster but a real and practising angler who believed, rightly, that good casting helps good fishing. He fished in Scotland, Norway and Iceland and took thousands of salmon over a long and successful career. His skill at the waterside was important or his advice would not have been accepted in the way that it was for, after all, no man likes to be told that he is a bad caster. To be a bad caster is like being a bad lover – it is considered unmanly and ignominious – even if most do both rather badly!

Edwards was the World Professional Salmon Fly Distance Champion and the British Trout Fly Accuracy and Distance Champion. He also held British, French, Belgian and European Open Casting Championships. With Eric Horsfall Turner he wrote *The Angler's Cast* in 1960, which thirty years on has not been superseded.

CHAPTER 4
THE STILLWATER GREATS

*I*t was a warm day in mid May, warm enough to generate all the usual fragrant spring scents, but as I neared the trees a new smell mingled with the others and I knew I'd found what I was looking for. Heavy in the air was that unmistakeable, almost fruity tang of a weedy, reedy pond. I began to walk faster, wondering what the place would look like and whether I would see signs of fishy life.

Christopher Yates *Casting at the Sun*

PHOTO:
Redmire, the Willow, the Punt, Thomas and Walker . . .
and a big fish in the boat

*N*ever doubt for a moment that stillwater fishing has the most supreme attraction for any true angler. There is something about lakes, meres, pools and pits that stirs the emotion. Anybody doubting that still waters have this appeal and this charisma should read B.B.'s account of Swan Coot Pool that appeared in *The Fisherman's Bedside Book.*

We now come to Mr Frank Barker's account about how he and a friend did battle with a tremendous carp in a Warwickshire pool . . .

This story of his perhaps stirs me more than most because after reading it I made a pilgrimage to this historic water on the last day of July of this year, 1944 . . .

Burdened with basket and rods I journeyed thither through an early morning mist and a lifeless, close atmosphere. It was one of those days so typical of late summer. The cottage gardens were gay with phlox and hollyhock, the hay smelt richly, bird song was stilled. I was soon in a remote and magic countryside, where the roads were gated and the farms amidst their orchards were in the old rose-red half-timbered Warwickshire style, and ancient men plied their scythes among the roadside weeds.

The lane became more rutty and sequestered, dipping down into a bowl of heavy elms and elder, and suddenly, there was Swan Coot pool, differing a good deal to the place I had in my mind.

It was very large, almost completely embowered with willows, elms, and oaks. It was square, its edges fringed with a wide carpet of yellow water lilies. For the centre, a very large area, was clear. The water was black, as black as ink, and by the sluice gate which figures in Mr Barker's narrative, and on which he rested his rod, it was very deep. Indeed it looked bottomless until I plumbed it and found it to be 8 or 9 feet close into the dam wall.

I must confess that I was spellbound by the beauty of this pool, never have I seen such an exciting place. Moorhens and coots tripped or preened among the lily leaves and over-all was that smell of ancient lily-girt water, some would call it a miasma, but to me it was a fruity yet thrilling smell. One solitary man was regarding his float as it swung at anchor by a lily bed. His eyes had the unmistakable dreamy gaze of the carp fisher, or, shall I say, the carp addict.

I asked him, in lowered tones, whether he had heard of any big carp taken from this place.

'There are carp in here, mister, as big as a man – ah, as big as a man. I've seed 'em, I'm afeared to 'ook one on 'em.' His voice was husky with emotion. . .

I fished as intently and silently as a heron, right through that steamy noon and into dusk. But my float never stirred, nor did the float of my fellow sufferer. And when at last night came and the wild ducks circled over the trees we both packed up our tackle. I have not got rid of the smell of that place yet, it haunts me. I know that I shall return again and yet again and I may never have even a small carp, but I shall return.

Waters like Swan Coot Pool and writers like B.B. together have inspired generations of men to fish still waters. And certainly for many decades their prime objective has been carp.

The twentieth-century carping achievement has to be put in context. It is doubtful whether such progress has been made with any other species. Remember that the fish, the carp, is not indigenous to the British Isles. Probably there were none in this country in the eleventh century. By the end of the fifteenth century Dame Juliana Berners mentions 'a few in England'. These were probably by now a developing species in the stew-ponds of religious houses, in all probability brought over from the Continent.

It was not until 1836 that a 20lb carp was seen in this country. This monster weighed 22lb and was netted, not caught on rod and line, from a pond in Surrey. For a true rod and line twenty-pounder we must wait a further half century until 1883, when one was taken from the Thames. A. J. Holden had a second nineteenth-century monster at 23lb but not until 1911, when the Red Spinners Club began to fish Cheshunt reservoir, did carp fishing lift off in a way reminiscent of the modern era. By 1928, the Red Spinners had taken twenty-two fish of over 10lb including the Andrews fish of 20lb 3oz – a massive wild carp or, at least, a naturally fully-scaled fish in 1916.

Mummery was the Cheshunt expert. He began to foster the legend of the wily carp and stated that the newcomer must expect 100 hours fishing before his first carp would bite. Albert Buckley became the next famous carp angler by catching the then record fish of 26lb in July 1930. He too influenced carp lore by landing the fish on very delicate

A typical long, lean, fully-scaled carp of the nineteenth to early twentieth century when the legend of their cunning grew up.

The Fisherman's Tables – Carp
One Day = eighteen hours
Eighteen Hours = one potato
Ten Years = one carp
H. T. Sheringham

Maurice Ingham in those heady
early Redmire days

tackle. Buckley was using 250yd of number one gauge line, the breaking strain of which he guessed would not be more than 3lb 8oz. His bottom tackle was even thinner and the hook was a number ten. In fact Buckley's tackle was roach gear, and it is hardly surprising that the battle with the fish was prolonged for well over an hour. It was the lessons of Buckley and Mummery that indicated that carp were almost impossible to hook and then it could only be on the lightest gear which would give them every chance of escape. This was the situation before World War II.

And before Richard Walker, Peter Thomas, Maurice Ingham, B.B. and the Carp Catchers' Club. B.B. was its president, Richard Walker was its secretary and the membership was made up of Peter Thomas, Maurice Ingham, Jack Smith, Harry Grief, John Norman, Gerry Berth Jones, Bob Richards, Dick Kefford, Fred Taylor and Bernard Venables. Richard Walker explains how the Carp Catchers' Club came about:

In 1946 I had a book given me, B.B.'s The Fisherman's Bedside Book. *This was full of stories of exceptional captures that fired our enthusiasm; I suppose natural human vanity was involved when we said 'Why, we've caught fish as big as some of these!'*

It must be difficult for the angler of today to realise what communications between anglers were like then. There were angling journals, it is true, but I doubt if their total circulation exceeded twenty-thousand copies. Their contributors were limited in number and, often, in knowledge and experience, and there was no real system for collecting reports of outstanding captures. Discussion was not very progressive, being confined, as I remember it, to debates about the value of nylon and fierce tirades against the fixed spool reel which was then beginning to achieve wider popularity.

Because of this atmosphere Peter Thomas and I were much more affected by the accounts of big fish in B.B.'s book than would be today's angler, who reads about several such captures every week. This was especially true of the carp, for two reasons. One was that at that time the carp record stood at 26lb and only four or five carp over 20lb in weight had been caught in Britain. The other was that Pete and I rather fancied our chances with carp, having caught quite a number of double-figure fish up to some 16lb in weight. Since the author of The Fisherman's Bedside Book *had expressed special interest in carp and clearly set great store by fish of the calibre that we had been catching, I invited him to come and share our sport. This he did in the summer of 1947 and from this joint operation, I believe, grew what we call specimen hunting today.*

B.B., Pete and I planned and carried out hunts for big carp. We corresponded. How we corresponded! Later, we were joined by others on similar quests. Maurice Ingham of Louth, Harry Grief of Dagenham, Gerry Berth Jones, John Norman and Jack Smith. While we were fishing at Mapperley (the home of Albert Buckley's biggest fish), someone came up with the idea of forming a club with a regular rotary letter. I said 'Let's call it the Carp Fishers' Club!' B.B. said, 'We are doing more than fish for carp, we're catching them! Call it the Carp Catchers' Club!' We did.

This was the first of many specialist groups formed to combine the ideas and knowledge of several anglers in an attempt to catch big fish.

The Carp Catchers' Club revolutionised carp fishing. Its tackle and approach were both different from the pre-war attempts of Buckley and the Cheshunt reservoir men. Dick Walker designed rods and hooks and landing nets for the quest. The members used a new strong nylon line and applied logic and experience to the process of catching carp. There was an element of fortune, of course, in the Carp Catchers' Club's rise to fame. The members' inventiveness and their dynamic wish to succeed coincided with their access to a new, exciting water on the Welsh borderlands.

The Carp Catchers' Club and the lake called Redmire combined to smash carp angling records. In October 1951 Bob Richards caught a 31lb 4oz mirror carp. In June 1952 Peter Thomas caught a 28lb 10oz mirror carp. In July 1952 Maurice Ingham caught a 24lb 12oz mirror carp. And then finally, historically, in September 1952, Richard Walker caught a 44lb common carp and in June 1954 followed it up with a second fish of 31lb 4oz. Carp fishing would never be the same again. By the end of

'Take my bait, O King of Fishes.' Hiawatha
Pete Thomas – bosom friend of Dick Walker – with the 44lb record carp

the 1950s carp fishing was recognisable as the sport it is today. These men had in every way effected a revolution. There is hardly a carp angler today who does not look back at the 1950s with the greatest of nostalgia. There was an openness then and a generosity of spirit that does not always show through today. The carp fishing scene progressed quickly in the 1960s and, towards the end of the sixties and into the seventies a new era began which, for sake of brevity, I will call the Hilton era.

In 1972 an important book was published – *Quest for Carp* by Jack Hilton. In it the progression from local waters to Ashlea Lake and then to Redmire was made. The dedication of Hilton was enormous. There is a chapter that describes a 1200 hour vigil that he put in at a local lake. The statistics are equally amazing; 1230 hours fished; 8020 miles travelled to and from the pool; 270 loaves of bread used; 750 freshwater mussels used; 40lb of processed meat used; carp caught, nil! Thus despite the work done by Walker and the Carp Catchers' Club, carp were still not easy and Hilton had to learn his own tortuous way. Yet, the carping scene in the 1970s was obviously buoyant. Hilton became the centre of a vast network of talented, rising young anglers: Peter Frost, Ken Ewington, Tom Mintram, Roger Smith and, more than anyone, Bill Quinlan.

At the height of his fame and at the height of his powers, Jack Hilton gave up fishing. The intensity and passion that he had shown for fishing were transferred to religion and he became a Jehovah's Witness. In much the same way one of his contemporaries, an equally masterful carp man, Lenny Bunn, also packed up his rods. The story he told me goes that, at Redmire, he put back a particularly beautiful fish, and watched it swim off to the depths of the lake. He turned round, viewed the beautiful world around him, and vowed never again to fish. He is now an ornithologist of note.

The way was now open for the rising generation of carp anglers who had benefitted from the work done by the Carp Catchers' Club in the fifties and the progress forged by Hilton and his friends in the sixties and seventies. I am fortunate in having met and talked deeply with many of the men who followed. Four better examples cannot be given than Rod Hutchinson, Chris Yates, Richie MacDonald and Tim Paisley. Between these four men, every skill in carp fishing is revealed.

Perhaps more than anything these men personify opportunism on the bankside. Not one of them fishes blindly. Not one of them is fast asleep in his tent from dawn till dusk and through the night, ignorant of what is going on, blind to the movement of the fish and the moods of the lake by his feet. Chris Yates, for example, got off his groundsheet and stalked his 51lb record fish. He was not a man to be glued behind rods and buzzer bars. Richie MacDonald, I know, values binoculars as one of his most valuable aids.

Richie constantly scans the water and a necklace of bubbles on the skyline will attract a cast and often produce a fish. Rod Hutchinson is one of the most fervent listeners to weather reports. Whenever a forecast sounds good for one of his waters he is up and away, sometimes hundreds of miles, even if he is already on a lake and catching fish.

Intimate knowledge of fish is something else that all the men share. In Chris Yates' case, this seems to be quite instinctive. For no logical reason, he seems to be able to feel when fish will be present in the shallows or when a carp will decide to come on the feed. It is said that he can predict a fish's route and place a bait in front of it. I have watched Chris at work on the Avon, where he has the most acute awareness of where a barbel will be hiding under weeds, hidden by a snag, or in a millrace. Simply, Chris Yates is

Yates and the Ultimate

totally at one with any carp or barbel water where he may be placed. I remember him fishing the Wensum in Norfolk for barbel for the first time. He patrolled the beat for a good 20 minutes before deciding where to fish. We had not told him the best swims but unerringly his experience led him to one of the prime areas of the river. Watercraft is a much used term, but it falls short of describing Chris' natural ability. Of course, he is quiet and merges into his surroundings. Of course he reads swims well, but his understanding goes deeper than this. It is uncanny; it is as though Chris, tall and lean, becomes like a reed or a willow by the carp lake, bending to breezes, responsive to the mood of the waters in a way only known deep within nature itself.

Something very similar exists in the psyche of Rod Hutchinson and this probably explains why he and Chris Yates, though very different in temperament, have fished happily and successfully together in the quiet confines of Redmire Pool. Rod

Hutchinson . . . the 'big man'
of the modern carp scene

consistently catches more fish than those around him. His tackle, rigs and baits are good, but not significantly different. Rather, like Chris, something tells him when and where and upon what the carp will be feeding. It is a gift nurtured by experience and confidence. Rod used to fish for a famous Norfolk carp by the name of Eric. I do not think that Rod caught Eric – hardly anyone did – yet Rod's knowledge of Eric was immense. I met Rod on one of his quests and spoke to him about Eric on the phone more than once and it seemed that Rod just about knew even when and what Eric was having for his breakfast! As I got into the chase myself for the big fish, I learned from my own observations how right Rod had been, and how generous in passing on that hard-earned knowledge gained on a difficult water pursuing semi-impossible fish.

Tim Paisley I find extraordinary but for different reasons. By fishing the very hardest of British carp waters – and that means the hardest in the world – he has come to recognise all manner of carp behaviour and defensive techniques. His knowledge of the fish is so profound that he can interpret a knock on the rod tip and tell what the carp has just done to avoid the bait at 60, 80 or 100yd. This type of knowledge has equipped him to scrap old rigs and design, test and be successful with a host of new ones. Tim once asked an audience at one of his talks, 'Do you take your tackle with you into the bath?' Tim does. He sees how lines lie and how hooks come to rest. Through his experiments, his knowledge of fish has become truly three-dimensional.

All these men share a careful, planned approach. It might not show at once in all of them. For example, Chris Yates is always, it seems, late! Yet, read Tim Paisley's book, *Carp Season* and you will see the enormous attention to detail that goes into the work of a top man. Similarly, when Rod Hutchinson was developing the particle bait approach he neglected nothing to make his ideas work. When shrimps were given their turn, he took half a hundredweight with him from Yorkshire to Wales. They thawed out and for the last 50 miles of the journey Rod had to wear wellingtons to drive dry footed!

With tackle too, these four modern maestros have points of contact. Admittedly, Chris Yates uses cane rods and centre pins still and thinks that modern carbon rods are only good for pea sticks, but his gear is as sound in itself as the modern high-tech materials that Richie, Tim and Rod use. Perhaps the point is that they all have confidence in their tackle, that they test knots, check the line for fraying and keep their hooks needle-sharp. They do not worry about tackle or bait but rather keep their minds free for the all-important jobs of location and deception.

To accomplish everything that these four men have done in their extraordinary careers requires the most exceptional amounts of time and patience. All these men are willing to spend huge lengths of time by the waterside, away from home, hygiene, and proper food. Chris Yates' book, *Casting at the Sun*, describes his early days at a lake in Wales where he lived a whole summer through. Trying to track Rod Hutchinson down in some months is impossible. He packs and leaves and no one knows where he goes; England, Wales, the Continent, he could be anywhere and no one expects to hear a word from him for weeks. Simply, for periods of their lives, if not the whole of their lives, these men have worked not to live as much as to fish for carp.

To lead such a life can cause immense problems. Some of those who have invested equal commitment have suffered, sometimes mentally, as in the sad case of Ray Webb the northern plumber who retired to fish in his middle age. What keeps all these four men so approachable, so easy, so generously relaxed is their sense of humour. On a river trip, Chris Yates leaves a little paper trail of green men drawn by his daughter so that friends can find him. Rod Hutchinson and Richie MacDonald are amusing men who can dominate any company with their tales and their personal charisma. Tim Paisley has a quieter, drier wit with the charming gift of being able to laugh gently at himself and at others.

No other species has inspired the intensity of effort seen in the past forty years of carp fishing. The strides forward in bait, tackle, rigs and understanding of carp have been immense. Any number of anglers deserve inclusion in this chapter. Fred Wilton is an excellent example for his development of high-protein baits. Lenny Middleton and Kevin Maddocks have changed the face of angling with their invention and development of the hair rigs.

Rudd are a stillwater species primarily. In fact they are the most beautiful stillwater species, with their golden scales and vivid red fins. Yet beauty has never made them as fashionable as many other larger species. This century has seen few successful rudd fishermen. Dennis Pye caught very large fish from the Broads in the 1950s and 1960s. In later years Brian Culley and Alan Rawden have had massive 3 or 4lb fish, from Midlands reservoirs. However, the fact remains that rudd specialists have been few and far between and there is one name only that stands out in the annals of rudd fishing history.

It was Fred Buller who supplied me with the information on the former rudd and tench record holder. Fred had been fortunate enough to make the Reverend E. C. Alston's acquaintance before his death in 1977, and presented me with a whole sheaf of correspondence that had passed between them for a decade. I read the letters on a golden summer day beside a lake, by chance in Norfolk, where Edward Constable Alston died. Generosity. Freedom from secrecy, ignorance of jealousy, love of the sport of angling, love of Ireland, love of life full of warm and rich memories – it was all these of which the letters spoke. Edward Alston was one of the most successful yet least known anglers of this century. He never published a word. He is famous only as a few lines in old record books. Yet he lives in the lives and memories of many, of whom Fred Buller is only one. It was Fred who wrote one of the obituaries of the great man.

When during the late 1960s I first got to know the Reverend E. C. Alston, he was Church of Ireland, Rector of Cliffdon and Roundstone – those . . . townlets on the wild Connemara coast.

In those days, when I was collecting material for a book, we corresponded on sundry matters often about curious and sometimes splendidly practical items of tackle from a past age . . . always in our correspondence we discussed pike that were his and my favourite sporting fish. To be more precise we discussed big pike – who had caught them, where they were caught from . . .

Last summer, during his 82nd year, when we were in Ireland driving around and fishing together, I drew him out on the subject of his earlier experiences. He had started his working career as a boy seaman on a sailing ship. Life was pretty hard below decks but the worst privation for Edward, who loved good food, was the awful dreary diet. When war was declared on Germany in 1914, Edward's ship was docked in Australia. Volunteering for the Australian army got him out of that particular frying pan only to land him in the fire that engulfed the Anzac army at Gallipoli. Edward remembered with great humility the sergeant who nursed him and other young recruits through the days and nights of terror when every officer of his unit was killed and when men who died around him could not be buried . . .

During one leave from France, Edward caught his first big pike, and he took it to Homer's, the famous taxidermist and tacklemakers in Forest Gate – only to be told that stuffing fish had ceased for the duration. Edward prevailed on them to make an exception for a fighting soldier.

After the war Alston went to Caius College, Cambridge (Walker's future college) where he chose the Church for his profession. This decision contrasts so much with his earlier choice that one is bound to think that his experiences in the trenches were the cause of him rethinking his future lifestyle . . .

As an angler, little was heard of Alston except that his name kept appearing in lists of record fish during the postwar years. He broke no more records . . . He never wrote an article for an angling magazine nor did he even write a book . . . Alston continued to fish at every opportunity, of which there were more than ever once he moved to Ireland. His first living over there was in County Cork but later he moved to Clifton where, as he said, the fishing was much better or at least more varied. He soon settled to his unconscious role of being a kind and sincere, and much loved, sporting parson . . .

Edward's favourite lake in Ireland was Lough Nafooey in Connemara. He always kept brown paper silhouettes of all his big pike and if you ever get the chance to see them you will see that many came from Nafooey.

Mention of Alston's collection reminds me of a dream of his that we constantly discussed. He had hoped to see, before he died, the establishment of a national angling museum, that would house all his treasures and the treasures that he knew to be dispersed around the country. You see, Alston distrusted regional museums, because of their tendency to accept and subsequently store out of sight, items that could not compete for limited gallery space . . .

Last summer Edward Alston caught his last pike out on the Nafooey – a 7 pounder. We made fishcakes with its meat and Edward sat at my table in my little fisherman's cottage with five other fishermen – we drank his health. Next year we shall drink to the memory of a gentle Englishman.

The Grand Old Man of freshwater angling – E. C. Alston – captured by Fred Buller during a last angling holiday

It was in Ireland that another great angler, Bernard Venables, met the Reverend Alston. What follows is Venables' account of Alston's exploits with rudd far away to the east in Norfolk.

The last light had gone from the harsh fangs of the mountains; they turned deep blue, then black, against the darkening sky. The lake's water was chiselled into leadened facets by the wind winding thinly through the pass at the eastern end. The boat's keel grated on the stones of the margin . . . This was the twilight end of a day of pike fishing on Lough Nafooey in the west of Ireland. From the shore to the road high above on the mountain's flank was a steep rise of rock and boggy tussock. A man could be seen picking his way down.

Presently he was near, and it could be seen that he was a big man, and that under his tweed hat was the quiet face and placid eyes of one whose life had been spent in remote countryside. He wore a clergyman's collar . . . 'You are Mr Venables I believe. My name is Alston.'

Perhaps that should have been identification enough in the ears of any fisherman and might have been but for the place. But could there be a farther cry within these islands than from Norfolk to this echoing shore of Lough Nafooey? Then Mr Alston made a passing reference to rudd, and at once a truth so strangely improbable became clear. This was the Reverend E C Alston, captor of the record rudd that weighed 4 pounds 8 ounces, and captor as well of the tench of 7 pounds that was for so long the record tench. When the tackle had been taken down, and stamping feet and flailing arms begun a warmer coursing of the blood, I went with Mr Alston over the mountains, through the dark, past the Twelve Pins of Connemara, by the hidden glimmer of lakes across the road, down to his house above the sea. There Mr Alston lit the oil lamps. 'Only for 3 years in all my life,' he said 'have I had the luxury of electricity. I have lived so much in out-of-the-way places, and this has always been the penalty.'

The small flames grew and strengthened, light climbed up the walls and glinted back from the glass fronts of cases that hung everywhere. On every wall there were fish, roach and perch and trout and pike, huge fish of all kinds and among them one case in which were 2 great rudd, one of 4 pounds 8 ounces, one of 4 pounds 4 ounces, both caught on that July day of 1933, the rudd record and the only one that has ever approached it. In another case was a great tench, the one of 7 pounds, that, with another of the same weight, was for so long the record. Mr Alston held up a lamp to each in turn and the faltering yellow light drew gleams from the varnish of the fish that had made one month so memorable so many years ago. He recalled that epic July.

At that time . . . he was rector of Wrethem in Norfolk, and, for one of his tastes, the district must have been an agreeable one. Many ponds and meres lay about it, and it is possible that in that area, very little frequented then as now, they received only small attention from anglers, and possibly none at all from any but local people. One such pool was Ring Mere, by which there had been a battle in Saxon times; but which . . . had always gone dry every 20 years or so. Such pools, unless adversely affected by some other factor, have the capacity to make quick growth in fish that live in them. The recurrent fallowing of them while dry, and the subsequent re-inundation, greatly enriched the food that they provide. Ring Mere, at the time Mr Alston turned his attention to it, contained no fish, and it may be guessed how richly stored it was for the reception of the fish he presently brought to it. From Stamford Mere, a few miles away, he brought rudd and tench, about 50 rudd and 15 tench. The weight of the rudd were from half a pound to 2 pounds and the tench 3 to 4 pounds. He also put in a few small pike and a few roach. This stocking he did about the year 1930, though after so long a lapse of time it cannot be certain within a year . . . But after his stocking, until July 1933 he gave no more attention to Ring Mere, turning his activities elsewhere.

In the month of that year his attention was sharply re-engaged. A boy in the neighbourhood, named Hunt, went to the mere, and in it caught a rudd that weighed 3 and a half pounds. Mr Alston says 'I went at once to the mere' but you can imagine how dry an understatement that is. He went in the evening. In that year, which was a warm one, there was no doubt a heavy midsummer magic on the evening – the strong dank smell of the water to intoxicate him with anticipation, the lush exuberance of the rushes, the scent of dew on meadowsweet, the sensuous warm of the evening air . . . Whatever the prelude, what followed justified the most fanciful hopes an angler could entertain. Mr Alston cannot remember exactly how many rudd he caught that evening, but he knows it was about 30.

Though that is a large number of rudd to catch in an evening, it was their sizes that made this certainly the finest catch of rudd ever made. The weights ranged from 2 pounds to 4 and a half pounds. Several of them weighed over 3 pounds, one or two of 4 pounds and the two that now stare from their case in Connemara. All were caught on worm. All except those two were given to a boy to convey to another small mere nearby which was not subject to drying up. But, as Mr Alston now says sorrowfully, it is plain that he still grieves at the memory, the boy threw them on the mud, rather than putting them in the water, and there

Alan Rawden with just a couple of his immense rudd

they died. But it had been a wonderful night's fishing, and as he walked home in that midsummer twilight, preoccupied with his retrospects and a mellow drawing of his pipe, the hay in the meadow smelt sweetly and he was a contented man.

Had there been no more fishing of any great consequence in that summer it could have been a glowing one, but in that same memorable month from the same Ring Mere, there came his record tench. He had seen tench as he fished for rudd, seen them going their placid ways through the reeds, and been excited by what he saw. Some of the tench, he said, were monsters, from 7 pounds to 10 pounds.

'I tried for them a lot and did hook some of them, but they went into the weeds.' So briefly, in his quiet way, Mr Alston dismisses what must have been prodigious adventures on those summer evenings with the huge brownish amber fish plunging heavily through the weed beds until the rod straightened and the line came limply back. Some indeed he did land and one of them was that famous one of 7 pounds.

To the true angler, the tench has been one of the most special of fish. His unique beauty has always been instantly apparent. The tench is golden nut brown. His scales are small and delicate and give the skin a silken gloss. His vivid red eyes glow like fire and his great fins are scooped like paddles out of mahogany wood. The tench has muscles that ripple electric under your touch. And the tench is so game. He tips up and he feeds boldly at dawn and his runs have always pulled to the limit rods from lancewood to the boron of today. For many a lad, the tench is the first fish to tussle, to strip line, to force the rod tip to the water . . . and all too often to break free in shattering grief. The thrill never palls, and old boys of seventy years or more visit those same lakes, those same swims, for those successors to the fish of their angling baptism. Summer dawns, soft weather, clustered bubbles, dipping floats, hooped rods, great fishing – tench are a part of the universal angling memory.

And yet, for a great while, tench fishing did not noticeably progress from the Walton era. J. W. Martin in 1906 has virtually nothing to say about them. Sheringham in his book, *Coarse Fishing*, in 1912, has even less to add. There is a paragraph on swim preparation, ten lines on baits and then he passes on to other species. Not until the 1950s do tench appear to merit the serious attention given to barbel, roach or pike. The Tench Fishers' Club was founded in 1954 and anglers like John Ellis and Terence Coulson began to take major interest in the species. John Ellis was the secretary. He contributed to an important book in 1957, *Coarse Fishing with the Experts*, and certainly advanced tench fishing from its pages. He examined the effects of weather minutely and discussed pre-baiting, swim preparation, tench preoccupation and even touches on the 1970s' revolutionary concept of particle baits. Night fishing, swan mussels and rods designed specifically for tench are all covered. Yet it is dry stuff and without photographs, without any personalisation. Still, tench fishing was now well on the map of coarse angling and the next explorers would be classic.

The year 1964 saw the publication of the specialist angler's earliest true work – *In Search of Big Fish* by Frank Guttfield. Frank had already won fame when at sixteen and as a schoolboy, he caught a large trout from the Ivel in Bedfordshire. Trout there were few and far between and yet in the mayfly's brief fortnight they could be caught, and very often they were large ones. In April 1956, Frank went down to the river to spy out the land. He saw three trout, the smallest one, he guessed, weighing 5lb and the largest one possibly 12lb. Even at that early age, he set himself to catch one of those fish with the type of dedication and steadfastness that he was to show when writing his book. He tied the fly himself, a large white moth, which was chosen to copy those that were about on the water like ghosts at twilight. He set up his tackle and wandered the green banks of the river. He saw his trout. It was the second-largest of those he had seen before. He crouched in the undergrowth. He put out a line. The fly dropped perfectly. The trout tilted and came at the fly. Frank played the fish like a man of many years of experience. For virtually half an hour he kept his head and controlled the fish's rushes. The fish was beaten. He was beautiful and he weighed 6lb 14oz. It was Frank's first trout of the season and an absolute monster for the environment. Even as a young man, it was obvious that Frank had a great future in fishing ahead of him. His first book would prove this absolutely.

In Search of Big Fish is a spellbinding mix of angling progress, technique and anecdote. Frank and his circle of friends showed a passion and an approach that was novel then, even if now the norm. The book certainly pioneered a new style of angling writing. The diary form built up the leading anglers as flesh and blood personalities. There was drama, disappointment, success, humour and a great deal of experiment within the pages. It is, however, in the months of June, July and August that the book reaches a peak. Frank was an excellent tench man. By the 1970s when a 5lb tench was still considered large on a national scale, he had taken a hundred such fish. In this 1960s book, it was apparent he would allow little to come between him and the species. At Black Squirrel's and Twitchalot pools in particular he experimented with baits, methods, gear and twitchers (tench that don't give a full-blooded bite) to great effect. What is ever-apparent is that failure simply meant renewed effort. There was no fatalism, little luck, and resignation was condemned. Problems were there to be solved and tench swam to be put on the bank. It is significant that Frank's almost constant companion in those tench days, showing the same determination and composure he would when carping, was Jack Hilton. In the course of July 1962, Frank broke a real barrier of those days when he landed a 6lb tench. For the young men of today, brought up on 8 and 10lb fish, it is hard to understand how important a tench of 6lb was thirty years ago. Certainly then a six-pounder had the importance of a double-figure fish today and was a remarkable feat.

For the first hour there was no activity on either rod, nor were there any signs of tench in the swim. At 4.30 there came a spell of bites, all of them on the twitched worm. In order to get any bites, it seemed imperative to cast and draw the worm, as close to the weed beds as possible. By close, I mean less than 6 inches. In order to do this consistently I took advantage of the thick lily pads, purposely casting the worm on top of them and then drawing the worm back and dropping it just over the edge. The accidental cast of the previous evening had given me this idea. Casting the bait thus it was also possible to hang it over the edge of the lilies, suspending it off the bottom. The first take came at 4.30, a deep solid fish of 5 pounds 2 ounces. The next two bites came while I was actually twitching the worm, and both were missed. Then came a fish of 3 pounds, followed by another little terror that tried to make out it was a salmon, of just about 2 pounds. All this time the stationary worm had been neglected. The movement of the worm certainly seemed to do the trick, as it had done with other species in the past. Each of the three bites resulting in hooked fish came immediately after the worm had been given a short pull or twitch. My two young friends, Mike Day and Pete Jones, were fishing the centre pool and at about 6.30 Mike paid me a social visit. They hadn't fared very well and on seeing my fish in the net Mike gasped, 'How do you do it?' So 'big head' says, 'Well, I'll have to show you then.' Within 5 minutes I was into another fish which on hooking felt like a 2 or 3 pounder. I proceeded to try and bully this fish in at great speed as I don't believe in giving small fish swimming lessons. Whether Mike could see this fish as I was playing it I don't know but he was looking at me as though I had gone mad. Until the fish was almost under my rod tip I had had things my own way. Now he objected and the fireworks really started. It was then that I got my first glimpse of him and knew that he was certainly no 3 pounder. He didn't make any long spectacular runs, just boring and jabbing in circles at close quarters. It was about 4 minutes before I had him in the net, as I heaved him clear I knew that my long vigil was over. It was a 6 pounder at last, of this I had no doubt! It was a beautiful fish in every respect and it wasn't a spawnbound fish either, which greatly pleased me. Mike and Pete weighed the fish, also helping me take some photographs. It scaled 6 pounds 4 ounces. Before the capture of this fish I had often thought to myself, and said to Jack, 'If I ever get that 6 pounder, I'll give tench fishing a long rest and go after some big carp.' On the contrary, my keenness didn't falter – now I had the urge to catch bigger tench still. And bigger tench. And bigger tench.

Frank Guttfield *In Search of Big Fish*

All the leading tench fishers of today mention two early influences in the same breath; the young, passionate Frank Guttfield and the older, more relaxed but equally prolific Fred J. Taylor. Fred J. Taylor was, and indeed still is, a remarkable character beloved by all who meet him. Perhaps to an extent he lived in Richard Walker's shadow, perhaps he never scaled the heights of fame and media coverage of the great man, but his contribution to tench fishing is vitally important.

It was to the Richard Walker Angling Library series that, in 1971, Fred contributed the volume on tench. No man was better equipped to write on tench, and like Frank Guttfield, Fred used a conservational water-by-water approach to his species. The discovery of the legendary lift method and its development in the great days of Wotton Lake fishing are discussed. News of the catches of Fred, brother Ken and cousin Joe Taylor regularly made the angling press. The chapter on the Saw Mills Lake is definitive. The gang of three fished from an old pontoon. They baited with over six dozen loaves laced with cans of ox blood from the abattoirs. They fished for days at a time, feeding swims to a climax. Colossal bags were taken – eighty tench on an opening morning and seventy-one tench over 4lb, with many over 5lb amongst them. The chapter, just like a feature on them in the *Angling Times*, is fabulous, inspirational stuff even today. In the time and effort of the preparation, the 'Taylor brothers' seemed to hark back to the thoroughness of the nineteenth century barbel fishers but with vital advances in tackle, method and thinking to add.

In the 1970s I was fortunate enough to meet Frank Guttfield. He, a childhood hero, approached me to write two chapters in his book *The Big Fish Scene*. It was a landmark in big-fish hunting and in it Frank gave the chapter on tench to Len Head from Suffolk. Like Fred Taylor, Len Head is part of an angling family team and the brothers Len, Ted and Phil have been formidable for years. In 1987 Len wrote an important book, *Tench*, but it was in *The Big Fish Scene* edited by Frank in 1978 that he broke such new ground. Len described in detail how he came to grips with the super tench of Bures Lake in Suffolk.

Alan Wilson cradles the one-time record tench from Wilstone reservoir

Len's attention to detail was immense as he set about conquering a water that had defeated so many before him. He drew a complex map of the lake, plotting all the depths and bottom contours. He got himself afloat to investigate features in more detail. When weed failed to grow and hold the fish, he constructed his own beds of reed-mace weighted with large stones as a counter-balance to keep them upright. He pre-baited intensely with casters, a relatively new bait for tench in the 1970s. He experimented endlessly to find the best available hooks of the day – VMC 9284 spade-ends. He made his own special rods, delicate on the strike but with power in the battle. He designed a ledger stop for fly lines so soft it would not damage the line and constructed an advance link ledger to stand proud of the bottom. He developed the once all-popular plastic ring butt indicator and he succeeded beyond all dreams of any sane angler in the seventies. He landed tench of 7lb 13oz, 7lb 10oz, 7lb 9oz, 7lb 3oz and a historic brace of 8lb 2oz and 7lb 1oz. These fish revolutionised accepted standards.

Len brought the same freshness to tenching as Frank and Fred had done earlier but, more than either of them, he proved how sensitive a species tench are and how very difficult the very biggest fish can be to hook and land. This last point has been taken up by the last of the tenching masters that I wish to mention. His name is Len Arbery. In 1989, he published a book *Catching Big Tench* and within its pages are vital clues to baits, ground baiting and the most modern techniques to overcome the shyness of a species now continually under the microscope and under pressure. Sections in the book on ledgering, float fishing, baits, pre-baiting, ground baiting, and the senses of tench, particularly smell, sight and hearing, are all revolutionary and set the standards for the 1990s. It is of course interesting that Len, the master tench fisherman of the day, has around him his own school of marvellous anglers who have aided and abetted him in this book – anglers like Bob Buteux, Bill Quinlan and, above all, that most excellent all-round angler Kevin Clifford.

One major stillwater species remains to be covered, the bream. To many the appeal of the bream might be difficult to understand. It is not a hard-fighting fish and there are times when it swims in vast shoals and is very easy to hook and land. Indeed a small bream can be covered in slime and as exciting as a sack of manure. A big bream, however, is something entirely different. It is difficult in the extreme to trace. It is hard

Peter Stone, first of the modern bream masters, holds a lovely specimen

to fool and frequently it fights as hard as any big tench or even smaller carp. There are men who have made a lifetime study of big bream and their results have revolutionised fishing for the species. Amongst them is Alastair Nicholson. He is representative of a new breed of coarse angler. He is articulate and brings a keen mind to old problems. His list of big bream is immense and he deserves every fish. At night he takes a boat out onto the difficult pits of the South and, with a headlamp from a car rigged up to a battery, peers into the crystal-clear waters to gain clues to the bream's behaviour. He examines gravel bars and the troughs between them. He looks for any disturbance kicked up by small fish that will attract bream to feed over the area. He is aware that plateaux in pits, especially if sparsely weeded, are very important feeding areas for bream. Some of the pits that he fishes are immense and hold bream stocks measured in dozens or at the most scores. Fishing is slow. The bream are difficult because the food stocks are immense. And yet he has succeeded against all the odds and his list of 14 and 15lb fish would have been quite unimaginable a century ago, when J. W. Martin was talking about 7lb bream as the ultimate of any man's ambitions.

Following Alastair Nicholson very closely is Tony Miles. Tony is probably one of the deepest-thinking of today's specialist anglers. His approach is painstaking and his techniques and feeding patterns show elements of genius. It was Tony above all people who realised the importance of undertows in big still waters, where he has highlighted this for roach as well as for bream.

In Cheshire no man has done more for the understanding of bream behaviour than Graham Marsden. It was Graham who discovered that bream are creatures of habit and that shoals follow well defined patrol routes around the large reeded meres of the North West. Graham popularised his findings in the sixties and seventies and as a result bream fishing became more predictable and less a hit and miss affair.

CHAPTER 5

THE GREAT PREDATOR MEN

*D*issolve Gum of Ivy in Oyl of Spike, and therewith anoynt your dead bait for a Pike, and then cast it into a likely place, and when it has lain a short time at the bottom, draw it towards the top of the water and so up the stream, and it is more than likely that you have a pike follow with more than common eagerness.

Izaak Walton *The Compleat Angler*

PHOTO:
Martin Gay and Barrie Rickards enjoy the bleak Fenland landscape

*O*bviously when anyone thinks of predators in this country, pike immediately spring to mind. They have entered the national imagination in a way no other fish apart from salmon have done. In angling terms, Fred Buller has done pike a service that sets them apart from all other species. Only pike have their 'Domesday Book' – Fred's list of 230 meticulously researched British pike of over 35lb. Fred Buller is a professional gunsmith, an all-round angler, a longtime giant on the angling and piking scene and a scholar. His researches to produce the 'Domesday Book' took him fifteen years, involved hundreds of letters and led him over thousands of miles on the often long-buried trail of some rumoured Victorian monster. Earlier in the 1970s, Fred also published his all-encompassing textbook on the species – *Pike* joined a whole group of works of the sixties and seventies period which helped to form the new attitude towards angling in the seventies and eighties. Buller's books stand alongside those of Barrie Rickards, Ray Webb, Jack Hilton and Frank Guttfield, and the Walker and Taylor books, in their impact on the modern angling world.

Probably though, it is the 'Domesday Book' that has endowed Fred with immortality. It is written with the assurance that comes from complete knowledge and a wealth of experience. The book is an absolute storehouse of stories and piscatorial fact. Once he and Richard Walker went to call on an old major and his wife, the ancient guardians of the revered pike relic, the Endrick skull. In their minds, as they approached, were all the doubts about whether it existed still, and, if so, how large a skull would it appear and how big could have been the pike that once possessed it? 'As we approached the priory, we were aware of a tingling anticipation. All the ingredients were there. The history of the ancient property lent something to the atmosphere and the threatening dark purples of the loch and mountain scene added more as daylight grew weak.' The pike skull was produced. Walker handled it, as Fred concluded, unforgettably: 'Walker came out with the big one first time – as the American long jumper, Robert Beaman, had done at the 1968 Olympic games – and in so doing he likewise scattered the field. Seventy pounds!' There is also deep research into other monsters of the British pike fishing past; the Dowdeswell pike, John Murray's pike, John Garvin's pike, Tommy Morgan's one-time record pike and last, but not least, the captures of Alfred Jardine.

Alfred Jardine, otherwise known as Jack the Giant-Slayer, was the master of Victorian and Edwardian pike fishermen. He was the captor of many twenty-pounders and of three pike over 30lb, including one of 35lb 8oz and a longtime record fish of 37lb. He was the author of the excellent book *Pike and Perch* in 1896 and he contributed regularly to that classic of angling journals the *Fishing Gazette*.

It could seem heresy to doubt such a man, and to cast suspicion on his catches over half a century after Jardine's death in 1910 is brave of Fred. Yet from an 1878 volume by Francis Francis, it seems that the 35lb 8oz fish was in fact lost, found dead three days later and claimed as a true capture by Jardine! Further researches in the late Victorian issues of *Fishing Gazette* and into articles by Brougham and J. W. Martin also prove the record thirty-seven pounder in fact weighed 34lb 12oz! Jardine added 2lb

A reflective Fred Buller – one of the intellectual angling giants of this century

4oz to compensate for the fish drying out in the hours between bank and scales . . . and also, it seems, to clinch the record.

Fred Buller finishes his study of Alfred Jardine thus: 'Because he was guilty of slight exaggeration his reputation is also slightly diminished. Even so, it is likely that he will always be regarded (rightly in my opinion) as a very great pike fisherman – perhaps the best that ever lived.' This is a generous comment from Fred, who at the very worst calls Jardine 'an old humbug!'

Poor old Alfred Jardine has been fairly gaffed by Buller but it does not do to call a man a liar too quickly. In the 1980s, there were many who wanted to call Norfolk's Derrick Amies' first 41lb pike a figment of his imagination. I have seen a photograph of that 41lb fish and it looked huge. No one now doubts Derrick, whose reputation is absolutely watertight. One major pike hoax was, however, exposed and it makes a further fascinating detective story.

Record Pike Expose. *The stuffed body of the pike with which London taxidermist Roy Whitehall secured the British Pike Record was not that of a 43lb fish from Lockwood Reservoir. The stuffed fish in fact weighed 32lb and was caught in Hampshire two days before Mr Whitehall claims he caught a 43-pounder at Lockwood . . .*

Among the evidence we collected were copies of Angler's Mail *dated June 12, 1974 and August 22 following. In the June 12 issue the newspaper revealed that two of its reporters had stumbled across the stuffed skin and head of a 42.¼lb pike in Mr Whitehall's studio in Dalston Lane. It was pictured held by Miss Alex Hunt, who works at the studio, and said to have been caught in Hampshire the previous season. The captor, for whom the fish was being set up, did not want publicity . . .*

Mr Whitehall was pictured in colour on the front page, holding the stuffed fish, then having had its weight altered to 42.¾lb. The report added that the weight given in the paper on June 12 at 42.¼lb had been wrong. Mr Whitehall had allowed for possible inaccuracy of his spring balance by putting the weight at 42.¾lb . . .

The stories were that Roy Whitehall and Alex Hunt had suddenly decided to go to Lockwood Reservoir on the morning of January 3, 1974, and invited a friend Richard Willis, whose photograph appeared alongside Miss Hunt's, and who subsequently went to work for Mr Whitehall. The two witnesses told Mail *reporters that they saw the fish caught and weighed.*

However, the fish died and was put into deep-freeze at the studio. And later it was carefully preserved, said the paper, at which point its men went to the studio on other business and told Mr Whitehall it was a record fish.

To cut a long story short, the claim went to the British Record Fish Committee, where it

was discussed at length, together with numbers of comments from anglers objecting to it being accepted. Among those objections was a petition signed by many well known pike anglers and presented by Martin Gay, one of this country's recognised top pike men and himself the captor of a pike just over 30lb.

It was Martin whose article raising several apparent discrepancies, including weather conditions on the day of the alleged capture, appeared in Angling *last March and brought an urgent telephone call to the office from a reader. That reader was Alec Baker of Bolle Road, Alton, Hants. Could we arrange for him to meet Martin Gay at the office?*

The meeting took place on March 15 and included Martin, Alec Baker, his clubmate Ian Cooke, Editor Brian Harris, and Art Editor Terry Hill, who made a tape recording.

Alec Baker there revealed that when he saw Alex Hunt holding the pike caught by the mystery angler in Hampshire in the Angler's Mail *of June 12, 1974, he assumed it was his pike and that it was 'nothing more than a publicity stunt'. He added that he did not mind his name being published since it had already been done when he won several prizes for catching his 32lb pike from his club's pond near Alton on January 1, 1974.*

He told us he immediately recognised the photograph as his pike.

The reason for his belief was that he had delivered his thirty-two-pounder to the Dalston Lane studio on January 12, 1974, where he went with his wife. Miss Hunt took it, gave him a receipt for his £10 deposit and said it was the largest fish they had ever had in the studios and would send an estimate for setting it up . . .

In fact Alec Baker never did get his pike back stuffed. Instead he was told that his pike – having already been told it was nearing completion – had deteriorated, gone out of shape and he was given a plaster cast. He brought it to the meeting: it was very poorly done and painted in a very amateur manner . . .

Mr Baker also told us at the meeting that he found the belly markings of his 32lb pike and the subsequent Angler's Mail *photographs similar, which he understood from experts were like human fingerprints, never identical. The only thing that appeared to be entirely different to his fish was the shape of the head, which gave the impression of being smaller. 'The impression I get is that it has been stretched, with its head pointing upwards.'*

He added that Miss Hunt had told him the body of his pike had been disposed of, in a telephone call about July 1974.

It was at this meeting in the Angling *office that Alec Baker produced various documents and a large colour print of himself in his home and holding his 32lb pike.*

It was this photograph that we handed to Alwyne Wheeler in April, together with a dossier which included the previously mentioned copies of Angler's Mail. *He was asked to examine all the evidence, cuttings, photographs and various comments on pike made by Martin Gay.*

And on May 5 Mr Wheeler gave his findings to the Editor and Martin Gay.

He explained how pike could be positively identified from photographs which clearly showed body markings. He had taken five small pike at random from a sample of 70 and had had two different photographs taken of each fish, in the tail fin to pelvic fins area. Five different photographs were marked A to E and five duplicates were supplied. All five could be matched up in pairs by non-experts as well as himself. Subsequently we tested several non-anglers and anglers, all but one of whom attained 100 per cent success rate.

Then Mr Wheeler told us how he had examined all the photographs in the two issues of

Angler's Mail, *the ones of Roy Whitehall holding a pike, on the centre pages spread, of Miss Hunt holding a pike and the colour print, plus a black and white print of Alec Baker holding his pike.*

He had, he told us, no difficulty in tracing at least 10 points of similarity between the root of the tail and a point midway between the anal and pelvic fins of all the photographs, where he stopped, though he could have continued noting other marks . . .

Alec Baker's fish, measured by him on his lawn on the evening of the day of capture from snout to tail fork was 45 inches; the stuffed fish pictured in the newspaper was 47 inches over the same extremities.

'Mr Baker's fish has been accepted as the record,' said Mr Wheeler. 'It has grown somewhat in the process.' A museum taxidermist had pointed out that increasing the length of a pike when setting it up was easy but it would tend to show in the gill-cover region. The give-away was the space between the preopercular bone and the rear edge of the gill cover.

'On the photograph of Mr Whitehall with the set-up fish the size of the opercular region has increased enormously – it is too big for any pike's to be, a point picked up by Neville Fickling,' added Mr Wheeler . . .

'There is no doubt,' concluded Mr Wheeler, 'that the fish with which Alec Baker has been photographed – photographs I have examined closely – is the same fish in the photographs I have also seen in the Angler's Mail *with Mr Whitehall and Miss Hunt, and in the photograph which Mr Whitehall sent to the Record Fish Committee.' . . .*

Angling Magazine, *1967*

Martin Gay worked tirelessly to expose this fraud. He travelled miles retracing the supposed journey of Whitehall to Lockwood Reservoir. He interviewed witnesses and he prepared a cast iron case to present to Alwyne Wheeler. Wheeler himself showed great bravery in his stance towards the British Record Fish Committee and put his professional reputation firmly on the line with his conclusive support for Gay. The *Angling* editorial staff must also be praised for the effort they put into the search for the truth. Thanks to all of them, Whitehall disappeared 'without comment' and his 'pike' no longer appears on any list of monsters today.

Barry Rickards found his place here in the predator chapter of this book if only because of his pike captures, his work to re-establish lure fishing and because of the fact that nine of his eighteen books deal with pike. He would however be at home in many other areas; his book *Angling: The Fundamental Principles* confirmed his as one of the most thoughtful and dominant minds on the angling scene. His book *Fishing for Big Tench*, published with Ray Webb in 1976, remains a classic work on that species. Indeed in every area of the angling world Barry has dominated for twenty years.

In 1971 he published (with Ray Webb) *Fishing for Big Pike* – a book of innovation and inspiration that motivated many of the young specialist anglers of that era. It was a mixture of Barry's incisive brain – he lectures in geology at Cambridge University – and Ray Webb's eccentric character and natural ability. The end product was far more than a mere textbook.

Barry will always be remembered for his work in establishing the Pike Anglers' Club. This group was the first of the major specialist groups and it came just in time to rationalise piking, to argue its case with the water authorities and environmental bodies, to educate the flock of novices into the sport and to help protect the pike themselves with a list of unhooking commandments. I remember a Pike Anglers' Club teach-in ten or more years ago, conducted by Barry and Hugh Reynolds on a freezing fenland morning. It was a splendidly run affair that began with fishing itself, moved on to casting and unhooking and ended with a seminar and coffee. I came away impressed that men should sacrifice their Sundays for the good of their sport and it was a glimpse of the very best of the angling spirit. In later years Barry has promoted lure fishing for pike through a major 'Coarse Fisherman' series. His *Text Book of Spinning* with Ken Whitehead has also gone a long way to make lure fishing one of the most acceptable ways of catching pike. There is no doubt that lure fishing is important at this stage of fishing in Britain. Live baiting is under pressure and dead baiting is not successful on certain water types. Spinners and plugs fulfil a need and yet have not been fully understood by the majority of pikers. After Barry's work, there is no real excuse for ignorance.

One of the greatest piking areas of Europe must be those acres of Norfolk marshland known as the Thurne system. The area is a wilderness of reedbed and of waterway lying close to the North Sea. For the angler the main attractions are Hickling Broad, Horsey Broad, Heigham Sound, Martham North and South Broad and the tidal River Thurne itself. Here is a vast, flat landscape of reed and water, marsh and pasture. The skies are magnificent, the wildlife is superb and rarely does an angler fail to see the harriers hunting, hear the bittern call or watch the great flocks of starlings roost at dusk. The great Broads are never still and the cool north winds generally rake them at some point in the day. To the newcomer, coping with the boat only increases the problems of fishing these small oceans of water. Yet, anglers have always made pilgrimages to the system. Its potential rewards are enormous. This environment, vast and harsh in winter, has produced more huge pike this century than any other British waterway. Over the generations, nowhere has been able to come close to it, despite the frequent disasters the system has suffered. Sea floods in the 1930s have been followed since 1969 by frequent outbreaks of prymnesium.

Prymnesium is an alga that thrives in the summer in the slightly saline water of the system. When the algae die they release a toxin which is lethal to the pike and the fodder fish in the water. Fatalities have been enormous, with fish of well over 40lb being found dead after the more serious outbreaks. Since the turn of the 1980s outbreaks of prymnesium have occurred virtually annually. Yet, nature is extraordinarily resilient. Although the number of pike is far lower than in previous years the system still has monsters in it, though they are few and far between.

There has been a long line of Norfolk men with the will and the knowledge to catch pike from the Thurne system. Angling history has lost record of the experts between the thirteenth century when the system was dug out for peat and the nineteenth century when records began to be made. It is impossible to tell what giant-slayers existed in medieval times but a solid record exists of masters of the system since Victorian England.

Jim Vincent was the first of these countrymen and the one who made the first real impact that we know of on the system's pike stocks. Jim was the warden of the marshes and famous as an ornithologist. He became known all over the country for his work in preservation but what is little known is his ability with the rod. His captures were great and his son Edwin, who fished throughout half the twentieth century, only dying in the 1960s, carried on a fine family tradition. Edwin Vincent teamed up with perhaps the greatest of all Thurne pike anglers, Dennis Pye.

Dennis Pye set the angling world ablaze in the 1950s and 1960s. He was an ex-army sergeant and he went into his fishing with the same type of organisation and approach that he had employed in the services. He gathered a team around him and directed it season after season. It was Dennis who decided when the boats would be repaired, when the baits would be caught, and which bays would be fished. He fished three days a week and only wanted the biggest fish that the system could give him. His talk was constantly about record fish and he believed utterly that the system could produce one. He was, of course, proved right when Peter Hancock landed his 40lb fish in 1967. Fish smaller than 30lb were of little interest to Dennis.

It is this that provides a clue to the confusions concerning Pye's honesty. Dennis was after a 40lb pike. As a result he did not bother about fish less than 25lb and certainly he did not weigh obviously lesser pike. Thus 17 or 18lb pike could easily be rounded up to the 20lb mark. This was not through any wish to deceive but simply through a lack of precision and interest in smaller pike. All decent twenty-pounders were weighed and recorded accurately. The rest Dennis regarded as mere irrelevancies. To those men who have followed Dennis, men who were more interested in small and unimportant details, these discrepancies seem dishonest. These men have used Dennis' slackness as a way to cast doubt on the authenticity of his legendary and properly verified monsters.

Dennis had many skills. His method was the correct one for the shallow, clear waters of the system. He used live baits that were allowed to roam as freely as possible under floats and on a greased line that could catch and harness the wind. Above all, he knew the system better than any other man. He knew all its moods; the effect of fish migrations, of the winds upon the vast acres of water, of the tides and especially the high salt tides that came in the spring, of the frosts and of the effects of the plummeting water temperatures. In fact Dennis knew everything about the hundreds of factors contributing to the location of pike on these waters. Dennis had plans and he followed them rationally towards success with pike, and also with big tench and rudd in the system's broads.

There are many still who remember the Norwich fish and chip shop owner and recall a small man with vibrant personality, a great belief in his powers and a tongue that was quite up to explaining them. The angler today who is probably closest to the memory was the junior member of Dennis' old team, the lad who boated so many specimens for Dennis twenty-five years ago or more – Derrick Amies.

To visit Derrick Amies at home, in his own study, is an experience a pike angler will never forget. The system's past is there in photographs, newspaper cuttings and glass cases. Nearly all of the big system pike that were killed and set up are there on display, adorning Derrick's walls. There is Jackson's big fish for example and Derrick Amies' own record fish, Dora, is there as a huge cast. There is a giant photograph of his first 40lb pike – at 41lb a pound less than his eventual record. In fact, 'the boy' has in the 1980s come to better the now departed master. Using what Dennis told and showed him, Derrick has added his own skills, knowledge and observations to complete the jigsaw.

Bill Giles – another of the legendary Broadland pike men

He has come as near as anyone to solving the riddles of the system. Yet despite having caught two forty-pounders and several thirty-pounders, Derrick still believes bigger fish do exist. Derrick obviously possesses Dennis Pye's drive. Fifty blanks will not deter him. Indeed five hundred in cold, in wind, in bad weather, would not drive him off. The line of men that has gone down from Jim Vincent to Derrick Amies takes pike fishing on the system with a deadly seriousness. Derrick Amies has both the advantages of a century of pike knowledge on the system and also of modern-day tackle and techniques. He has combined both these to prove a formidable force.

Mention must be made of Neville Fickling as the last of these Broadland masters. It is perhaps unfair to link Neville with any one area of the United Kingdom for he is one of the modern band of specimen anglers who will travel relentlessly for their sport. He has been successful in Ireland, Scotland, on lakes and pits and even on the Continent. In fact Neville has mastered water upon water, but it is with the Thurne system that he is most associated. Indeed it was here in the mid-1980s that he briefly held the pike record with that same fish landed by Derrick Amies. In fact it was not the first time that Dora had fallen. Paul Belton had taken her at 35lb some years earlier but no one had expected this record growth that was to take Neville, the fish's captor, to brief national fame.

I met him on the banks of the Thurne shortly after the news of the capture had featured in angling and national press alike. The monster fish had caused an uproar, far removed from the serene reed-fringed river home of the pike that sunset. The sky was completely clear and a frost was falling though it was only late afternoon. Despite taking this huge fish, Neville had returned to the river and had been on it a week, living on a cold, damp houseboat. His plan was to remain for several days further. This, in part at least, is the key to Neville's success. He obviously knows the best methods, understands the species, and has located the waters, but it is his undying determination that so fires these gifts with success.

Talking to Neville and reading his columns in newspapers you get the impression of a man determined to get his pike! Neville is one of those men to look the discomforts of piking firmly between the eyes and ignore them. Make no mistake – to live on the Thurne in a freezing mid-winter is far from pleasant. The weather comes in either wet and gloomy from the west or bitingly cold from the north-east coast only a handful of miles away. There is no shelter from wind or rain in these huge marshes and fishing is slow enough to provide little diversion. Days can crawl by with nothing to anticipate but the misery of a cramped cabin, a damp night and precious little in the way of food and drink. Neville has lived like this and he fully deserves the rewards that travelling and living rough have brought him.

Neville Fickling – experienced, dedicated . . . successful

Neville has been no stranger to controversy, like other pike masters such as Jardine before him. He openly dislikes fools and this tendency has led to savage criticism. His suspicions and his outspoken opinions have often attracted desperate arguments. His detractors have accused him of many things, from poaching to rule breaking, but he has always fought back successfully. He is a man of high education but that has not smoothed the rougher edges of his character. But few good pikers are bland; their ways are forthright and they develop a directness that some find embarrassing. There are those still critical of Neville in the pike world, but you cannot ignore him. His record and his constant probing for innovation see to that.

It is inevitable that with such a popular species as pike there are many successful men on our waters today. However, my admiration really goes out to those who troll the great Irish loughs and the vast Scottish lochs for the big pike that both are known to hold. These vast waterways so close to the Atlantic seaboard are the wildest possible places to fish. Waters like Lough Mask and Lough Corrib in Ireland and Loch Awe and Loch Lomond in Scotland can become fatally rough in a matter of minutes. Danger is ever-present and the risk of capsizing and even drowning is a constant menace which the men who brave these waters must learn to live with. The man who trolls must have absolute control over his boat, both in calms and in storms. He must also know the lochs intimately and have a good idea of where the fish holding features are likely to be. He must have absolute confidence in his gear and an excellent knowledge of spoons and plugs and the depths and speeds at which they work best. The troller also knows solitude and must be quite prepared for long, hard, lonely days when he might see no one else on the loch. However, the rewards are exhilarating. The pike are frequently very large and they fight better than fish from any other habitat. It is for these reasons that experts, great trolling men like George Higgins from Ireland and Gord Burton who fishes constantly up in Scotland, put up with the discomforts and dangers on a season to season basis.

Pike fishermen are not always the only men out trolling a loch.

In both Scotland and Ireland there exists a strain of brown trout known for a century as the ferox. The ferox is a big cannibal trout and has the potential of reaching 25, even 30lb. In Victorian times a pinnacle of trouting achievement was to land a ferox and the better off came northwards, making the long journey by rail and carriage to Loch Awe, Loch Ness, Loch Rannoch, Loch Garry and a host of personal, favourite, remote lochs to troll their holiday through. They were rowed by renowned gillies and they watched the hills while they waited for the screech of the clutch that could indicate what would be the fight of a lifetime and the fish to be immortalised in their ancestral halls.

The last serious ferox fishing took place in the 1930s. World War II seems to have been the watershed. After it, the world speeded up; there was not the time, the money, or the inclination to devote the entire annual holiday to trolling a bait after a legend. Also, 'the fly' became the paramount, the exclusive art of the trout man. In Victorian times, purism was not rife and it only became so in the modern age. It is a fact that there are no ferox that will ascend 40 to 50ft for a tiny gnat. Even if one were hooked, there are very few that could be landed on a 2 or 3lb leader. As a result ferox became increasingly a dream from the past.

In a very few men, however, the desire for ferox still burned brightly. In the far north

'For those willing to travel, to explore and to experiment, there is a fish arguably more charismatic than the pike.' John Bailey – *In Wild Waters*

Bobby Tarr holds a monster ferox

of Scotland, John MacDonald and Bobby Tarr of Inverness set themselves to read, to learn, and to fish loch upon loch, perfecting their techniques as they went. They showed both massive patience and a massive effort. The trial of sitting in a boat all day, every free day, through long periods of failure, is immense. It was only during the mid-eighties that they began to taste success. Even now they are lucky to catch two or three big fish a season, but what fish they are. They are frequently above 10lb in weight and are the most magnificent wild brown trout imaginable.

Above all, men like MacDonald and Tarr show dedication. I myself have become a ferox fanatic and in March 1989 I fished the month through. It was my tenth year of ferox fishing and I still remain largely unsuccessful though I have lost three very large fish. The March in question saw a period of heavy snow and freezing weather. I managed to be out four or six hours a day on the water but then I could do no more and retired to the little hotel for baths, warmth and dinner. John MacDonald, however, was up there at the same time. He fished all week from dawn to dusk. Added to this is an hour or two both before and after for preparing and dismantling. From the water he went to a crude bothy every night where the water remained frozen and just to cook a simple meal took massive effort. Despite all this he failed that week to find any ferox whatsoever. Not that he was deterred. When I was back in the Highlands in May, the first boat that I saw was piloted by John MacDonald continuing in his quest. Later that summer he was phenomenally successful and landed a monstrous 17lb fish. The record now is only just 2lb away from him and I have little doubt that it will fall to his rod.

For many years, until the 1950s or 1960s at least, few men took perch fishing very seriously. Where perch existed, they were frequently abundant and generally not too hard to catch. As a result perch had few specialist anglers in their pursuit and little was written about them. Everyone, naturally, appreciated their looks and the bold, bristling vigour a 2lb fish has in plenty, and many therefore were pleased to catch them. Not least was my own grandfather who took splendid fish to 4lb plus from Midland lakes during Edwardian times. He spun for them or used worms, the methods advised in the few books of the day that gave perch mention. Notable is J. W. Martin's book *My Days Amongst the Pike and Perch* and Alfred Jardine's book *Pike and Perch*. In both volumes perch, however, are very much the junior partners and perch literature has remained comparatively rare. Mansfield (1954), Venables (1961), Rickards (1974) and Bailey and Miller (1989) have written the only books dedicated to an often neglected species. Where big perch have shown in the past, several anglers have had the presence of mind to capitalise on them. An excellent example would be of course one of the most famous; Richard Walker's blitzing of Arlesey Lake in the 1950s. There, Walker heard tell of large perch and developed long casting techniques to the deep areas of the water. Several perch of over 4lb fell in his time on the water as once again he showed that large fish could be caught by design.

Also in the 1950s, arguably the best perch water of all time began to make headlines in East Anglia. Oulton Broad is near Lowestoft and had for years produced fish to over 3lb. However, it was only after World War II that the locals really got to grips with the water. The most notorious of the perch anglers of Oulton Broad was Sid Baker, a Norwich man of some character. Once when I happened upon him carp fishing in a late October morning he challenged me to a fight! I was twenty-five and he was in his sixties and he was angry simply because I watched him fish! Sid actually held the record with a fish of 4lb 13oz caught in the mid-sixties. For that fish he became nationally known but whether he was a great perch angler I rather doubt. The story of the angler was told to me by his boat partner on the day in question.

They had rowed to one of their favourite bays on Oulton Broad and had begun to fish as usual with small live baits. It was very early on in the session that Sid found himself in a dreadful tangle. He sat cursing loudly in the boat's well undoing the knots in his line. His boat partner, my informant, was left watching the floats and saw Sid's go down. Sid was duly informed but ignored the bite while he continued to undo the birds' nest. The float began to move away and the line to the rod grew tight. Annoyed, Sid left the tangle of line and struck. He played the fish for a few seconds and dismissed it contemptuously as a jack pike and went back to his task. After a few minutes he had the birds' nest sorted out and he prepared to reel in, hoping the 'jack' had worked itself free of the hooks. Of course, it had not. The perch was netted and Sid became a hero!

A much more accomplished Oulton Broad angler was a Lowestoft man, Les

Walker – one of the great modern perch fishers (Kevin Clifford)

Proudfoot, who had numerous big perch over many, many years. Proudfoot, who was a modest, quiet man, evaded all spotlights upon him and until recently the angling world had heard little of his captures. In the 1970s all perch waters declined, hit by a deadly disease that decimated numbers. Only in the 1980s did perch begin to return slowly on a nationwide basis and in 1987 a group, The Perch Fishers, was organised to pursue them on a more rational basis. Several outstanding perch men like Pete Rogers and Stuart Allum belonged to the movement but possibly pride of place belonged to Vic Bellars and Pete Garvan. In fact Pete Garvan's record of fish over 4 and even into the 5lb bracket is unequalled.

Vic Bellars however is one of the most charismatic statesmen in angling today. Around seventy years of age, he reminds me somewhat of a hobbit. He is on the short side and his long white locks fall over a tanned, mischievous face and small twinkling eyes. Vic is always busy, always thinking, always talking with elaborate twists and turns of his lively hands. He laughs a great deal and smokes and drinks far into the night. He is a man who has friends in every quarter of the world and, I believe, even if the Martians landed he would know half of them before the evening was out!

Vic has fished constantly for well over sixty years. He writes about angling, he lectures about it and appears on videos. He designs tackle for his company Marvic and has recently even opened a tackle shop. He is a unique gentleman with his roots in the pre-war idyll of unspoilt fishing and his present in high technology. He travels constantly, especially to the Low Countries where he can develop his own special skills as a predator fisherman. There Vic has made contact with the Dutch pike expert Bert Rozemeijer who knows where big pike are and why during every month of the year. Bert has showed Vic how to use an electronic graph recorder properly and develop careful study of the readings obtained. Bert has proved that large pike hang around the thermocline (the area where cold and warm water meet) while they digest their prey before moving up towards the surface on another hunting foray.

However there is little doubt that the Dutch perch scene excites Vic as much as the pike. The large waters are a challenge and he has explored new techniques of trolling small live bait on suspended paternosters, moving slowly behind electric engined boats. The method is quiet, delicate and will convert well to British waters.

If pike, perch and ferox are the major predators of this country there are also imported alien exotics that make the predator hunter's life that little bit more glamorous. In America the black bass is one of the gamest of predators and attempts were made in 1878 to bring it to Great Britain. A Scot named Pegge who was then living near Lake Huron sent a few specimens from the St Lawrence river. Some of them were placed in a lake near Oxford and the remainder went to Dunrobin Castle. In the same year W. C. Silk made a trip to America, secured his own supply of black bass and returned with 153 of them to this country. Here they were placed in a small reservoir. In 1879 Silk again crossed the Atlantic and this time managed to purchase 1,200 small bass of which 812 survived the journey home. Again the fish found their way into reservoirs and into the Nene and the Welland. Silk continued with these efforts throughout the 1880s, yet there was very little evidence that the black bass spawned successfully and few fish were caught in this country on rod and line. In 1936, a hundred bass were introduced into Coombe Abbey lake near Coventry but none of these fish was ever seen.

Another unsuccessful stocking of foreign predators was the attempt to introduce the Huchen or the Danubian salmon to this country. The last consignment to reach England arrived in 1905 when Herr Paulze brought over a large number of eggs packed in ice. After a journey of over 40 hours the precious cargo eventually reached a hatchery at Uxbridge where the fry commenced a hatch on the day after their arrival. A year later they were placed in the Thames and were never seen again!

However, despite these setbacks, two European predators were introduced to this country and have proved to be a controversial success story. In Germany, Austria and south Russia, the European catfish reaches a weight of 100lb and well over. Some consider it an ugly voracious brute that is long, sinewy and rather like an eel but with feelers like massive cats' whiskers. The first catfish were purchased in 1872 and put into a water in Somerset. Then in 1880, seventy small catfish were sent to the waters on the estate of the Duke of Bedford. Here the fish seemed to disappear but they were to resurface many, many years later in dramatic form. In 1906 Lord Rothschild placed two or three big catfish of up to 30lb in Marsworth reservoir at Tring. Again nothing more was seen of these fish until in 1928 a 3lb specimen was caught by a Mr W. Roberts while he was roach fishing. That might have seen the end of the Tring catfish were it not for a later sensation.   It was in the 1950s that Peter Frost, a Bedfordshire man, began to pursue catfish in these waters that had been stocked in the nineteenth century.

It was a dull day in October back in the fifties. The scene was the middle lake in Claydon Park and I had the water to myself. Armed with a short crank-handled spinning rod of American design, multiplier reel and a three-inch spoon of a type that flip-flopped its way through the water, I slowly worked my way along the bank, pausing at each gap in the rushes to cover the area in front with fan-shaped casts. Suddenly the spoon stopped with a vicious jerk. For a second or two the rod remained arched and immobile. Then came a wrench that slammed the rod tip nearly into the water which almost had me off my balance. At the same time an enormous boil appeared on the surface of the swim, which was only about three feet deep. Pulling like a tank, the fish moved to the left for a dozen yards or so, then came another tremendous jerk as it about-turned and the lashing body fouled the line. When it reached the spot where the spoon had been seized it turned yet again and then, seeming at last to realise that something was wrong, it set off with increasing speed for the far end of the lake, at which stage the hook came away. Thirty yards out the swirling patch of muddy water, with little vortices spinning themselves into oblivion, marked the spot where briefly I had been in contact with the biggest catfish it has yet been my fortune to hook.

The loss of this fish spurred him and others to strenuous efforts in the 1960s. Finally a fish of 33lb 12oz was caught in 1961 by Reg Hutt. It was recognised as a record but not a fish to hold the title for long.

We move back now to the Tring reservoirs. In 1967 Frank Guttfield, the tench maestro, had been fishing at Wilstone, one of the Tring reservoirs. He had been pursuing bream in September when the fog was so thick he could only just see his silver foil bite indicator. Frank apparently was experimenting with a cheese paste bait when slowly his indicator appeared to rise. Frank struck into a fish which could not be moved at first and then put up a thunderous but dogged fight that lasted several minutes. The fight was totally one sided and soon the 6lb line parted. It came back minus a hook and the last few inches of line were rasped. Shortly after this, in September 1970 at Wilstone, a 43lb 8oz catfish was taken by Richard Bray.

In the 1980s there have been strenuous attempts to spread catfish throughout British waters. Men like Kevin Maddocks, Bob Baldock and Shaun Harrison have between them done wonders for the reputation of this fine fighting fish. I have never landed a catfish personally but I have seen my good friend Martyn Page hook, play and successfully land a 20lb fish. To say the fight was sensational is an understatement. There were times when the fish had complete control of events and Martyn was reduced to stripping off and entering the lake after it. Even when the fish neared the net the battle was by no means over and I have rarely seen any species capable of swimming backwards as quickly as it can swim forwards!

Another European import is the zander. The first attempts to introduce it began in 1878 when twenty specimens of about 2lb each were sent from northern Germany to a pool again on the Duke of Bedford's estate. In 1925 some twenty fingerlings were placed in the River Ouse and on 10 March 1934 a Cambridge angler hooked a zander of nearly 12lb in the River Delfe at Welney in the Ouse basin. However, it was the stocking of the relief channel by the Great Ouse River Authority in 1963 that was to really open the way for zander fishing in this country. By 1966 pike anglers were experiencing fast abortive runs as they fished the relief channel. At first the culprits were a mystery until a tiny zander of a mere pound or two was landed. By the 1970s however, these small zander had grown and waxed fat on the plentiful supplies of small roach and bream that the relief channel then held. The zander was a new and exciting predator and it attracted a great deal of attention from many skilled enthusiasts.

Amongst the leaders were men that we have already met on the pike scene – Rickards and Fickling. Between them they caught many fish over 10lb and once Fickling even held the record briefly. They were accompanied on the channel by other fine anglers like Bill Chillingworth and Laurie Manns. These fen men were also joined by Norfolk predator hunters John Wilson, Martyn Page, Steve Harper and Terry Houseago. The relief channel went through a golden period and the sport could be fast and furious. The record was broken again and again, going up to 16lb and then finally to a shattering 17lb 8oz. After this fish taken by Dave Litton, again from the relief channel, the heyday of zander fishing was virtually over. Various washouts hit the relief channel and many fish were swept out into the North Sea.

Fishing began to suffer and the water authority was heavily criticised for introducing zander in the 1960s. It was believed, by matchmen in particular, that the zander were eating fry and fingerlings and were denuding the channel of fish. Whatever the real cause, war was waged on the zander and the water authority conducted a campaign to remove them. For some years zander fishing went into the doldrums and even now as we move into the 1990s the zander is certainly not as prolific as it once was. However some enthusiasts continue to flog these fenland drains for a species that exercises its own charm upon them. One of the more successful is Mick Brown. He works hard at location and travels miles along the winter waterways looking for the few remaining, isolated zander shoals. In the winter, on these bleak wind-blasted plains, this is a lonesome task that should not be underestimated.

CHAPTER 6

THE RIVER GREATS

*I*t is easily possible to love rivers, just as easily in fact as human beings themselves. Both have beauty, character and both have good and bad moods. You can feel at ease in the company of rivers. They can soothe like a mother, interest like a teacher or even excite at times like a lover. Rivers roll on through history and make their own marvellous legends. They give off a charisma. They can, simply, be magical.

John Bailey *In Wild Waters* (1989)

PHOTO:
Weirpools – traditional home of big Thames trout and barbel

A River Never Sleeps, Beloved River, Summer on the Test, By Dancing Streams, Where Bright Waters Meet, At the Tail of the Weir, and *The Path by the Water*; a whole list of angling books pays testimony to the power of rivers over the mind of man. Fascination lies in the river's ever-changing face, in the challenge of reading the water, looking for swims along miles of tempting bankside, and in the difficulty of mastering the current and presenting the bait in a natural manner. The fish themselves have a dash and a vigour that corresponds well with moving water. An angler expects them to be dynamic and almost always from fast clear waters they are so. This is never more true than with the barbel.

I really thought for half an hour that I had hooked the very Jabberwock himself. I could not get on terms with him at all. He hung to the bottom like grim death. His tugging and his boring were terrific. Getting his head up was utterly out of the question.　　J. W. Martin.

You had a terrific bite and you tried to play him with the rod and he's broken you? And it was a 9 pound barbel! My good sir, I didn't tell you to grasp the rod with both hands and hold on with your eyes starting out of your head!　　Hugh Tempest Sheringham.

Ten times I got that float above the water and nine times he dragged it down again and dragged and dragged until I thought I should never see it again.　　J. W. Martin.

Of the barbel, it is hard to speak with too much praise.　　Bernard Venables.

But best of all I love the barbels . . . because they roll like big brown and white cats in the golden shallows and sing in the moonlight with the joie de vivre of June. And because, too, they are all Thame to me and wild rose time and the streams running down to the weir.
　　Patrick Chalmers.

Very very slowly, I gained a few feet of line but then the rod was wrenched ferociously down and I had no option but to back wind as fast as I could as the fish set off down the stream. Again and again, I retrieved line by straining the tackle to the limit but always the response was an awesome retaliatory surge of power.　　Andy Orme.

Nothing further need be said; barbel are big, beautiful and fight like beasts in the rapid water. They have captivated anglers, exhilarated them and left them devastated too. In contrast to many other species, a great deal was known about barbel before what we can call the modern age of specialist hunting – from 1960 onwards. Certainly catches in the past have been fabulous, especially when the Royalty ran at its peak. In September 1933 F. W. K. Wallis landed ten double-figure fish including one of over 14lb and a second of 13lb 8oz. Four years later, with Claud Taylor, Wallis shared a haul including four barbel in the 12–13lb range. Twenty years on, Bill Warren took twenty-one fish over 10lb to 13lb 4oz, in a single four-month period. The Trent produced equally great catches with fish recorded by the Trent Otter to nearly 15lb and Robert

'The barbel possesses the furtive, hangdog expression of a priestly inquisitor. He has a hideous leathery mouth . . . you picture him enjoying the wriggling of a lusty worm before he swallows it.' Applin

Wells' catch of 123 fish in a single day. Also in the nineteenth century a 16lb 10oz barbel fell to a lamprey baited night line. The Trent, the Avon, the Kennet, the Thames and the Lee . . . There is no doubt that the earlier of the barbel men had the fish to pursue and they knew just how to catch them.

In 1906 J. W. Martin, better known under his writing name of the Trent Otter, published *Days Among the Barbel* that retold his life on the Trent, Thames and Kennet, his captures, and his acquaintances. Among these latter was Owen, the tackledealer from Newark, who '. . . showed me the barbel tackle used thirty years before then, tackle that is never seen nowadays and is scarcely dreamed about; bottoms of double twisted copper wire, a rod of solid timber weighing as much as three or more pounds; a line of hemp and cord and a ledger lead that would brain the first barbel that it dropped upon!' Martin worked hard for his fishing and it was nothing to him to collect a thousand lobs before a barbel campaign. The initial baiting alone meant the chopping up of some two hundred of them. Often, these worms would be introduced in the most massive of swim feeders – an old earthenware pot with tapering sides lowered from a boat. He took risks, too, for his favourite barbel.

My old friend Frank Sims was a believer in night fishing when the water was bright and low, ledgering with a good lump of white greaves. We went one night to a deep hole not far from Kelham bridge on the Trent; I got a 6-pounder that fought and splashed in the darkness like a fury. The water had hardly settled after the commotion and we heard the tramp of the keeper along the gravel. We had no business there at night. Fortunately we were under an overhanging bank and the keeper had to make a detour above us. Just at that moment my big barbel gave a hoarse, sucking croak, enough to attract the attention at short distance. The keeper stopped, and appeared to listen for a minute, but hearing nothing further went on. It was a narrow escape.

Martin seems to have been at the centre of something like a late Victorian/ Edwardian specialist group. Tommy Sunman, George Wakeland, William Bailey, Tom Bentley and Andrew Broughton were '. . . old Trent barbel fishermen with whom I have spent many a day and whom I have assisted to land many a barbel.' Were Martin and these other men great? I think so. The Trent Otter himself had nothing but praise for these anglers:

. . . good men and true, barbel fishermen of the first rank, now sleeping their last long sleep, every one of them. Sunday after Sunday and sometimes once or twice in the week, we roamed those lower Trent waters. Many a hint did I find valuable coming from their lips and many an object lesson did I learn from their illustration. Twenty years have passed since some of them died but in my memory they still live.

In 1912, Hugh Tempest Sheringham published his book *Coarse Fishing*. There is a passage in it which anticipated many of the advanced experiments that were to take place sixty and seventy years later.

Obviously we ought to fish for barbel with the things that they eat normally. I believe water snails and freshwater shrimps and things like that are the barbel's natural food. The trouble is putting them on a hook. Shrimps are tiny little things and barbel hooks have to be pretty stout in the wire. Perhaps you could use some sticky stuff like seccatine and simply stick 4 or 5 shrimps to the hook. Snails might be tied on by fine thread. Frenchmen use aniseed cake and they tie it to their hooks with thread. We don't know everything about fishing in England – though we think we do.

A neater summary of the particle bait theory could hardly be imagined.

The twentieth century progresses and in 1948 *This Fishing* by Captain L. A. Parker comes onto the shelves. Parker was born in 1886, was the ace of the Hampshire Avon, for many years kept The Bull at Downton and finally retired into Weir Cottage at Bickton Mill. His life therefore spanned the days of Martin and those of many anglers of the present. Roach made him famous above all, but his development of clay ball fishing

OPPOSITE
John and Tony Pawson – a great team (Bill Bachman)

'That man is richest whose pleasures are cheapest'
(THOREAU)

Alan Young casts a dry fly on the upper Garry

Another fabulous Fickling fish
(Neville Fickling)

LEFT
*John Sidley prepares to put two
very large eels back* (John Sidley)

RIGHT
*Martin·James – a courageous
angler* (M. James)

for barbel is classic. Although the clay ball concept was not new, Parker's principles advanced the method. His instructions are as follows: obtain clay; mix it in a bucket to the right consistency; make up golf-size balls and fill them with broken worms or maggots; seal the hole with a thin layer of clay and deposit a dozen of the balls in the exact spot to be fished. Eventually, the baits work through and the barbel take an interest. Soon they are nosing the clay balls like demons. This is when the angler acts. On a treble, he puts worms or maggots on each of the points. The whole is then covered with clay, perhaps with a few tails hanging loose.

Barbel love nosing into clay and eventually they start nosing into your clay balls and finding food. Then comes the most delightful thrill when you find one nosing into your special ball with the hook so beautifully concealed. There is no mistaking it for it is fast and vigorous and eventually, when the barbel has worked you up to fever pitch, bang goes your rod tip – and what a bang! – and you are fast into one of the gamest fish that swims. Don't strike at slight taps.

The captain's plan I decided to take up on the River Wensum. For those who don't know this stretch of prime barbel water you must realise it is a short beat and very heavily fished. All the barbel have been caught, often many times before. They like anglers' baits, but they are constantly wary of them. Also, every method of presentation has been used but this one. Accordingly in summer 1989 I tried it down there in the gin-clear water where the weed drapes the gravel. It would be nice to record instant success. The truth is that the barbel took three sessions before they began to investigate the clay balls, to which they were obviously quite unused. Finally at the end of this third session one barbel took my clay ball with true intent. I did not prolong the experiment. I feel I should have done, for it would have undoubtedly put me ahead in this very tight game.

By the 1970s interest in barbel was sweeping the specialist world and in 1977 John Everard contributed a chapter to *The Big Fish Scene* on barbel. The work was instantly recognised. Of the greatest importance was his approach to locating Thames fish. He discusses fishing the places of the fastest current, clay shelves, undercuts, pilings and water cabbages – all the usual places that writers before him had advocated. However, it is when he looks at these swims in meticulous detail that Everard breaks new ground.

Having located as many swims as I can, the next step is to plumb them all very carefully, recording the results. I look for variations in depth over small areas. The barbel are usually found where the bed suddenly starts to shallow. Where possible I plumb the whole width of the river in order to find any shelves. In this way I build up a mental picture of the cross section of the river bed. Barbel are often found in deep water over the shelf. I also take note of any minor depressions in the bed as barbel are known to lie in these.

Everard's other major contribution was his emphasis on holding the line and feeling for barbel bites.

When fishing in the dark I invariably held the rod. Barbel bites can vary considerably from a strong wrenching pull to a small positive pull of half an inch on the rod tip. At other times

Captain L. A. Parker – mine host at the 'Bull' where the kitchen was called The Board Room and where Mrs Parker held sway: 'I never saw her seated, except when she laughed . . . laughter poured from her like wine poured recklessly from a flagon . . . it filled the room, warm . . . intoxicating . . . to control herself she would fall into a chair, holding her sides, folding her arms across her breast whilst tears filled her eyes.' A. Applin – *The Philandering Angler*

Martyn Page with a near 11lb barbel – tackle designer, angling author and a modern-day big fish catcher

you can feel a sawing sensation on the rod top . . . I think that the feeding barbel descend on the bait, swallowing it on the spot. This has been proved on many occasions as a hook has been swallowed so far down that the line has had to be cut before returning the fish, since any attempt to remove the hook would have led to injury of the barbel.

In 1988 the Barbel Fishers' Group produced their book on the barbel rivers of England. Excellent as the book is, it does however lack the depth of Fred Crouch's earlier volume *Understanding Barbel*. Fred does something rather unique in angling literature and that is to relate the barbel's behaviour to that of other creatures in nature. These exercises show how deeply Fred has studied wildlife and how little he takes anything for granted. The following investigation into the life of the owl is typical.

Most people gather at least a basic knowledge of nature. The majority would have learned that the owl's feather and wing structure enable it to fly silently. They would also have learned that this benefits the owl by allowing it to approach its prey without being heard. You probably just accept this very valid point without further consideration. It is quite understandable, after all every book you have read on the subject would have reinforced your view. I didn't settle for that, not because I did not believe it, I needed to know if there were any further implications.

Here is a clue. If you stood next to a noisy machine and called to someone thirty yards away they would hear you clearly. If they called back you wouldn't hear a thing they said.

Look at a picture of a long-eared owl and you would be forgiven for thinking that the tufts of feathers on top of its head indicated the position of the ears. It is of course untrue and all owls have their ears situated adjacent to their eyes, so cleverly placed that the owl enjoys the added but vital asset of stereophonic hearing. When night falls and the owl's vision decreases it can not only determine the exact direction of a sound but the precise distance. So necessary is their acute hearing that any sound that might impede it would be an intolerable handicap. Any noise caused by their wings would so interfere with their own hearing that the detection of the barely audible sounds made by mice, voles etc would be impossible.

Roach fully deserve a chapter on their own. They are not large fish and do not fight hard, but they are beautiful, wary and have over the decades been Britain's most popular coarse fish. If anyone should doubt the importance of roach I need only quote Captain Parker from the 1940s:

In future, take much more care and pains, both in the use and the preparation of your ground bait. It is the very essence and secret of success, and success in roach fishing demands it, for your creel becomes heavier, you become happy, and you die happy because a 2-pounder hangs up on the wall.

A young Bailey and a fish to treasure

The importance of the 2lb roach cannot be overestimated. For every man who fishes coarse waters in this country the 2lb fish has been a fish of a lifetime. It is still the case today at the end of the 1980s when in many ways the specialist world has gone mad for big and yet bigger fish. Here I quote from a recent article by Chris Tabbron:

. . . despite the fact that carp, tench and bream, in particular, have grown in recent times causing the old targets for which the average specimen hunter realistically set his sights to become obsolete, the humble roach at least seems to have retained a quiet dignity making a 2-pounder still the weight most of us want to beat. A 2 pound roach is a big fish, much bigger than many anglers credit . . . To catch a 2 pound roach whilst actually fishing for roach is the pinnacle of success.

In 1988, Owen Wentworth died. He was the most charming, generous roach man imaginable. I do not say, along with Captain Parker, that he died happy because he had caught 2lb roach, but I do know how happy he was shortly before the sad day of his death. His lifetime ambition had been achieved. After the capture of hundreds of 2lb roach, Owen finally landed his first long-sought-for three-pounder. I remember I sent him a letter of congratulation and I have his lovely reply to this day.

Dear John

Many thanks for your letter of congratulations. You, of all people, know how marvellous a three pound roach is and you will therefore know exactly how I felt the day of the capture. Words just cannot explain it. It has been a long time coming, that fish, and I'll treasure the memory the rest of my life.

Kindest regards,

Owen.

Owen was a true roach man. Born in Wimborne with his feet quite literally in the Stour and the Allen, one of its tributary streams, he grew up with roach and never once looked like growing out of them. His catches became legendary from the 1940s onwards. As a young boy in the north, I worshipped him when his catches seemed to me beyond comprehension: huge bags, huge fish from exciting, weed-curling chalk rivers contrasted sharply with my gloomy canals and occasional 4oz fish. Another man also was making a name on these Wessex rivers – Gerry Swanton. Between them the two have kept alive the great tradition of Wessex roaching that stretches back well into the nineteenth century. Over a hundred years of experience was built up between the two of them and the day I met them in the summer of 1986 I realised the vast storehouse of knowledge they possessed.

Scrapbooks, photograph albums and diaries and never-ending memories flooded through our talk together. Atmospheric changes, water temperatures, float designs, ground bait recipes, swim choice, roach behaviour – there was little or nothing that the pair had not investigated over their years on the banks of the Avon and the Stour. So much of what they said I could instantly agree with – nowhere more so than with their choice of bread flake as a primary big roach bait. Neither Gerry nor Owen would budge from their belief in float fishing as the most efficient roach catching method, even though I myself have found on the River Wensum in Norfolk that ledgering consistently produces a bigger fish. Even though we were talking about the same species, our deep wells of experience led us into friendly conflict. 'Expert' seems to be a term to be used carefully, even with the single species. The great angler bears in mind that very frequently the longer he fishes the less he knows for certain.

Roach fishing, of course, goes back beyond these two fine men. Grenville, Faddist, Gordonian, Captain Parker and the Trent Otter all wrote in-depth descriptions of river roaching. Their large floats, silk lines, 12ft rods and whirling centre pin reels I would love to have seen in glorious action. All the men liked to fish from punts, filling the holds with their catches, some of which were prodigious. Parker himself landed 162 fish of over 2lb in weight during his lifetime and probably thousands of roach over the pound. The rivers of those days seem to have been headily prolific and a blank day even in the coldest of winter weather, Parker's diaries make clear, was rare.

Such was not the case when I found myself at the beginning of the 1970s in East Anglia, fishing the Rivers Wensum, Bure, Yare and Waveney. Disease in the 1960s had decimated the numbers of roach on these rivers but a bonanza of large fish survived. A successful angler in a situation like this fishes desperately hard and improves his techniques and understanding as he goes, and that is how my own roaching developed in 1970–85. For long periods, I fished seven nights a week with frequent dawn sessions included. I fished on my wedding night even. I felt guilty if I were not on a riverbank somewhere; roaching was just the breath of life to me in those days.

To some extent, I made advances in my methods and my knowledge of roach. I proved to my own satisfaction that the very biggest roach preferred to take a static bait. As a result I worked on my ledgering techniques and brought them to a state of near perfection. I also came to believe that dawn, but to a far greater extent dusk and true night, are the times when the biggest roach feed. Therefore I fished on ever later, finding that on the very coldest of nights a feeding spell might begin as late as 10pm and continue to well after midnight. Over years of constant observation, I discovered where the roach shoaled at certain times of the year before spawning and how the change of the seasons affected their movements in and out of certain swims and areas.

All this knowledge, all this effort, produced sensational results. If records mean anything, it is probable that my roach tally is unsurpassed. Over four hundred 2lb roach and five fish from 3lb to 3lb 10oz is a great haul, yet I would never claim to be an exceptional roach angler. I was dedicated in my attitude, professional in my approach and the fish could not but have come to my rod. Yes, I may have handled more big roach than any living angler and I may know a great deal about them but any competent, very keen man could have done as much. Perhaps in this I am an object lesson; records by themselves do not necessarily indicate any exceptional fishing skill. There is more to the great angler than a list of catches alone.

OPPOSITE:
Bailey with a 3lb 5oz roach . . . a disciple of the greats, Wentworth, Swanton, Wilfred Cutting and, of course, Bill Penney, the man who caught over two hundred 2-pounders and two of 3lb 14oz (the long-time record) and 3lb 1oz in one day

In my favour, I think I realised this during those heady days and always gave the prime credit for my catches to the rivers themselves. And how I loved them – the Wensum in particular. To some, the East Anglian rivers may look bleak but to one who knows them so intimately they are nothing but lonely beauty. Their decline over the past decade I cannot forgive. Agriculture, industry, development and the inland drainage boards have all combined to destroy by nitrate infiltration, pollution, abstraction and dredging the great roaching I once knew. I fear it will never fully return and I suspect that my so-called records will long stand.

The chub is a true river species and one which has inspired great affection for centuries. Chub have been written about, praised and generally held up as a good river-type chum who will make a round mouth and oblige in any season, in any level of river, to any type of bait and to every way of fishing it.

Now as in the past, a big chub is a very difficult fish to catch for two reasons. Firstly they have always been rare, and secondly, at a size of over 5lb 8oz, they are very cunning beasts indeed. I knew one once, partially white and dubbed Moby Dick, that was at least 6lb in weight and flaunted himself happily to all. However, to put a hook in him seemed to be all but impossible. He was in fact a typical big chub and as wise a fish as one could ever meet.

Just once did I deceive him – unfairly really, by using the thinnest of lines and smallest of hooks. I now realised a third reason that big chub are so hard to land; they are powerful. Moby just went. Scalded. Fearful and unstoppable. As I reeled in a fluttering line at least I could remember that other great chubbers had witnessed the same thing in the past.

In 1928 A. Courtney Williams wrote

. . . a Londoner was fishing just above me at Christchurch when his float literally whipped out of sight when he was least expecting any movement. The fish dashed across the river ripping out 40 yards of the line as it went, and was back under the angler's feet in less time than it takes a tail. Frantic recovery of the loose line followed, and not a little joy, also, when it was found that the fish was still hooked . . .

The rod, of built cane and steel at that, was bent well nigh double. Once again the reel screeched as the fish made off down the stream . . . Out of the pool and round a sharp bend in which the water was fast and shallow, and then into a long, and deep glide, went the man and fish – a distance of perhaps 150 yards. The angler . . . began to feel pleased with himself, for in this open water there was every probability of killing his fish. He wanted to very much, for it was the last day of his holiday, and so far the number and size of the fish he had grassed would have caused merriment amongst his friends! The only cloud in the sky was that after a quarter of an hour the rod was still bent and the fish had not tired; at any rate, not to the extent that any self respecting chub should do.

. . . Half an hour passed and he was a man who was growing tired, the fish being as fresh as ever. Just about that time, to make matters worse, the line became buried under a large bed of submerged weeds, the angler being on one side, and the fish on the other. It appeared to be a question of stalemate, for after another 15 minutes had passed by there was no change in their respective positions . . .

Having watched this protracted struggle from a distance. . . I left my own rod in order to see if I could offer any help to a brother angler who was obviously in difficulties. On arriving at the scene of the action . . . the fish was frequently coming up to the surface. What a fish too! Seven or eight pounds was my estimate, and it was a beautiful specimen, hooked right through the dorsal fin! Here of course lay the explanation of the long fight . . .

The council of war followed and all sorts of schemes were discussed. Giving the chub extra line in the hope that it might free itself from the weeds nearly provoked disasters. Gently pulling the fish downstream caused him to struggle violently and gave us some altogether too exciting and anxious moments . . . The only hope seemed to be to wade out and net the monster . . . It was a desperate case . . . so off came my boots, my socks, my coat and my waistcoat – and then the chub decided to take a part in the final act. One slight kick – and the frail hold on the fin gave way. The man from London town was left holding on like grim death to half a ton of weeds before he could be persuaded that the terrible thing had really happened.

The Trent Otter also witnessed a similar happening.

The water eddied round the willow, and flowed towards a thick bed of weeds that seemed to project from the old tree itself. The whole stream was not 6 feet wide. My friend the postman dropped one or two of his insects down and presently one of the largest chub I ever saw came out from cover. It was quite 7 pounds in weight and looked in magnificent condition. The postman was on his mettle and he alternated his hooked beetle with loose ones; but the one that had a hook in it was left severely alone. At last, on my whispered suggestion, when the fish refused it, he lifted it from the water and dropped it behind him close to his tail. I don't think I ever saw a chub take a bait quicker; he wheeled round in a moment, and had it like a flash. The rest of the adventure can be described in a few words. On feeling the steel, the chub made a headlong rush into the weeds below and half the tackle only came back the next moment; the water was ridged as though a steam plough had been driven beneath it.

Truly serious chubbing probably began with Martin and his friends, and again we witness the importance of geography. The Trent and the nearby Great Ouse were fabulous chub rivers and produced a near eight to Martin himself and great bags to him and his colleagues. He records twenty fish for 88lb and forty-two fish from 1 to 4lb 12oz and to his friend Coxon once forty-four fish in a few hours averaging 1lb 8oz apiece. These fish were '. . . arranged still alive and kicking on four square tables at the Crown Inn and were given away to anyone that cared to beg them.'

Into the twentieth century the Avon system takes up the challenge from the declining, polluted Trent and Midland rivers. Again it is Captain Parker who leads the way. He invents an underwater telescope with which he researches the Thames. There he finds that things white attract chub and therefore begins to incorporate crushed eggshells into his ground bait.

So get your good lady to save them and dry them off in the oven. She may, of course, say a few kind words, but anglers don't care. Collect a good quantity and put them in a sack and stamp on them; now shake the sack up and stamp on them again and they will soon be in very small particles and ready for use as required. Mix 2 or 3 very large handfuls with your ground bait and throw in liberally at first to form a sort of carpet over which your hook bait will travel.

The captain was succeeded on the Avon by one of the great chubbers, Bill Warren, longtime holder of the chub record and captor of numerous six-pounders and scores of over 5lb. Warren haunted the river, built up a deserved reputation and became a guru to many who flocked to the great man on the great river. One of Warren's disciples was the young Peter Stone who himself developed into one of the most successful chub anglers of the sixties and seventies. Peter learned his skills on all the southern rivers and then fished with Walker and the Taylors on the Upper Ouse. As a result he gained vast experience of different river types and different methods and soon became a great and generous teacher in books and articles for over twenty years.

The 1980s have seen four real chub experts. John Etherington is one, a vastly bearded, low-profile angler whose detailed approach and meticulous takings of water and air temperatures first appeared in print in his book *Fishing for Roach and Chub*. Trevor West and Tony Miles, like Peter Stone, have travelled the Midlands, East Anglia and the South to take vast numbers of 5lb plus fish. The pair, who have often teamed up together in the past, are proficient in every method and have at their fingertips a vast storehouse of chub knowledge. A great deal of this was put down in Tony's book *My Way with Chub*, published in the late 1980s.

We finally come to the last and possibly most underexposed of chub experts in history – Alan Rawden, the quiet lorry driver from the Midlands.

'Chub will often take flies as large as humming birds.' J. H. R. Bazley – *Coarse Fishing*
The mouth of Peter Stone's monster confirms this is still possible

Alan Rawden with one of his enormous 6lb chub

For many years he used to frequent the Wensum and would sleep in his car as the frost crackled down around him. Strength of character is not Alan's only gift for, as he says, 'I feel I have been bestowed with a gift of both spotting fish and finding fish. I do not want to sound big headed by making this statement but it is one of those things I am gifted with and I would be a liar if I denied it'. Numerous other anglers do catch chub at night and John Wilson promulgated the method in the 1970s, but it is true to say that Alan has developed the acceptability of night fishing for chub more than anybody else. He has made it clear also that extreme cold does not put the fish off.

Alan is a modest man and details of his chub record have yet to reach the angling press in full: only Bill Warren can claim parity. Alan has sent me his top chub list and it makes awe-inspiring reading. The top four are shattering: 6lb, 6lb 2oz, 6lb 4oz and a final devastating 6lb 14oz fish. As Alan says, '. . . as for my biggest chub of 6lb 14oz I feel that this is probably one of the biggest genuine river-caught chub since the last war.'

It is not possible to end this chapter on river fish without a mention of the trout; not the delicate trout of Halford or Skues that sit in spinners or nymphs, but the great old browns who have grown into old age and turned predator as their sizes increased. Legend often has it that such trout grown dark, lean and hook-jawed, are out of condition, are frequently blind and are approaching death. Such is sometimes the case with the oldest, most tired of fish, but it is rare in my experience. My own biggest brown river trout weighed 10lb 8oz and it was magnificent in shape and colour and it fought wildly. I have seen larger fish, equally majestic, that I have failed to land in England's lowland rivers, chasing fry in and around the tails of weirs. One man, Jimmy Sapey, for

A great river trout – from the Avon and caught by E. W. Gawthorne. The record barbel lies to the rear

years made these big river fish his objective and had great success with monsters in the 6–8lb region, all on minnow. I remember seeing photographs of these fish and every single one looked mint-fresh and beautiful.

The master river troutman of them all however must be A. E. Hobbs, the Henley man who made the Thames fish his lifework. For years he was a constant sight on the river, with his boatman, rods and baits, moving up and down the stretches that he knew so well. He always carried with him a diary, kept in his waistcoat pocket where he made notes of all his days on the river. He published these eventually, spanning the years 1890–1941. During that time he caught no fewer than 856 trout of over 3lb each. Ten of these were of an average weight of 9lb 12oz and exactly fifty weighed between 6 and 8lb 8oz. Importantly, nearly all the fish were taken in the open river and not from just below the weirs, as are most Thames trout. The book is an absorbing record of one man, one species, and one river. The knowledge of brown trout in the Thames is absolute.

Of course controversy followed him and his results. There were those at the time who criticised Hobbs. Remember that the 1930s were the peak of the dry fly versus nymph fishing debate and to use minnows and dace for trout on spinning flights seemed heresy to many. Practicality, though, is all-important and Hobbs realised it. Hobbs was after fish that were over 3lb and were totally disinclined at that weight to feed off insects. Courtney Williams sums up Hobb's career.

The magnitude of Mr Hobb's performance can perhaps be appreciated the better if one recollects that to most of us a 3-pounder represents a very big trout indeed. In fact there must be many hundreds of trout fishermen who have never killed even one trout of that weight in their lives; for one man to get well over 800 is a remarkable feat!

CHAPTER 7
THE GUARDIANS
OF THE STREAM

*A*s I look from the window of the train my heart aches, for there below me I see acres and acres of watercress beds, laid out with a ghastly precision between long lines of concrete walls, like some nightmare sewage farm, with only the remnant of the lagoon to tell me that here I once had sport fit for kings; and the solitary pollard tree, sole survivor of the creek of old days, standing like a sentinel to mark the spot where on August 31st 1903 the little Bourne and the little iron blue and I made merriest of all.

Plunket Greene

PHOTO:
'That man is richest whose pleasures are cheapest.' THOREAU

*I*t is one thing to catch fish successfully but it is another and a far greater thing to fight successfully for the waters and for the fish themselves. At no other time in history has the environment come under so much pressure and the very existence of fishing in this country hangs by a thread. Since the Industrial Revolution, inroads have been made on our green and pleasant land and in the nineteenth and early twentieth century far-sighted anglers responded by supporting the Mundella Act and the Clean Rivers Act and by forming the Pure Rivers Society. Francis Francis, Hugh Tempest Sheringham and William Senior are three important angling editors who believed strongly in clean water and the wellbeing of all fish species; since then, dangers have intensified. Those men who have taken their places at local, national and even international levels, deserve every measure of support and merit every epithet of greatness. It is a crying shame that the Anglers' Co-operative Association (ACA) is not supported by every angler in the United Kingdom, adult or juvenile. Subscriptions of £5 and £1 per year respectively are a pittance set beside the work done by the association for the sport that so many are supposed to love. Money spent on timeshare salmon rivers, on weeks in sporting hotels or on matching carbon rods would all come to naught without the ACA and yet cost many times over the meagre association joining fee.

The history of the ACA is heroic. In 1948 John Eastwood, KC, persuaded a few friends that using the common law would be a far more effective way of fighting water pollution than parliamentary laws could ever provide. His singleminded enthusiasm and persistence were responsible in that year for the formation of the ACA. John Eastwood's primary task was to persuade anglers to support his idea that if all of them paid a little, it would enable the ACA to use the common law to turn back the tide of pollution that was threatening so many rivers. As a King's Counsel himself he well knew the residual strength of the common law. But he also knew that if the association went into court with a carelessly prepared case it would lead to collapse and financial ruin.

Take the Gade case for instance. The Gade is a small Hertfordshire river which rises on the county's western border, then flows some 16 miles to join the River Colne near Rickmansworth. It holds both trout and coarse fish. At least, it does now! In 1930–50 the river was continually polluted, and although statutory proceedings were taken against the polluters the Watford bench refused to convict. At the time the ACA decided to take action, the pollution had turned the water brown, opaque, frothy and stinking. No anglers went near it, but its waters seriously affected the fishing on the Colne and the canal near Rickmansworth. On 1 May 1952, the action began.

The hearing was expected to take three weeks, which meant that the entire resources of the ACA were committed to the case. Defeat would have meant bankruptcy. It is easy to imagine the anxiety of the ACA's committee and council members that day, and easy to envisage their stunned surprise at the result, because the case was finished in hours. Halfway through the opening speech by the ACA's counsel Mr G. R. Upjohn KC, the case was stopped. Stopped because the defendants decided they would no longer defend the action. They submitted to the injunction demanded, and agreed to pay all damages and costs. It was by no means the only legal case the ACA was involved in at that time nearly forty years ago, but it certainly enthused its members with the confidence in the common law rights against polluters that has led to the description of the ACA's actions as 'the most successful war ever waged against pollution by any voluntary body in the world.'

Stratton Gerrish, the ACA's first brilliant solicitor who died in 1970, wrote at about that time,

> *. . . there is a section of industry which takes a view that rivers should be regarded simply and solely as public conveniences and should be subject only to the jurisdiction of the river boards; in their view, providing they can persuade the river board to allow them to discharge their effluent into the river nobody else should be entitled to stop them however much damage their effluent may do.*

The debt owed by the ACA to Stratton Gerrish was immeasurable. For nearly twenty years he steered its legal activities not merely through a succession of High Court and Appeal Court victories, because it was he who assembled and presented the evidence for council use, but also presented sound evidence to parliamentary committees concerned with no fewer than five major acts. When he died of cancer after a long illness, his absence halted the ACA's legal activities. There was an interregnum, so to speak, while various solicitors strove to cope with the stream of legal cases. The association was fortunate when Jansons appointed Simon Jackson as solicitor for its legal cases. His success for the ACA was immediate and continues to this day.

The ACA has had many successful chairmen and one of them was Dermot Wilson, son of the previous chairman Major General T. N. F. Wilson. Dermot Wilson was faced with several tasks, chief of which was the parliamentary threat to erode some of the common law rights of clean water. His appeal to members to write to their MPs was so successful that it brought the rueful comment from one minister 'It's as if we proposed to revoke Magna Carta!'

ACA's successes over the years attracted wide support and the list of fundraisers is formidable. Possibly chief of these must be Walker's of Trowell, the famous tackle shop. Mr John Walker is now a vice-president. Using the wide resources of Walker's, John promoted a series of anglers' evenings at Nottingham's Festival Inn that raised some thousands of pounds for the funds. Pike matches around the country have also been successful promotions. Final matches, supported and organised by *Angling Times,* with scores of qualifying matches organised by the ACA, have become record fundraisers. One of the best known supporters of the ACA was Richard Walker. In 1985, when he died of cancer, the association lost one of its most firm and generous supporters. The popularity of Richard Walker can be gauged by the fact that the response to the request he made before his death that donations should be sent to the ACA instead of flowers raised an astonishing £2000.

These are just a few of the heroes of the ACA's inspirational story. Today the director of the ACA is Allen Edwards. He is highly competent and highly conscientious and his appearance at tackle shows and meetings all round the country has made him a respected and well known figure. His drive has motivated many anglers to join the ACA and membership now stands at over ten thousand. Of course this ten thousand is

Allen Edwards receives the Dick Walker memorial bust for services to angling from Bruno Broughton . . . Three men who have given their all to the preservation of the environment

nowhere near enough, as Allen Edwards is constantly repeating in his talks around the country. Not until every angler is a member of the ACA will the future of our fishing be truly safe.

Equally important to the conservation of fishing in this country is the Salmon and Trout Association. The association was formed in 1903 to safeguard the salmon and trout fishers of the United Kingdom. Today, individual membership is over eleven thousand together with a hundred and fifty affiliated clubs and associations representing over a hundred thousand more. The association campaigns for the end of drift netting in England and Wales and for more equitable laws, to represent game fishers and their interests in parliament and at a local level. It is also active against industrial and agricultural pollution and the increasing demands for water abstraction. The association publishes an excellent quarterly magazine at present under the editorship of Dick Orton. Content shows a nice balance between articles to entertain and articles to instruct. Those to instruct are essential. They reveal the depth of scientific back-up to which the association has access. It is this type of knowledge that is essential if the Salmon and Trout Association, and others like it, are to combat polluters and the negligence of certain water authorities.

The association is split into forty-eight local branches which provide angling and other facilities for members. An excellent example is the Norfolk branch. In Norfolk there are several figures who have been outstanding in promoting the Salmon and

Trout Association and in providing fishing for hundreds of keen game anglers. Messrs Bramall, Temple Richards, Clarke and Robbins are examples of landowners, organisers and workers on the riverbank who have strained to produce the type of fishing that Norfolk members of the Salmon and Trout Association now enjoy. Their effort has been colossal and fishing is provided on three rivers and on a still water.

The Atlantic Salmon Trust battles just as hard. This charitable trust, whose patron is the Prince of Wales, aims to conserve wild Atlantic salmon for the good of the community and to present the true facts concerning salmon to the public and to government. The trust publishes progress reports twice a year which are sent out to subscribers, and it also holds workshops and conferences from time to time. The Atlantic Salmon Trust is another organisation that has total belief in facts. Like the Salmon and Trout Association, it combines science with passion to make its voice heard both loudly and with authority. Over the years the Atlantic Salmon Trust has been fortunate in having a line of distinguished chairmen, directors and council members. There are too many to mention individually but David Clarke, the retiring chairman, was the member picked out by his successor Sir David Nickson. Sir David writes:

David Clarke relaxing at home

David Clarke has had a lifetime's interest in angling and particularly in the Atlantic salmon. As chairman of the appeals committee he was instrumental in raising finance for the Atlantic Salmon Trust. He became chairman of this organisation in 1979 and it is largely due to his tireless efforts that the Atlantic Salmon Trust is regarded as the premier conservation organisation for the Atlantic salmon. He has an international reputation for funding research and publishing and distributing scientific information. During his period as chairman until he retired in 1988, David Clarke devoted an enormous amount of time and personal commitment to the Atlantic Salmon trust, travelling in Europe and North America, organising an international symposium at Biarritz, and keeping in constant touch with ministers, politicians and officials in the interest of salmon conservation. He gave an inspiring speech at the annual dinner of the Fly Fishers' Club – of which he is a member – in 1986 and is widely regarded as someone who has played an outstanding part in the interests of the Atlantic salmon over the past 10 years.

It is as well that there are men of dedication and commitment like this to fight for the Atlantic salmon because the list of problems still facing the species is enormous. At present there are eight schemes in England and Wales for barrages at river mouths.

One of the most serious is a proposed barrage on the Severn which will seriously affect runs of salmon up the Wye, the Severn and the Usk. Barrages alter tidal regimes, change the water turbidity, and because there is less flushing of water the water quality is bound to change. They also present a physical obstruction to migrating fish, not just salmon but also sea trout, shad, lampreys and eels. There is also little known about fish mortalities as they pass through the turbines placed on the barrages. Changes in forestry also present problems, particularly in Scotland. The massive growth of salmon fishfarming is of major concern as the threat of disease is ever-present. Acid rain continues to be a menace on all the salmon rivers in this country. Drift netting, legal and illegal, continues to play havoc with salmon stocks at sea as they return to their native rivers to spawn. When asked what the future problems were that the Atlantic Salmon Trust had to face David Clarke replied simply, 'Do you want it in a nutshell? Man's greed! That covers nearly bloody everything!'

Certainly there is a need to ration the number of salmon taken even on rod and line. One fish per rod per day ought to suffice and even that over a week's holiday could amount to more than is needed. Anglers are fishermen and not fishmongers. No arguments can gainsay moderation at this moment in time. Anglers' friends will have to do with a part of a fish instead of a half of one or a whole one. Fish that are a little black must go back into the river rather than into a smokehouse. The angling press still carries photographs and stories of mammoth bags of salmon taken and killed by anglers. These appalling evidences of slaughter must cease. When politicians see them they believe that the rivers are in no need of protection. They also ask why salmon should not be exploited at sea if they are to be exploited like this in their home rivers. And consider how morale-sapping such sights are for men like Sir David Nickson, David Clarke, Allen Edwards and the others. They spend their lifetime and energy fighting for the salmon only to see them cudgelled to death in vast numbers by greedy, so-called sportsmen.

Mike Tomkies is known as a naturalist who lives in isolation in the north of Scotland rather than as an angler. However in one of his books, *A Last Wild Place*, Tomkies does hook a salmon:

> *What right, I thought, have I to wrench this poor old fellow from his natural world? He put up a courageous fight for a longer life, beyond that of most of his kind, for a second chance. I let the rod tip down and watched him lying under the surface, gulping to recover more strength. I could see myself in this old fish and I knew I would let him go. I slid the gaff down the line after turning it round, inserted a gentle downward poke, plucked it out – Go on you old bugger.*

In the late 1980s the Thames Salmon Trust was established to help restore a substantial self-spawning population of salmon in the River Thames. The trust has identified three principal requirements. Firstly, to allow access to nursery areas, some of the obstacles man has put in the way must be overcome. A series of fish passes at weirs between Sunbury and Whitchurch will allow returning adults to reach spawning beds without difficulty. Secondly, because the truly natural population will take some years to get established, artificial support will be required. The trust will develop a

A time when big bags were not damaging

hatchery where the progeny of returning Thames salmon can be reared to augment natural breeding. And finally, to monitor progress against the target of one thousand fish per year, an accurate fish counting device will be required.

Launched at the start of the European Year of the Environment to capitalise on what has been called 'the achievement of a generation', the trust offers the opportunity to redress some of the damage man has done to the environment in the name of progress. It is probable that the Thames will never be a salmon river in the true sense of the word but the symbolic importance of the trust is great. The list of trustees shows just how environmentalists, politicians and media men have combined to make all this possible. Environmentalists like the Duke of Wellington and David Clarke have joined with politicians such as Sir Geoffrey Johnson Smith and Cranley Onslow and with men from the media like John Humphries to present a strong argument for conservation. More and more politicians like Roy Mason and Sir Hector Munroe in Scotland are joining the fight to preserve salmon. 'The salmon runs are a visible symbol of life, death and regeneration, plain for all to see and share . . . If there is ever a time when the salmon no longer returns, man will know he has failed again and moved one step nearer to his own final disappearance' (R. Haig Brown).

Coarse angling also fights for fish and for waterways. The National Federation of Anglers was founded in 1903 and is the biggest of Britain's angling organisations and

Graham Gamble stocks a prime
bream into Buss Creek

the national organisation for coarse fishermen. The aims of the federation are to promote measures for the improvement of the freshwater fisheries laws, to fight against water pollution, to safeguard anglers' rights and privileges, to develop common fishing waters and to deal with other matters concerning fisheries and angling in general.

NASA (National Association of Specialist Anglers) began life in 1965 as the National Association of Specimen Groups and changed its name in 1982. The aims of NASA are similar to those of the NFA but include the promotion of comradeship and the interchange of information between anglers, and also the important role of encouraging the young into angling and educating them to appreciate and respect fish and fisheries. During the 1980s NASA has won a great deal of respect, largely because of the hard work of such men as Bruno Broughton, Neville Fickling, Keith Barker and others. The association has proved itself very active in supporting campaigns all around the country.

Indeed the 1980s has seen a proliferation of actions by anglers in different localities against water authorities and against polluters. Campaigns for the Avon, Wensum and Derwent all proved that anglers do have the organisational ability to challenge major abuses of waterways. All three campaigns have had great successes in pushing water authorities into rethinking plans and into laying down new guidelines on water quality. The Save the Wensum campaign spawned yet another development. In the late 1980s the Norfolk Anglers Conservation Association was founded, largely due to the work of men like Chris Turnbull and Mike Davison. NACA works hard in Norfolk to liaise with conservation bodies and to provide a wise voice on all manner of water questions. It has recently acquired a stretch of the River Wensum where it will put into practice all kinds of progressive river management techniques in an attempt to bring back the decimated roach shoals of that water.

Again and again coarse fishermen around the country are using their initiative to try and benefit the environment. In 1980, in Suffolk, the late Peter Sherwood devised an imaginative plan to develop Buss Creek as a new fishery. Observing the growing popularity of angling and seeing how few the resources were in this area of Suffolk, Peter realised that the existing Southwold Society waters would not meet the demands of the late 1980s. A restoration project was set up which involved dredging to clear the overgrown reed of Buss Creek to provide an average depth of 4ft of open water. Now Buss Creek is a thriving fishery which provides sport for many local anglers and especially encourages youngsters to take up angling. The importance of such projects has now been seen by industry. Buss Creek was supported by Shell, by Adnams Brewery and by the Southwold Town Council itself.

Indeed, individuals are active at every level. John Sidley is a Midlander who has specialised in the fishing of eels. His own story is an interesting one.

On an August night in 1975 I was once again sitting on my chosen swim at Earlswood Lakes in Birmingham. A rod was baited with four lob worms and cast out near to a weed bed some thirty feet from the bank. By dawn I had landed my personal best eel weighing in then at 7 pounds and 1 ounce. Pictures were taken by the Anglers Mail *and I made a decision that was to change my whole life, to change the attitude most anglers have for the freshwater eel. That decision was to kill my 7 pound eel and to have it set up. I took it to the*

Eels have, traditionally, been victimised – even by Plunket Greene: 'I used to spear eels and asked my instructor how I could accelerate their end. He told me that the best way to kill them was to bite their tails. I tried it once and no more for it promptly turned round and bit me on the lip.'

Birmingham museum who were to put the fish in a case. A few months later the job was completed and I went to pick up my prize. I was told then by the people who had carried out the work that they had estimated the eel to be at least 68 years old. It was then that I swore that I would never kill another eel for the table or for a trophy and I pledged that I would do my utmost to win for the eel the protection it needed. My respect for that fish grew and grew when I researched its life cycle and I realised just what a remarkable fish it in fact was. As a result I originated the Put Eels Back campaign. I wrote letters to all the angling publications and out of my own pocket paid for thousands of car stickers to be distributed through their pages. After a while I received a flood of letters in support and I learnt that there were more anglers who really took an interest in the freshwater eel than had ever been realised before. From there in 1980, the British Eel Anglers Club was formed and now the membership has well over 600 anglers, some of whom live in Germany, Holland and Sweden. Just like the pike, the eel is now looked upon as a worthy opponent and a species that must be protected. I am very proud to say that because of my help, the eel is now being protected not just by today's anglers but by many of the water authorities. These water authorities have now realised that our eels are under threat because of overnetting by commercial trappers and byelaws are being brought in to control this activity.

The point has been made that without expert knowledge all these organisations would founder. It is vitally important that they have reliable scientific statistics at their disposal when it comes to court cases and to challenging water authorities or polluters. This is the reason why the Freshwater Biological Association is so important. The FBA has been researching the ecology and biology of freshwater organisms worldwide since 1929. It advises angling clubs on the practical management of reservoirs, lakes and rivers. Its library is probably the finest in the world for freshwater biology and is a constant source of reference for all conservation organisations. The love of fishing leads men in different ways. Some decide to write like Haig Brown or J. W. Hills. In some it leads to invention, like Illingworth or Coxon. With some, the love of angling leads to the desire to paint like Russell or Armstrong. In yet others, the love of fish leads them into a desire to investigate them for themselves. Most if not all great fishing naturalists have fished. Scientific enquiry happened to be their particular bent. Fishing naturalists have helped angling infinitely and have profoundly changed our sport.

This country has always had a background of monastic stew-ponds but true fishery knowledge really began in 1713 when Roger North published his discourse on fish and fish-ponds. His work was taken up by Ebenezer Albin who added plates to the original North book. The work stimulated interest in fisheries and it coincided with the estate lake boom from the 1740s onwards. Because of North's work the lakes were stocked with fish and different species were transported from different parts of the country. In 1836 Yarrel published a history of British fisheries and pushed the art of fish biology still further. Yarrel was an amateur and by profession a newsagent at St James' in London. His book was excellent for the time, and part of a whole natural history series. Yarrel knew the fish as a fisherman and put tremendous care and love into the plates and descriptions. Indeed so time-consuming was Yarrel's love for fish that he let his business decline. Yarrel was a bachelor, gave his life to natural history and really was the inspiration to the burgeoning Victorian fascination with fish biology.

Nineteenth-century fishing research developed quickly

In the 1880s Francis Day, a surgeon, published *The Fisheries of Great Britain and Ireland*. His professional approach was mirrored in the standard of his work which provoked great debate and controversy. In 1887 James Maitland published a history of the Howie Town fish hatchery which produced salmon and trout for rivers. This book was the inspiration behind vast stocking programmes around the world. The work of Maitland combined with the development of trains, with steam ships and with refrigeration to allow trout eggs to be taken to India and to New Zealand. These projects benefitted fishing not only in this country but the world over.

Probably the greatest name in the nineteenth-century world of fish biology was that of Frank Buckland. In 1873 he published his familiar *History of the British Fishes* which was expanded greatly in 1883. He was a popular writer who contributed frequently to *The Field* before setting up his rival magazine *Gleanings from Natural History*. Buckland was a populariser of fish, and adopted the work of Maitland and spread it to other species. He became heavily involved in restocking programmes and tried to bring the Austrian salmon, the huchen, to the Thames. Buckland was the first Inspector of Fisheries in the British Isles and as such the first public official to be involved with angling. His vitality spread into every sphere of fish and angling.

The story goes that he was taking home a sturgeon from Billingsgate to be stuffed. As he was carrying it into his house, he lost control of the fish which slid straight down the stairs, crashed through the doors into the kitchen and so terrified his cook that she passed out on the table. Yet, Buckland's life was scarred by domestic tragedy. As a result of an amorous liaison he was forced into marrying a chambermaid. The resulting son died at the age of three and for the rest of Buckland's life he had a wife uninterested in her work and one who was going to long outlive him. He felt shackled by her and did not even have the pleasure of raising his son. Equally sadly for posterity, much of the research work that Buckland did on the fishes at his disposal was in plaster and very little survives to this day. Furthermore, in his Will he set aside money for the Buckland Foundation and to provide a professorship in fisheries. However, the longevity of his widow led to a decline in the value of his money. It was not until later in the twentieth century that the post was properly started and even then it collapsed because of lack of funds. Buckland, however, remains a vital figure in the nineteenth-century interest in fish and fisheries. His name was constantly linked with preservation and he was a founder of the Thames Angling Preservation Society along with other giants of the day like Francis Francis.

Buckland was followed at the British Museum by the German expert Gunther and later by Tate Regan who took over the zoological department. Tate Regan had fished as a boy in Dorset and so, like Buckland, was a practising angler. In 1911 he published *The Freshwater Fishes of the British Isles* which is the first obviously modern history of fish. Regan died in the 1940s and is the clear link between Buckland and the fish biologists of today who do so much to help angling. In the 1960s Jack Jones organised the Liverpool coarse fish conferences which were eagerly attended by anglers' clubs and river boards. He was also an adviser to the newly set up British Record Fish Committee and it was he who looked at many of the record claims of the 1960s and 1970s. His position was taken by Alwyne Wheeler. Wheeler has brought home the importance of understanding fish and fisheries to all anglers and organisations. He is a courageous man who has no hesitation in standing up for what he believes is correct. This was demonstrated admirably in the case of the Whitehall record pike. The British Record Fish Committee hesitated before throwing the pike off the list but Wheeler forced the issue, threatening resignation unless this was done immediately.

Fishing biologists, committees, panels, scientific reports, magazines, and international conferences are all essential but must be harnessed to men actually on the waterside who will provide the sweat, tears and sometimes blood to put into effect the dictates from above. So in part, this chapter is in praise of hundreds of bailiffs who patrol salmon and sea trout rivers and estuaries at night, who risk bodily harm to preserve the fish that run in from the sea . . . also the keepers who have made the care of the rivers their life's work. Some of these men are professional, like Bernard Aldridge, Tom Williams and Frank Sawyer. One of the greatest was William Lunn.

William James Lunn was born in 1862 and in 1887 became keeper on the Test for the Houghton Club. Lunn was inspirational. He showed a knowledge of everything in the valley, of the water weeds, of the flowers, of the birds and of the fish. He was a born naturalist and even went as far as taming an eel and feeding it by hand for three and a half years. One of his gifts was a most acute observation and it was this that led to his discovery of flyboards. He realised that most small duns lay eggs on posts, on bridges or on reed stems where they are devastated by caddis larvae. However, Lunn realised, caddis cannot swim and hence the idea of floating boards was born. These are moored out in mid-river and therefore are immune to caddis attacks. A board that is impregnated with eggs can then be floated to restock barren areas of the river.

W. J. Lunn – the entymologist at work

It was this power of observation that Lunn used as a fisherman. His eyes never left the water and his mind and concentration never left the problems that he witnessed. He was continually changing flies until he found the right pattern and he hated mental or physical laziness in the anglers accompanying him. His eyesight was magnificent and allowed him into the world of the fish as nearly as a man can ever enter. When choosing flies he tried to put himself in the place of the trout and even improved on Halford's flies that look excellent from above the surface but less so from below. Lunn began to tie flies in 1916 and is remembered for forty patterns. Most famous are the Lunn's Particular – an imitation of an olive spinner – the Spent Gnat, the Houghton Ruby and the Hackle Caperer.

Dinner time at Houghton

Life at Stockbridge on the Test in 1887 was genteel and leisurely. There were no cars and little of the haste of the modern world. Lunn was an all-round fisherman and pursued grayling in the autumn and pike in the winter. He would use natural mayflies in their season and would spin at the weirs where he kept cans of live minnows for trout, perch and pike. Lunn's career spanned the crossover period between the up-and-downstream and wet fly debates. The whole style of fishing was changing and by the 1890s the modern school of dry fly fishing was well in vogue. Until 1914 however, the club still stuck to many of the old ways. For example Sunday fishing was forbidden, and in the meadow at Houghton a tent was erected within which at 6.30 the club dined before moving off to fish the evening rise. Lunn's career on the Test was a fine one and during it both the river and the fish improved immeasurably in quality. His family has continued the keepering tradition and, indeed, the Lunns and Stockbridge are woven together.

Michael Robbins – Robbie – now has time to fish his transformed River Bure

Amateur river keepers can have an equal impact on their waters. The work of Michael Robbins on the Upper River Bure is a case in point. I know now that I personally was lucky to be a part of his schemes. The phone would ring unfailingly, early morning, each and every Sunday of the winter and the spring. No matter what the weather, Robbie's eager, urgent tone would speak out: 'At the shed by 9am if you please. Wire cutters, yes! Oh yes, grand, a sledgehammer too if you have it.' That was all, and all it meant was a quick breakfast, a 20min drive and a walk through a bleakly dripping wood to the river. There a team of us worked until midday or sometimes, just occasionally, Robbie would call a halt by 11am if the weather was particularly foul. Lucky us. We could beat it off the river plain with the sleet gnashing at us and get back to a fire before all sense and feeling had quite gone. They were dire times, up to our waists in cold chalk stream water, hammering in the stakes that would support groynes, clearing the silt that would allow gravels to appear, planting the saplings that would bring shelter and food to future fish and eventually stocking the reborn river with brown trout.

All that happened around ten years ago and because of Robbie a great deal has taken place since. Today the beat is highly prized for its excellent brown trout that are again overwintering and breeding in what was once a moribund stream. Today there are mayfly hatches and great shells of bright green weed and lines of willow and alder

Whatever the weather, the gillie rowed on . . .

breaking out into new growth. The credit belongs to Robbie as the sergeant major, the visionary and the architect. Since those days Robbie has written a book on river management and possibly can no longer be classed as an amateur. It is an excellent book but for me the proof of his work will always be the Upper Bure where it twinkles, rejuvenated, over the heads of seemingly ever-feeding trout.

Of course, Robbie's work cannot be guaranteed for ever. Anglers must always be aware of future problems and be prepared to tackle afresh any invasion of the river. In the 1930s for example, A. C. Keith wrote a book *Trout Fishing in Norfolk* which described his work on a Wensum tributary. The things that he did half a century ago were very similar to the things that we helped Robbie do on the Bure. Yet over fifty years all Keith's work has been lost. The pools, the gravel, his trees and his weirs have all been destroyed by the work of the Inland Drainage Board.

To Charles Kingsley the river keeper was somebody to be held in some awe as '. . . the river God in coat of velveteen, elbow on knee and pipe in mouth.' Much the same can be said for the other men of the rivers, the gillies. Every game fisherman has his memories of a favourite gillie on a favourite beat, from a special week or so of life, and to mention them by name would mean a list impossibly long. The number of gillies today looks like rising again for, as bodies like the Atlantic Salmon Trust buy the nets off the rivers, the salmon runs strengthen, anglers increase and the one-time netsmen become smartly dressed gillies. On whom should these new gillies model themselves?

According to the late Terry Thomas it would be Bill Law, the man known as the best gillie in Scotland. Law combined many gifts. He was a great salmon and trout angler both. He was an exceptionally successful tournament caster. Thomas remembered him using a Mallock reel in the bait accuracy event at the Crystal Palace in 1935, changing the spool angle so quickly one could scarcely see what he was doing. A good gillie also knows the river and its flies and Law was a practical, first-class entomologist and a fly dresser who bred his own fowl for their hackles. Law also knew the river and its valley in all their various moods. Once, observing that a storm in the mountains was causing the river to rise, Law grabbed Thomas by the arm and ran him half a mile upstream where he had two salmon in the space of a few minutes.

Thomas saw in Bill Law the self-taught pragmatism that was possessed by William Lunn. Both, he said, went for the obvious. Law always wore army ammunition boots instead of canvas waders because on some of the stretches he fished they gave more ankle support, preventing strains or breaks. The relationship between Thomas and Law is very typical of that between many a salmon man and his gillie. As Thomas says,

Law knew me as a small boy. I shot my first rabbits with him – 'Shoot them in the lugs!', he said. I caught my first sea trout with him. But he did not pass on his wisdom easily. It took

---

OPPOSITE
Men of the waterside have always been appreciated by the true anglers who rub shoulders with them. H. T. Sheringham remembers: 'Old Billy has a face wrinkled like a winter apple yet he can paddle a heavy boat, lend a hand with the seine nets, can pull up his eel traps and carry a bucket full of fish as well as many a younger man.' *An Angler's Hours* (1905)

years and a World War, before, in a series of stages, I worked out his logical, obvious approach. Bill did not only keep his cards close to his chest; he kept them there for a long time.

This was Bill Law, just one of a brave line of gillies over the centuries. They are men of the waterside who know their rivers, their flies, their fish and all the natural world that surrounds them. They can be gruff and forbidding but beneath that they are kindly and often take young anglers firmly under their capacious wings. They are brave men who will see off poachers and support the good of their river come what may. There is quite a gulf between the president of the Atlantic Salmon Trust and a humble Scottish gillie on a far-flung river but both men are absolutely essential to the sport of angling in the British Isles, and both men make the greatest possible contribution to the sport that both so obviously love.

CHAPTER 8
THE FEMININE ANGLE

See how she makes the trembling angle shake
Touched by those hands that would make all men quake.
See how numerous fishes of the brook
(for now the armour of their scales
Nothing against her charms prevails)
Willingly hang themselves upon her hook.
See how they crowd and thronging wait
Greedy to catch the proffered bait;
In her more bright and smoother hands content
Rather to die, than live in their own watery element.

Edmund Waller

PHOTO:
'I am not ashamed to own that, although I have for many years enjoyed the higher excitement of trout and salmon fishing – I can find much pleasure in taking a young friend with me for a day's gudgeon fishing at Hampton.' T. C. Hofland (1839)

A little lady preparing, perhaps, for a future on the Tweed or Spey . . .

As I earlier explained, the first angler I ever knew was a lady angler, my grandmother. The fact that an old greying lady should walk me miles to pools and canals, explain floats, rods, reels, show me how to cast and hook on my worms meant a great deal to me then, just as the memory and the legacy of these acts of love do still. I imagine we made a quaint sight; a bowed, seventy-year-old lady and a toddler of three or four, hand in hand, our eyes staring at the water with the same passion and intensity, though one pair was bright and the other dimmed and faded. That her elderly eagerness was as keen as my youthful one I do not doubt; I remember well her horror at a particularly fine perch that broke free. I guessed it at a pound and she at three ounces. Whatever, I tell you, it was a whopper! When she was once ill, I took home a roach, alive, in a bucket to show her. She rallied. When I was ill, she told me tales of her fishing days, before World War I, with the grandfather I never knew. I recovered. Within the week we would be fishing again. I like to think our greatest triumph was when I won a club championship series of matches in 1960. She was bedridden by then so could not attend the dinner and see me carry off my prizes but the first thing I did on my return home was to lay the cups by her on the counterpane and fall into deep sleep amongst them all. I have had nearly a dozen fishing partners over thirty-five years but grandmother was the first, the best and the most beloved. From the first day I held the rod, it seemed to me that women anglers are very fine indeed.

7 October 1922: a date very important in the annals of British game fishing, for on that day a woman caught a 64lb salmon from the River Tay and set a record that has lasted for approaching 70 years.

Miss Georgina Ballantine was born, lived and died in a cottage only a good cast from the pool above Caputh Bridge, near Murthly, where she did battle with this huge fish. Her father had taught her to fish and, as registrar to the area and friend to the local landowner Sir Alexander Lyle, could introduce his daughter to excellent salmon beats.

It was a Saturday and late in the afternoon when Miss Ballantine began to fish with a small natural bait, a 2in dace, on her line. Darkness was pulling in. Indeed her father had just looked at his watch and said it was near time to leave when the salmon took hold. The time was 6.15pm.

For a while, the fish moved slowly downriver, tempting Mr Ballantine to land the boat to beach the fish ashore. Once on the bank, however, Miss Ballantine knew she had a fight on her hands. In a surging two hundred yard run the salmon went down through the Caputh Bridge, cutting her fingers as she gamely tried to slow the line down. Thank God the salmon passed through the nearside arch of the bridge and she was able to stumble after him along the shore.

It was nearly dark and the salmon continued its downriver journey, slower it is true, but still with such inexorable power that Mr Ballantine returned for the boat so that they could follow it – all night if need be!

By now, Miss Ballantine was calling the fish the 'Beast' and feeling the strain. She pleaded with her father to take the rod from her aching arms, but he refused. Always a believer in strict fishing disipline, he would force his daughter to complete the job.

At that stage, without the boat the fish would have been lost for it took off irresistibly to the other side of the river, towards an island a quarter of a mile downstream. All the Ballantines could do was to follow over the darkening Tay. They landed again on the island above the Burnbane Pool and though there was no light to see the salmon, by the arch in the rod and the angle of the line they knew it was close to them now.

Mr Ballantine felt along the line until he came to the swivel. He knew the length of the cast beneath, estimated the position of the fish, and took the risk to gaff the salmon unseen. His judgement was unerring. The time now was 8.20pm and the fight had been played out over half a mile of the River Tay.

The fish was only slightly pink along its flanks and still had traces of sea lice, so it was a true fresh run October giant and no stale spring fish.

So much is known to everyone but perhaps only women can understand the full significance of that snap of an Atlantic salmon's jaws. Men of course acknowledge Miss Ballantine's achievement but tend to pass it by, and even dismiss it as luck. Women, sensibly, know better; the capture was fated and was not luck in any way. Miss Ballantine hooked the fish, played it throughout and in every way deserved to land it. Moreover, the capture of that one salmon has meant that for by far the greater part of the twentieth century a woman has landed the biggest authenticated British freshwater fish. Every ounce of its 64lb frame speaks of glory, muscle and power – and it capitulated to a woman only a little larger than itself. To see a cast of the fish is a revelation. Stunning, awe-inspiring, use whatever expression you like, the fish is simply huge, with scales and fins such as you have never seen before.

There are many excellent women anglers, especially in the game world. Many of these ladies have been fortunate to have been born to or married into wealth and position and have exploited it in angling terms to the full. There are few better salmon anglers than Her Majesty the Queen Mother who over the years has caught many salmon with aplomb, but she is far from being alone. I quote Bill McEwan who in his book *Angling on Lomond* writes, 'In 1927, women's lib took hold and so did a 36 and a half pound salmon! A Mrs Leckie-Ewing, who fished out from Luss with her husband, an ex-army major, tolerated a fearsome gale off the north eastern lip of Inchfad and was duly rewarded with this sizeable prize.' In 1924, a Mrs Morrison took a fly-caught 51lb salmon on the Deveron. In 1923 Miss Doreen Davey took, by spinning, a fish of 59lb 8oz from the Wye. In 1924, Miss Radclyffe accounted for two fish of over 40lb in two days on the Tay. Both were caught on the fly. In 1935 Lady Joan Joicey, when spinning in the Tweed in February, killed twenty-six salmon and two sea trout during a single day's fishing. And again, in 1930, Mrs Barbara Williams caught two Wye salmon on consecutive days which weighed between them 86lb. Like Miss Ballantine, she too had a fishing father – a Mr Wyndham Smith who once took a brace of fish from the Wye within half an hour of each other which weighed a staggering 94lb. There cannot have been many double catches any greater within a single family.

Today there are other successful lady game anglers. I know that Grace Oglesby, the wife of well known Arthur, catches a good number of fish, as does her great friend from Norfolk, Shirley Deterding. Other notable ladies to add to this list are Mrs Hugh Blakeney and Frances Shand Kydd.

For several years I stayed at the Tilmouth Park Hotel on the Tweed and once I was

RECORD TAY SALMON
64 lbs.
Length 4ft. 6ins. Girth 28½ ins.
Caught on Glendelvine Water by Miss Ballantine
with "Malloch" Rod and Tackle.
7th October 1922.

The Lady and The Fish

Mrs Florence Miller, justly proud of another excellent salmon

LEFT:
Lovely fish: lovely lady. Shirley Deterding has fished successfully for years

fortunate enough to watch the owner of the hotel and estate, Lady David Burnett, cast for, hook and play a large salmon. My vantage point was from a cliff face twenty yards above the river and every action that was carried out beneath me was neat, precise and utterly controlled. The fact that Lady Burnett lost the fish at the net was simple misfortune and detracted nothing from her legend. Certainly the hallway of that famous and excellent hotel bears testimony to her skill in the past: the cast of an enormous salmon caught by Lady Burnett looks down on every visitor.

I have heard the secret of such ladies' successes explained away by their willingness to listen to the advice of their gillies and carry it out to the letter. It is argued that ladies are denied the experience that male anglers build up over a lifetime's fishing. As a result, it is suggested, they simply and sensibly use the props provided for them. Whatever the gillie says, the lady angler does and she is therefore sometimes more successful than the male angler who cares to go his own, rather pigheaded way. So runs this argument but I feel it is oversimplistic. It is male condescension all over again and it denies women any real place in the angling world.

At another extreme, I believe that research is being carried out to prove that women are better salmon anglers than men. This is being attributed to something in their genes, their vibrations, their pysche, their scent or something that finds a response in the salmon. It is being seriously suggested that in some way the salmon, the fresh run fish, relates or identifies in some strange fashion better with a female than with a male. I cannot pretend to understand this without seeing the argument in full and assessing the facts for myself. However, I do not dismiss it because I do know that women frequently make better game anglers than do men. Certainly when it comes to casting, for example, women have a natural rhythm and ability that frequently outstrips that of men.

The history of angling is full of great women casters. An excellent example from the early part of the century was the Honourable Mrs Cooper, the sister of Lord Glanusk, who proved to be an excellent salmon fly caster. On the Usk in the 1930s a Miss Mary Dawson was a disciple of the tackle shop owner and casting champion Lionel Sweet and proved herself successful at competitions. Also in the 1930s a Miss N. V. Tufnel, a Kennet fisherlady was the winner of several fly distance competitions. It seems that in the 1920s and 1930s when women did move to the casting arenas they frequently approached the distances achieved by men despite the obvious disadvantages of lesser natural strength and bodily muscle.

Anne Voss Bark is the owner of the Arundell Arms, the Westcountry fishing hotel. However, few people realise the storms that she has weathered to reach a position now that seems so assured and well established. Her problems began when her first husband, Gerald Fox Edwards, developed a lung complaint. Mrs Voss Bark says

We didn't know how many years Gerald could take of his present life so we made the big decision to leave London. I found the Arundell Arms in Lifton. The rivers were wild. Within a mile of the hotel they joined the Tamar, the frontier river to Cornwall. It was excellent for fishing there but the hotel pub was run down. Gerald had to work on in London at first, so I went down to start running the hotel; I knew nothing about hotels and I had never held a fishing rod.

Anne Voss Bark

Men seemed to come down and go off fishing together. If their wives came they were not expected to join them on the bank. They were not given a chance. I thought it might encourage the women if the hotel was more comfortable.

Eighteen months later Gerald retired to Devon and their second child was born. Soon after, when the struggle with the hotel, her husband's illness and two small children was beginning to seem over, Gerald died. Anne continues.

I knew it was coming but it's always a shock. Gerald died of a heart attack on my 45th birthday. The children had become so used to him at home with them all day he left a large empty space in their lives. I felt I could not uproot their home as well so I stayed on and told myself I'd just have to learn about water and fish.

Roy Buckingham, a Welsh open fly fishing champion, had joined us in 1969. He gave guests and me lessons. I remember exactly where I was standing when I caught my first trout. It was on a dry fly, a half pound brownie. Roy hit it on the head for me. The excitement remained in my blood.

Conrad Voss Bark, former BBC commentator and then parliamentary lobbyist for the public relations company Charles Barker, was a passionate fly fisherman. He'd stay at the hotel while looking for a retirement cottage. He wrote books on fishing, was 60, and looked forward to living in Devon. He came to Devon again and stayed at the hotel during his cottage hunt. Within the year we were married. He had four children. The youngest was 14 and the eldest was married. That Christmas the two families gathered. It all just worked. My daughter Jane would write essays at school talking about her five brothers and sisters.

On our three-day honeymoon in London, Conrad made a special lunch booking at the great and grand Fly Fishers' Club. Women were not allowed; there was a separate small room for us. The president, Sir Julian Paget, heard we were there. He had visited the Arundell Arms with his father when he was 12 for a memorable holiday while he learnt to fish. When he heard about Conrad and me, he, like everyone, was happy for us. The inevitable joke going around was – trust Conrad to marry the best 20 miles of trout water in Devon.

Now Anne's hotel is the model for angling hotels in this country. Its comfort is legendary and its fishing has improved over the years out of all recognition. Anne has made game fishing accessible and attractive not only to men but also to scores of women anglers who visit the waters year after year. Anne Voss Bark is a lady of boundless energy and intelligence. She is a local JP and a campaigner on all manner of countryside issues, like her friend Jean Howman, who is a council member for the Salmon and Trout Association. Thank goodness that Anne Voss Bark has recently been appointed one of the first ladies to the new Rivers Advisory Council that will hopefully safeguard our waters well into the next century.

Why there are few lady coarse anglers did mystify me, stupidly, for a while. With typical chauvinism, I put the fact down to the feminine dislike of maggots and worms, their sensitivity to the cold or their dislike of mud, slime and general discomfort. Then the penny dropped; the simple fact is that women work harder than men – perhaps not on a nine-to-five basis, but the home is a constant chore. A lady can go salmon fishing a few times – even twenty times a year – with her husband on holiday, but to accompany him once or twice a week for eight or fourteen hours a day every month of the season is something else. Whilst it has been long accepted that the husband, the male coarse angler, has Sunday at the very least by the waterside, it has rarely been possible for his wife to leave the children, ignore the mealtimes and desert the home on such a regular time-consuming basis. Should she work as well, then the problem is merely compounded. Never has it been accepted that the family woman has the right to time called her own. If a woman has made demands then the typical characterisation of her as a hairnetted harridan has come into play, 'Her indoors', 'Her at home'. Stereotyping of this sort has probably denied coarse angling to many a good lady practitioner.

The situation has been historically different for ladies of the upper-middle and upper classes. Through the nineteenth century and right until the mid-twentieth century at least more money, generally higher education, more leisure time, more freedom to travel and far greater help in the home have bestowed more freedoms on ladies of sufficiently independent spirit to seize them. Now, though, in the later twentieth century, we are witnessing a change, though a slow one, as is inevitable in the changing status of women. I was well aware from the 1970s that more ladies were seen on the pits,

'For beauty is never constant and continually she will present a new shape to delight your eyes.' Applin

ponds and rivers of southern England. Not a few of them began to take to match fishing in that period, many to pleasure fishing and some even to specialist angling. I think that the most successful of these latter was Maureen Clarke who formed such an admirable partnership with her well known husband, Arthur. From the mid-1970s to the early 1980s Maureen caught fish of every species. She fished throughout the winter. She camped by the waterside. She wrote in the angling press. She appeared at tackle shops, at angling meetings and in anglers' bars. She was a lovely lady who brought a rational influence to the more competitive ways of men. Her enthusiasm for the sport and her generosity for everybody's successes were important characteristics in a time when areas of the specialist angling scene were becoming increasingly petty, niggling and unpleasant. It took a lady to make a lot of so-called great male anglers see an element of sense. When Maureen's local river, the Wensum, came under threat from abstraction and pollution, she took a vital role behind the scenes, raising money, writing letters, making phone calls and arranging accommodation, often at her own house, for visiting fellow-fighters. She was a beacon of energy, optimism and intelligence.

I have used the past tense talking about Maureen only because at present she and Arthur are working on the Continent, where I hear they are still fishing and I know Maureen will still be catching big fish, developing her skills and generally championing the cause of the lady angler for the future.

CHAPTER 9
MATCH FISHING

*I*n an All-England match, nearly every section of the community seems to be represented. There are lawyers and accountants, school masters, and newspaper editors, side by side with miners, mill workers, cotton-spinners and others. Here they are all on equal terms. There is none of that stupid class-consciousness we read about in other places. They are all anglers, all sportsmen, and that is all that counts. A man who puts on side at a fishing match would soon be taught the folly of it.

Ernest Phillips *Float Fishing*

PHOTO:
Billy Lane, captain of the famous Coventry team, collects another trophy

Match fishing is generally seen as a branch of coarse fishing which began in the North and the Midlands during the later Victorian period. It was the result of many different social and economic trends. The 50 hour week was commonplace then amongst working men in the mills and the factories. The depression of the 1840s was behind and living standards improved in the 1850s and 1860s to allow a certain amount of spare money to be spent upon leisure. The working class men of the northern cities developed a desire for angling but the canals and rivers to which they had access were frequently polluted or could only produce small roach, gudgeon and other sprats of the coarse world. Clubs began to spring up in workshops and factories, in even the smaller towns. As a result, matches became natural. Small fish by themselves provided little inspiration but the chance to beat a fellow worker or neighbour was irresistible. It also ought to be remembered that these men had limited time for their fishing. Matches could be contained and were the ideal outlet for these urban anglers. Matches were also splendid social occasions, as an article from the *Fishing Gazette* in 1878 makes plain.

On Her Majesty's birthday ... the memorial fishing sweepstakes took place ... The affair was formulated at an old-fashioned public house, which I think was the Red Lion, in a village near Manchester. My friend, my brother and myself, eager for the fray, left the cotton city ... and arrived at the scene of action at about 2pm on a glorious afternoon, the sun threatening to bake us.

Indeed, my friend, Alfred Mills by name, and a very good 'Doctor' advised us to partake freely of the good country ale, saying that it could not possibly do us any harm and that it would keep us from becoming 'dried up'. His advice was followed conscientiously, and to all appearances, many others were adopting the same tactics, the house being alive with anglers taking their beer after the manner of a fish taking water.

Immediately in front of the house was a fixed flagstaff, decorated in the most gorgeous manner, with ribbons, hanging at intervals of a foot or so. The prizes! Ye Gods! What a sight! Hams, legs of mutton, tea and coffee pots, pewters, spoons, and whatnot. There was enough on that pole to make everyone's mouth water, and you could see the competitors licking their lips as they made their way to the house. None of your 'half pint of your ale' there; the style was 'here, lassie, give me a quart of ale.'

At about 3 o'clock, the one hundred and sixty anglers repaired to the back of the inn for the draw. The entrance fee was one shilling [5p], but one half of this amount was returned in beer or bread and cheese. The draw took about an hour, during which time, the motto seemed to be more ale!

After the pegging down business had been arranged, a move was made to the water, which consisted of a dirty little pool near to the house. It was so small that the competitors had to be divided into two lots, pegged down about three yards apart. It was difficult to cast, so close were the rods together, but what matter as long as you are happy?

The allotted time for fishing was an hour and a half, but before that period had elapsed, half the fishermen were fast asleep. The salubrious atmosphere, together with the 'home brew', had evidently worked the oracle, for all around the pool, one could see victims of slumber with their rods in the water, or on the bank. The fishing was brought to a conclusion by a gun shot. The total catch consisted of five very fine fish, of which one had fallen to my rod.

The heaviest, I think, was a dace of one and a quarter ounces, and the other four were small gudgeon. Mine which took fourth prize – a teapot – turned the scales at a fraction over a quarter of an ounce, or to be exact, quarter of an ounce plus two rabbit shot!

The second batch of competitors were rewarded by a catch of seven fish, all of which fell short of the one and a quarter ounces and it was thus the great angling sweepstakes ended.

After the prizes had been distributed we departed homewards, or at least that was our intention, but we did not get there until the next morning. My friend Mills must need 'wet' the teapot, so we visited the house of the well known Joe Sheppard. When inside the parlour, our amiable Mr Mills immediately challenged old Joe to fill the pot with whisky and promised that he would do the same. This challenge was accepted and the teapot was twice or thrice filled. And to wind up, cigars were smoked all round. Such is the true history of this great Lancashire angling sweepstakes.

Prizes in those early days of matchfishing were of mixed sort. A typical example of a prize list is that of the Barnsley Fitzwilliam Club which had a match in the year 1877. The first prize was 27 shillings (£1.35p), the second a mirror and the third 14 shillings

The weigh-in . . . always a serious moment

(70p). Then came a live pig, a sewing machine, a timepiece, a bottle of whisky, cricketers' boots, a canary and cage, a felt hat, a drinking flask, a bottle of rum and one of gin, a woollen shirt, a pair of ladies' boots, and a velvet smoking cap. Next to last was a rolling pin and the forty-sixth prize was a calf's head!

When I began match fishing in the North West in the 1950s things were not too different. The coach would grind out of Stockport at 6am and the whole crew would be made up of factory workers sitting on crates of Guinness or brown ale. Most, by the time the Trent or other rivers were reached, were far too 'gone' to think of fishing and spent the whole day stretched out in a meadow. Prizes were frequently of the domestic sort and many times they were more in number than the fish actually caught, and had to be distributed by lot. It was only in the 1960s when my match fishing career began to flourish, very briefly, that I saw more of the modern side of match angling. Once I moved from my homely little club into the world of open matches I found a very different situation indeed. It was during the early to mid-sixties that my admiration for match anglers grew. Now, I doubt whether any other branch of sport is more highly developed and the skills of the modern match anglers are phenomenal.

My hero in the late fifties and through the sixties was Billy Lane, the father in many ways of modern match angling. He was from Coventry where he had a tackle shop and developed, almost from scratch, modern float fishing. Billy Lane destroyed the myths of the 'old' fine and far-off approach, where the heaviest float considered possible was a light crow quill. Billy Lane began to use battleships of floats to present the bait correctly. A heavily weighted float overcomes a wind, a drag and a current far better than the light floats that match anglers were then in the habit of using. Billy Lane won the world match championship in 1963 and went on to become the most famous match angler of his era. He became a father-figure to any number of young and aspiring anglers and even in his later days wrote a column in *Coarse Angler* where 'Uncle Bill' would answer questions from youngsters nationwide. Though his skills were most recognised in the match sphere, Billy Lane was also an accomplished big fish angler and even pursued salmon on the rivers of Wales and Scotland, catching a thirty-six-and-a-half-pounder from the River Wye.

Benny Ashurst is the second of the modern giants of the match angling scene. To no man would the phrase 'true northern grit' better apply. He was a miner for a quarter of a century and a serious leg injury once kept him in hospital for eight months. During that time he planned his return to the match scene and, heavily encased in plaster was half carried to Fir Tree Flash at Leigh. He fished a match there barely able to sit upright, propped against his basket, but he still won. He experienced a horrific car crash in 1951 when he broke a wrist, his leg was snapped around the knee and he suffered severe head injuries. As he was being dragged from the wreckage, his first words were 'I'll never fish again'. Yet, Benny did live and only two months later, fishing one-handed, was placed fourth in a match where there were five hundred competitors.

Benny was brought up in the hard school of the North before and after the war. There was little money at that time and there were restrictions on the amount of ground bait that could be used during rationing. Tackle was of the poorest quality, especially the lines. There was little or no petrol for pleasure travel and matches had to be fished in the immediate locality. This type of background bred a desire to succeed and a passion

Dan Leary holds one of the largest ever English pike – 39lb 8oz (John Wilson)

Uncle Bill – how sadly missed . . .

OPPOSITE
Tim Paisley with a wondrous common carp (Tim Paisley)

to win. Benny began to look at match angling in a new light and analysed its failures and successes. He moved towards the use of the stick float, employing a buoyant balsa tip and heavy tonkin cane stem that settled fast and registered bites from shy fish as the bait was falling. Also he experimented with two-piece peacock quill floats to counteract the drift on the canals when his bait was on the bottom. Both these float developments revolutionised match fishing in the North and soon began to spread throughout the Midlands.

Benny was a great bait man and was brought up in Leigh where men knew all about the maggot types – pinkies, gossers, squats and anattos. These men could tell good flies from bad and knew exactly upon which meats to feed the maggots. Benny became a bait breeder in part so his bait would be supreme. His maggots were famous throughout the North West but his name became known for the development of the sinking chrysalid – better known as the caster. This was a massive breakthrough in match fishing bait and he experimented from 1953 onwards. By 1956 Benny Ashurst was sweeping the Lancashire canal scene and the River Weaver with his new bait. By the 1960s the caster was the most commonly used match bait and every modern match man must know how to use it effectively.

And, of course, Benny is father to Kevin – the greatest all-round match angler in the world. He is recognised as such by that shrewdest of judges Colin Dyson who said 'If I had to elect somebody to fish for my life, I would undoubtedly choose Kevin Ashurst.' Kevin has also effected a revolution, as his father did. From infancy, Kevin was brought up to think deeply about angling. Father and son became a famous team in the 1950s and 1960s. In 1969, Benny captained Stoke City AA to the national championship on the Trent. Kevin took the team's highest weight and was therefore chosen to represent Stoke in the 1970 world championship team. The match was fished on a Dutch canal and the English team fished typical British rod and line tactics. The team was annihilated in a match dominated by Continental pole and bloodworm tactics. Kevin himself came in forty-seventh out of sixty with five fish that weighed together less than a pound.

He felt humiliated initially, but as the devastation cleared from his mind a new determination crept in. Moving totally against the current trends of thought, he decided to master the pole and set out on a colossal course of self-tuition on the canals of the North West. In 1972, Kevin was again selected for England in the world championship in Czechoslovakia. The river here was ideally suited to English methods but the team was pushed into second place behind the French one, all of whose members were using the pole. The lesson could not have been clearer and Kevin's learning curve was upped even further in 1973 when the Belgian and French pole men beat English rod and lines into third place.

In 1974 England for the first time tackled the world championships on the pole. The team came in sixth but the die had been cast and the match pushed Kevin personally into the final stage of his development as a leading world pole angler. It was in this

OPPOSITE
Two Greats. 'There's nowt like a few bream to cheer you up,' says Fred Foster as he poses with his old friend, Benny Ashurst of Leigh

Kevin . . . World Champion. The Irish
look every bit as happy as Ashurst himself

match that he analysed minutely the French pole tackle. He modified it slightly for English waters and now he began to win matches on canals and rivers in the North and Midlands. Between 1974 and 1978, Kevin's successes reached the consciousness of thousands and by the turn of the decade the pole had become a firm part of the English match fishing scene. Even if Kevin hadn't been solely responsible for the pole movement, there can be little doubt that he directed it, masterminded it and endowed it with his personal charisma. It is so fitting that the first Englishman to become world champion using the pole was Kevin himself, in 1982, on the Newry in Northern Ireland.

Kevin's achievement should not be underrated. He gave match fishing the essential push to move towards the pole. This added a dimension domestically and made England far more competitive abroad. Kevin was fortunate in being the son of a decided 'gent' and of being taken immediately into the heart of the northern club scene, but he made the most of his advantages and lessons. He felt a great deal of doubt and faced a great deal of criticism and loneliness along the way of the pole, but he was proved right, he came through and is a deserved legend in his own lifetime today.

I consider myself fortunate to have heard Ivan Marks talk at two meetings and, even more vitally, to have seen him fish one misty morning nearly twenty-five years ago on the River Wensum. On each occasion I have appreciated the genius that radiates from this happy-go-lucky, impish man. His contribution is not immediately easy to set down. He has not personally masterminded changes in tackle or technique in the way of the Ashursts or Lanes. His success rather lies in his simple, sheer brilliance of fish catching. He is technically superb – flawless really – in every department and utterly equipped to tackle any challenge. Even this pales beside his essential ability. No man so absolutely understands the ways and the whims of fish as does Ivan. He has said himself that he thinks like a fish and it is this ability to 'see' under the water that he has talked about in

the times I have been his audience. He has discussed tackle and its application of course, but the real issue with Ivan is to set his mind against the fish before him. Ivan is a great angler because he can read waters rapidly and correctly. He can appreciate a changing swim intuitively and employ almost subconsciously any method to exploit it. All his intense effort of thought and will goes into understanding the water and not into struggling with tackle complexities.

In the 1960s, I suppose it could be said that the Upper Wensum was an easy roach river and I could always manage a few pounds of fish from almost any length. However, the bag that Ivan was to amass that particular morning staggered me. I hadn't actually considered his swim before but when I saw 70lb of big fish winkled from it I was there the next dawn and fished all day for about a quarter of Ivan's effortless weight. The fish had not moved for they topped constantly, but what Ivan could do, I obviously couldn't, even on a river I was beginning to know well. Thinking

Ivan Mark

like a fish, Ivan settled onto a water and read it instantly. Because of these gifts his match successes were widespread on the Severn, the Trent, all the Fenland drains and numerous still waters.

Ivan's talks showed him to be an open and natural teacher with no wish to hide anything from his pupils. The same desire to pass on knowledge shone through his marathon *Angling Times* series that reached tens of thousands of readers over many years. In them, he preached the concept of balanced tackle, a message especially important for ledgering methods. In conjunction with Roy Marlow, his angling and business partner, and a technical innovator himself, he produced the Persuader ledgering rod. This was soft and delicate on the strike and light and precise to hold and cast with. What it did for me, it must have done for countless others; simply, I began to hit bites with a frequency I found astonishing. Also, so forgiving was the Persuader that, even for big fish, I could use the lightest bottoms and smallest hooks. Ivan, through his teachings, example and rod had made ledgering an art form.

I have concentrated on these four men because they are legends and always will be. Their skills and their contributions have stood the test of time and no history of match fishing will ever omit their names. Today there are any number of brilliant anglers. Ian Heaps, Dick Clegg, Steve Gardener, Dickie Carr, Frank Barlow, Jan Porter, Johnny Rolfe, Billy Makins, Dave Thomas and many more are all anglers of exceptional ability. The standard of match angling and of their tackle is always improving. The top men now fish against each other constantly and their knowledge and experience thus progress in leaps and bounds. The stars also travel abroad and, like Kevin Ashurst, bring back all manner of knowledge from the Continent. The match scene today is rich in information. There are books and magazines full of knowledge. There is a phone network around the country which match anglers use to get the latest information on good waters. Equally there is a grapevine of methods, and it is rumoured that match secrets last anything up to two minutes! Matchmen as a whole are open and generous of spirit. There is little nonsense talked for after all the result is always up on the board in black and white.

Despite this increase in professionalism, the motivations in match fishing in the 1990s will not be vastly different from those at play in the 1860s and 1870s. The prizes are important only to an extent. The top men do earn thousands of pounds, but this only goes part way to paying off their enormous expenses. Matchmen do not fish for the prizes alone. Far more important is the fishing itself and, to a great extent, the social scene. There is a brotherhood of match anglers that gathers in the fishermen's bars after the matches and drinks and discusses the day and the results. Match anglers are a gregarious crew. In the main they enjoy each other's company. Fishing for many is a solitary sport but to the match angler it is something to be enjoyed in the company of others. A match angler likes to pit his wits against his mate one minute and then drink and talk with him the very next. I have not been involved in a match, a proper match, now for many years. However, I have been involved in a competition in the most unlikely of fashions and the most unusual of places.

I happened to be staying at a small Westcountry hotel that had a river with a few salmon in it. The owner was naturally keen for those fish that were moving to be caught, entered in his record book and reported in the *Trout and Salmon* magazine to draw in customers. I was one of the few fishing, a retired captain was another and the owner determined to keep us both fishing as effectively as possible. Without either the good captain or me ever knowing, we were steered into a polite, unannounced, yet keenly felt match.

'My word, the captain's good. You'll do well to keep up with him,' the owner would say over drinks. 'You know, if there are salmon in the river, captain, then Bailey will be the one to catch them', he could be heard telling the captain at breakfast. The result was that both of us were up before dawn, kept at it through the heat of the day and were the last in to dinner each night. We tramped, we waded, we crept and we crawled and between us we caught six salmon from the river that really should not have held a grilse! After four days, and honours even, I think we realised what was happening and tacitly the match was abandoned. Lovely as those soft Exmoor dawns were, it was good to lie in until breakfast when the smells of cooking wafted up the stairs.

Of course, match fishing in the game world is not new. The first fly fishing matches have a long history and date back to the formation of the Ellem Club in 1831. The following year the first fly fishing match on record was held on the Whitadder on the Borders. The first national match was held in Scotland on Loch Leven in 1880 and the first international was held there in 1928 between England and Scotland. Wales and Ireland joined the scene in 1932. The international was held once a year until 1971 but now there are autumn and spring matches that go round the four countries in turn. The teams are made up of fourteen members. England selects the top twenty from its previous year's national finals with the best four from the last international.

The English national final is a very competitive event. There are qualifying matches in all regions and a hundred men fish in the final each September. These hundred men represent some of the finest fly fishermen in this country. They exhibit all the skills necessary, they are fit and able to endure the foulest weather. They are excellent casters on both short or long lines with great feeling for the trout in front of them. They have mastered all-round skills and can fish loch-style from boats, from the bank on lakes and on rivers very commonly encountered overseas. They are masters of the dry fly, the wet fly and the waiting nymph. They are able to tie flies even on the bankside should something be hatching that needs to be copied. Psychologically, these men can blend concentration with relaxation and manage to maintain patience even when the fish are not being co-operative.

There are very many fine fly match fishermen in the country today. Brian Leadbetter is a world champion. Chris Ogborne, Peter Drennan's associate in the tacklemaking industry, is an England man and a writer of renown. Chris Howitt, Brian Thomas, Dennis Buck, John Horsey, Peter Cockwill and Bob Church are all well known.

However, the most successful partnership in match fly fishing consists of Tony and John Pawson. This father-and-son team has literally swept the board in the UK, in Europe and in the world through the 1980s. In 1979 Tony Pawson was selected to fish the home internationals on Chew Lake for the first time. In 1983 Tony was England's top rod in the world championships and in 1984 he was the individual champion in Spain where his son, John, was sixth. In 1985 in Poland Tony was again top rod in the England scene. John Pawson fished for England in 1987 when this country won for the first time. England's team of five filled the top six places that day, with Brian Leadbetter as world champion. Tony was European champion in 1984 and again in 1989 when John was runner-up in both. In 1988 John won the world championship in Tasmania and now they are unique as the only father-and-son team to win world championship titles within four years of each other. England cruised to success in Tasmania in 1988. The Australian press summed it up, saying

> *. . . the most impressive aspect of the English team was its professional approach in difficult conditions. While many people may say that fishing wet flies blind in rough water is based on luck, the fact that England caught 37 fish compared to France's next best of 16 and Australia's 15 shows there was much more to it.'*

John Pawson, the winner, was drawn on the same beat as John Rumpf – one of Australia's best anglers and the tackle firm Hardy's representative there. Rumpf fished the margins, catching one fish, but Pawson waded a hundred yards out with the water to his armpits. Pawson had appreciated that the strength of the wind would push the fish onto the bank of a deep channel cut by the river. Each cast was thirty yards and he retrieved slowly for just five before recasting. These were wild fish and took on the drop or in the first few yards before they were scared by the line. John won even despite

Frank Barlow, a modern, match maestro – and the man for a pint after the whistle

Another English Great – Ian Heaps, happy with the pole or the float (Paul Elliott)

losing an approximately 6lb trout after a long 10 minute fight. Between Tony and John there is a lovely friendly rivalry that is mixed with the deepest of pride: John was heard to comment recently, 'Technically dad's a bit of a mess, but for his age he is tremendously enthusiastic!'

Fly match fishing is likely to increase in popularity as the century progresses. Now each year the Benson and Hedges competition attracts well over ten thousand entries. There are going to be more matches from the bankside, on rivers and on small still waters. The European and the world championships are going to be better covered by the media, are going to be better organised with more teams and on a more formal basis. In short the future for this branch of match fishing will be explosive.

And who is the best match angler of all time? In my mind there can only be one answer – Jim (J. H. R.) Bazley. He is the only man to have won the national championship twice and his was the name revered round the match angling circles of the early twentieth century. Amongst the many words he wrote on match fishing appear the following:

> . . . the expert match fisher who can be relied upon consistently to do well anywhere is one who has made a long and careful study of the habits of the fish he desires to catch. He has practised in the most painstaking manner, casting, presenting the bait, and playing the fish he has hooked. And further he is always striving to obtain the best possible return in all sorts of adverse circumstances by giving meticulous attention to the multitude of details

that must be dealt with if success is to be achieved. Aided by a run of luck, almost any angler of moderate skill can make history for a short time, but unless he is, first of all, a person of real angling ability, he will never be heard of again.

A better description of the successful, great, match angler could not be found anywhere and Jim Bazley fits all his own guidelines.

But what makes Jim so great and so unique is the breadth of his experience and ability. As a Yorkshire specimen hunter he stood supreme during the early years of the twentieth century. He caught brown trout to 8lb 4oz, nine chub over 5lb, roach to 2lb 15.5oz, pike to 30lb, dace to 1lb, thousands of grayling to 2lb, barbel to nearly 8lb, rudd to 2lb, perch to 2lb 8oz and salmon to 23lb. For Jim Bazley's time these catches were phenomenal, not least because most of the fish were caught in Yorkshire, a county not famous for very big fish. Grayling fishing was one of his greatest loves and one of his friends recalls how, when the season was well advanced, they were all on tenterhooks for 'Baz' to announce his two-thousandth grayling of the season! He took most of the grayling from the Marsham reaches of the Ure and from his favourite angling spot of all, the Wharfe around Burnsall. A sharp bend in the river near here was so much to 'Baz' that it is still known by many today as Bazley's Corner. His best bag of grayling, however, was 161 in 12 hours on the Teviot, a tributary of the Tweed.

Bazley was also a writer on more than match angling. His books *Fishing Stunts* and *Fun with the Fishing Rod* are a fund of stories of his outings. The books were written in the 1930s and are now difficult to get hold of, but they show a tremendous sense of humour and everybody should read them if at all possible. Bazley was also a fly tier of renown and particularly enjoyed making patterns for his beloved Yorkshire trout and grayling. He corresponded with Courtney Williams when the latter was compiling a dictionary of trout flies. Bazley was a fund of knowledge on Yorkshire patterns and Yorkshire variations of standard flies.

But above all, what made Bazley great was his generosity. Few men were less forgetful of the people who gave him the chance to fish. Legend has it that from wherever Baz was returning to Leeds, he would leave a parcel of fish with the porter at nearly every station for those who gave him access to their fishing. Indeed some trains were known to be late because Baz had so much 'business' to contract on the journey home. If Baz always wanted to share his fish with others he also wanted to share his joys and his successes with his friends. When he caught his biggest pike – a Hornsea thirty-pounder – he was so excited he took a taxi all the way from Hornsea to Leeds so that he could display the fish, alive, to his friends at Leeds Anglers Club. People loved Bazley and his sense of humour. He played practical jokes on them and it was not unknown for the tables to be turned on him. One particular day he was bringing a pike back on the train from the Derwent. His fellow-passengers insisted on seeing the cargo. Agreeing, he warned them to keep their hands away from the fish's mouth, but one of the group bet him that he would not be frightened to put *his* hand in the fish's jaws. The bet was struck and the moment the gloved hand was placed between the pike's jaws, they closed with a snap. A worried Baz was just about to reach for the communication cord so help could be summoned when the gambler revealed his secret to him . . . there was no harm done for his hand was an artificial one.

CHAPTER 10
ANGLING AND ART

*C*rop-headed children spat upon us from the bridges as we went below, with a true conservative feeling. But even more conservative were the fishermen, intent upon their floats, who let us go by without one glance. They perched upon sterlings and buttresses and along the slope of the embankment, gently occupied. They were indifferent like pieces of dead nature. They did not move any more than if they had been fishing in an old Dutch print.

Robert Louis Stevenson *An Inland Voyage*

PHOTO:
A. Roland Knight – Whipping the Willows for Chub

*I*t is the morning of a sale at Bonhams, the auctioneers in south London. It is a sale of angling artefacts and there are seven hundred lots. The atmosphere is mixed – tension and massive interest combined. There are all manner of people swirling round the room with their catalogues, pencils, and with their minds firmly on their chequebooks and bank balances. Some of the men are in suits and some are elderly, but just as many are young men casually dressed. What unites them all is tremendous interest in angling's art. There is tackle on display, taxidermy and many angling paintings all in a room fifty yards long by perhaps twenty yards wide. The room is a treasure trove. It is full of history, memory and beauty. It is an extraordinary experience to be there, where all these wonderful relics of angling are housed.

It is also a good place to make an assessment of greatness in angling art. Here, where so many pictures and so many cases of stuffed fish are laid out, comparison is possible. The good glistens and the poor stands out equally sharply by contrast. Everything in the hall is undergoing the most intense scrutiny. Rods are being flexed and canes not used for half a century are groaning. Reels are clicking, dusty pieces of machinery that have not squealed to a fish for even double that time. Creels are being picked up, examined and tested on the shoulder and spiders are running away from the cobwebs. Labels are being checked on the back of cases, on reel seats and on rod butts.

Everyone is slightly in awe of a well known enthusiast, a writer, a man who is a true collector, sitting at a desk fingering fly wallets as though they were gold dust. It is rumoured that he will set the pace in the bidding. He looks around the room occasionally as if he has every awareness of the stir that he is making. It is a Friday. It is approaching lunchtime and the sale will start at 2pm. The number of people begins to mount as gentlemen from all over the City are coming in to spend their lunchtime in the room. Probably they will stretch their lunchtime to cover the last hours of the working day, as the weekend is looming. They are happy to be there even if they are not going to make a bid. The room has become a link with their favourite river. They can imagine that they will soon be heading north again to a mountain stream where they can fish for trout or salmon or to a pool deep in Dorset, perhaps, where the carp roll.

It is the cases of stuffed fish that immediately grab the attention. There can be no doubt that taxidermy is one of the highest art forms in the angling world. The work that goes into a beautiful stuffed fish is immense. Cases, even last century, were never cheap to complete because the manhours that they represent are enormous. In part this explains why there tend to be more cases of salmon and trout than of coarse fish; often there was simply not the money to send a chub, a barbel or a bream to be set up. A whole industry now surrounds the collecting of stuffed fish. When I began personally twenty years ago, they were seen as oddities, as curiosities, as cracked dusty pieces of occasional interest in the dark recesses of antique shops. Attitudes towards them began to change in the mid-1970s. They were seen as they truly are: beautiful pieces of craftsmanship that embrace angling history in the most perfect of fashions. Collectors came over from the Continent. Anglers in this country began to appreciate the worth of stuffed fish and together they forced prices up. The case that went for £5 in 1968 would undoubtedly have reached £500 ten years later. Moving now to the turn of the 1990s, prices are ever-rocketing. An exceptional case can now command prices well in excess of £1000.

The truly great cases in the angling world belong to John Cooper & Sons. This company operated for virtually a century and the art was passed down from father to son, and to the workers who joined them as the business grew. There are several Coopers in the room and in each case the colours are liquid and the light, delicate, bow fronted glass shines like the water tension itself. The shape of a Cooper fish is invariably perfect and the shading on the scales is exact. The heads of each fish, so difficult to get right, are invariably excellent. The mouth is always tight and accurately placed and the eye is always immaculate in both size and colouring. The fins are never frayed and always as proudly erect as if the fish is just coming across the waiting landing net. Moreover, the fins always carry the right tinges of colour. Before me in the room hangs a big chub, and its ventral and anal fins are the perfect mandarin that only an angler would recognise as being absolutely the right colour. Equally the tail fin is all edged with that characteristic black that again the angler recognises immediately the fish breaks surface. It is this attention to detail that makes Coopers so desirable and such marvellous examples of angling art. In each of the Cooper cases, the reed background cannot be said to be lifelike but artistically it is the perfect setting. Cooper never overdid things with the reeds, and the background is always delicate and set against a

Caught by D.TRUBY, Severn, Shrewsbury. Oct. 17th 1926. Wgt 1lb 11ozs 14dms.

A large roach – even cased – is a creature of beauty

A very lovely late period Cooper case

duck-egg-blue board. The overall effect cannot be perfection for that is the fish in the water but, and thousands have agreed with this over the centuries, a Cooper case is a near substitute.

Here is a case of four mirror carp. Their weight only averages 2lb apiece but they were big fish for 1901 when they were caught. In fact, they would have been large even for me when I had my second carp of 2lb 4oz in 1962. I held that fish and gloated over it by a cattle drink for minutes. Even though that capture is over a quarter of a century old I can remember every detail of the fish. It is a cameo that has sunk into my memory and is reflected now by these small carp in the case set up by Cooper's. They are marvellously done. Cooper's has caught their stockiness and their bull-shouldered power. Their colour is the exact deep mahogany that comes with the fish of the high summer from small ponds – and these were caught in June from a little mere, the case says. The scales are armoured into the flesh and they look like miniature battleship fish. The carp are small, I suppose, but they have presented a memory of a great angling achievement well on through the twentieth century.

Later Coopers continue to be fine but perhaps tend to be too highly coloured and the scales overbold. There is a case of roach here that Cooper's worked on around World War II when the firm was drawing to its close. The case is good, undoubtedly, but the art is beginning to wane. Everything about the case is a little overstated, but it still stands as a fine example compared with some of the cases that are littered around it.

There are fish species that are virtually unidentifiable and you need to check in the catalogue, which is even then a guess. Their fins are ragged and their scales are bleached. Their shape is unnatural even to a non angler and their heads and shoulders are discoloured, misshapen and in totally the wrong pose. Sometimes the flank is dented and the labelling on the case is poor or faded. The backgrounds are hideous creations and in short the whole case is a piscatorial nightmare. Perhaps they were once admired as presents or as memories but they were a travesty that can never be transferred to another person's wall.

There is a salmon in the far corner and the painting of the scales is the most wondrous I have ever seen. The label says it was caught by John Edward Jopson on the River Naver in Sutherland on 25 May 1927. Its weight is 12lb. Its length is 32in and its girth 17in and the fish was set up by Spicer. The background is quite superb and stands comparison with any of Spicer's famous bird cases. But it is the scales that draw me back and back. Each one is a drop of a pearl. It is translucent and reflects any colour put against it. It is exactly like the fish in the living stream that glow under blue skies. Its head is immaculate and its eye so liquid that then it surely moved to follow me across the room. But then, as I said, salmon very often attracted the very best work. There was the money available to set up a fish like this well – superlatively in fact.

It is much the same with the painting of fish. The centrepiece of the entire sale is a painting by John Russell, one of the important nineteenth-century artists. Here one wall is dominated by his painting of a 42lb 8oz cock salmon lying before the pool of its capture – Banff's Rock, Farglen House. The fish is lifesize and it glows and it is covered with the sheen from the sun that dances all along its upper vent and again

Sheer majesty, John Russell's study of a 42lb 8oz cock salmon, painted before the pool of its capture, Banff's Rock, Farglen House, in 1877

behind the gills. There is a trickle of blood, simply a smear that seeps from its gill flaps. It is a smudge that only a true fisherman would recognise. Again, like the set-up Spicer salmon, the eye is still alive. Deep in it you see the despair of the fish and the triumph of the scene for the angler both together. Lord Banff's Rock pool is in the background. It is painted fabulously. It is enticing, deep, black and mysterious. It has the feel of water that has just settled after a mammoth battle. And further behind still is a fine Scottish forest and the house itself appearing above, waiting for the fish to be taken in and laid out proudly in the hallway. It is a moment of Scottish sporting history caught forever on this magnificent 1500sq in of oil on canvas. Everybody in the room is happy just to have seen it and my only regret is that, with a price estimate of £20,000 I fear it will be the one, for me, that got away.

But there are other fine paintings, notably by the nineteenth-century artist H. L. Rolfe. There is a still-life study of four trout on a rocky lochside painted in 1859. Possibly the painting itself could have been renovated more carefully but this is no detraction from the fabulous quality of the artwork itself. Rolfe was a magician with light and here a shaft plays from behind a cloud, over a mountain top, illuminating the catch and bringing it to the freshest of life and vigour. The yellows of the fish are in death turning to deeper golds but the bellies are still cream and the fins only just done trembling. It is impossible to paint a trout's red spots better than Rolfe has done. There is no doubt that this painting is highly prized and will go for several thousands of pounds when the hammer comes down.

At the turn of the century A. Roland Knight was painting his series of angling scenes. In the saleroom is one of his more famous ones, 'Whipping the Willows for Chub'. The background to the painting is quite lovely. It is misty and gloomy both and

H. L. Rolfe – still-life study of four trout on a rocky lochside, 1859

the deep green river flows quietly along. The willows weep in beautiful fashion and emphasise the placid slowness of the water beneath. The chub are seen gurgling, just as they do, in the roots and the whole picture is reminiscent of a lazy dawn on the upper Thames or one of its tributaries. But the fish, compared with Rolfe or with Russell, are stiff as though they were painted on the scene afterwards. The mouths are not correct, the angle of their leap is awkward and the water is strangely limp as it falls from their sides. The painting is so near to being lovely and to a non-angler probably is so anyway. But to me, who has seen so many chub do this exact selfsame thing, the painting is not right, and the miss, to the dedicated, is as good as a mile. The angler should always trust his instinctive judgement and measure a painting by what he has seen in the real world and draw back if the two do not tally.

Today I fished the most insignificant little farm pond, one passed again and again by walkers who can never guess at the beauties that the dirty brown waters hide. Like the ramblers I saw and appreciated the wrens, the long-tailed tits, the first of the year's primroses and the heron coming into the bare tree at dusk. I, though, was alone in witnessing the perch from the pool itself. I had four of them; all over 2lb and all stunningly beautiful. Their humped, barred bodies are a vision unique I believe in all the world. Where else but on a perch's cordal fin can a human see such a sublime, fiery tangerine blazing red, so singular that language falls far short of describing it? As I laid the perch out on a wetted sack at dusk under the sighing poplar trees, I felt it strange that God should place such beauty where man could not see it, touch it, or ever guess at it. I alone was privileged to witness those perch and probably never again will I, even as an angler, see such a sight. This is why I revere the skill of the angling artist so highly. At his greatest he is almost a medium between God and man. He can reveal in part the beauty that only fishermen half guess at and non fishermen never even suspect. A great angling artist reinforces the angler's understanding of the fish by helping reinforce dim visions of the underwater world with such vivid light and clarity. And, ultimately, a great angling portrait is inspirational. The beauty of it drives us on and on in the foulest of weather in the hope of obtaining our own personal rainbow.

The twentieth century has seen several excellent angling artists and my own link with art and angling is strong. I first met one of the greats a near decade ago in his cottage on the fringe of a Norfolk estate. When Chris Turnbull was not fishing, I found that he was painting, and I loved to visit him at work, by the window that gave onto one of the long oak avenues into the park. That was where the idea for our first project together, *In Visible Waters*, was born. As our friendship grew, we realised that we were both drawn to the behaviour of fish just as much as the catching of them. Chris, like all good anglers, was first a naturalist and second a fish catcher, and this quality came out in the truly aquatic feel of his paintings. The contract for the book was negotiated and day after day for six months I watched as Chris' stock of pictures gradually grew up. Chris, I soon realised, was meticulous as well as talented. I well remember his painting of an autumnal rudd splashing on the waters of Felbrigg Lake. He walked to the local city graveyard and poked around under the trees until he found a leaf of the exact shape and colouring that he wanted to copy and place, floating, beside the leaping fish. For over an hour he mixed his watercolours until the precise shade was accomplished; only then did its fragility begin to appear on the paper. Finally, that one leaf, a detail many lesser artists would have ignored, took Chris over three hours' work.

I also witnessed Chris' utter obedience to the rules of the naturalist. Beside him as he worked were innumerable biological studies, for each fish that he drew had to have precise scale counts and fin ray numbers. He insisted on the exact colouration of an eye, on the perfect proportioning of a mouth and the size and placing of the gills. In the end every fish in *In Visible Waters* is a perfect creation, a true reflection of the wild. It is as though real fish swim in its pages, are caught a second and then glide on.

I could not count how many roughs Chris made of underwater scenes and then destroyed as inadequate. The intellectual problem was to superimpose his own angling and naturalist knowledge onto a vivid artistic imagination and convey the fish in their private lives beneath the water's surface. The sweeping fan of the barbel's tail, the flanks of the chub curving on the curls of the currents, the angles of the pike's strike, the dip of the bream shoal over a bream bed and the pair of trench pirouetting over a blood-worm colony are all the result of a vision that is true art.

A second twentieth-century artist who I admire is Robin Armstrong, who lives in an old cottage in a most secret Devonshire valley. Even when you know the address and find the village you can be a long while from arriving at his door. The day I met him first was a blisteringly hot one and, though it was only early July, the colours of the landscape had matured to give the look of August. Very shortly, we were where Robin wanted to be; down the hillside, walking in the shade of the valley along his river. We wandered miles and a multitude of Robin Armstrongs came to my view. First, I saw him as a water bailiff though now, having turned to full-time art, the job of a dozen years is not forgotten. He commented constantly on the state of the water-starved river. He knew the pools so intimately that he saw sea trout where I barely even saw the water itself. He knew all the bed's depressions and the bankside undercuts and realised that poachers knew them also. A couple of willow wands he discovered snapped off; poacher's rods. Some long grasses flattened; a poacher's seat. A smidgeon of dried slime on a leaf; the poachers had caught fish.

And accompanying this bailiff's easy way along the water bank was the long-acquired knowledge of a countryman and naturalist. He lamented an old and majestic pine debarked by cattle and doomed to die. Often he stopped to listen to a particular birdsong or to watch a butterfly or observe the behaviour of the dragonflies. Beyond all these things, he showed of course that he is an angler. Pool by pool we stopped and he marked the fish – two-pounders here, a six-pounder under a bank over there and a near four-pounder at the tail of a weir. And for each fish he worked out a strategy for the night when dinner would be done, the pub would be closed and the light summer darkness would be drawn in. For myself, I could hardly wait but I saw the sense in his call for patience. It was his river and he called its tune.

Above all things, however, I saw Robin Armstrong as an artist. He is fascinated by water as a substance. I watched him analyse it as it flowed over stones and bubbled in the rapids and boiled in the little weirs. He pointed out how water holds light and reflects it and how the surface film is an element that constantly changes under sun or cloud, breeze or calm, twilight or full day. We looked over a bridge. He pointed out the water running a couple of feet beneath thick alder leaves where the sun was striking here and there as the wind blew them back. Where the light hit the water it turned opaque, like a Milky Way in an otherwise clear, dark stream. An insect fell and struggled on the surface, floating slowly downriver towards us. It came close. It was a wasp and its legs and wings kicked out ripples that beat the water's film and cast rings of shadow on the gravel bed. The tiny moorland brown trout came up to it, nosed it, tugged and tore at it until finally it was no more. 'What a picture,' Armstrong said of its end.

It is such sights that Armstrong now wants to capture. His paintings have the very feel of the water and portray it as it really is, as probably only anglers know it. Now he wants a lake in his grounds – a still water of around two acres. On it, from his window virtually, he will be able to observe that special surface film a summer still water develops, especially in warm weather before a wind grows up in the morning. At dawn, the lake may well be thickly skinned by the shucks of hatched insects, by drifted weed, by the lazy bubbles of burrowing fish and by the oils from the feathers of the waterbirds. It is a face of water very different from a rushing Dartmoor stream but exciting and, each succeeding day, quite unique and irreplaceable.

Before Robin Armstrong, most if not all angling artists could be better described as illustrators. Water has been merely a background for their fish to be set upon and rarely existed in its own right. In Armstrong's paintings the fish is merely a focal point and, though brilliantly executed, is almost dispensable. The water itself, the tricks it plays, and the moods it assumes are taking over in importance for him. There is a great deal of excitement hanging about Robin's studio. This is pioneering stuff and so there must be trepidation. There are a great many things that can and do go wrong. Some canvasses lie overnight in a full bath to soak in water and sheen. Fish and weeds of great intricacy are doused in washes of colour that could obliterate them and ruin days of work. The fear of failure, though, is nothing compared with the elation of success.

Robin has achieved pictures that no one has tried before. His is pioneering work and will force angling artists of the future to look ever harder at what has been produced and, as a result, they might well strive ever harder like Robin himself to push one step beyond.

Every generation of anglers has its inspirations. Beginners especially need motivation for those long sequences of blank days, when only tangles seem frequent, when cold and boredom become nearly unbearable and when a bent rod and a singing reel seem far, far away. For those of us in the 1950s there were many influences; practically, few of us would deny K. P. Morritt and his fixed spool reels pride of place; intellectually, we must owe the greatest amount to R. S. Walker; emotionally and spiritually, we still dream along with Mr Crabtree and Peter, and the water world drawn for us by Bernard Venables.

Mr Crabtree Goes Fishing was published in 1953 for 5 shillings (25p). It was a *Daily Mirror* production based on cartoon form and covered excursions to the Royalty, to the Broads, to Slapton Ley, to canals, carp pools and chalk streams. Everywhere success was bound to come and young Peter, who was Mr Crabtree's disciple, found his eyes ever widening with amazement as monster fish followed their every footstep. Always, though, Mr Crabtree's pipe puffed contentedly. The combination of beauty, adventure and security was perfect and there was even a little practical knowledge thrown in besides.

Bernard Venables – angler, author, artist, editor – no one has inspired twentieth-century angling more powerfully

In the 1970s it became fashionable to criticise Crabtree. Yes, he was pompous, he was opinionated and egocentric. Peter did seem compliant to the point of foppishness! The fishing everywhere was fabulously, unrealistically good, but to point out all these failings from an adult standpoint ignores the view of a child eager for heroes. I do not want to pass strict judgement on the quality of Crabtree as art, but what the drawings did possess was a mesmeric quality, an ability to draw in the child, to fill his subconscious and stay with him forever. There are many times I have visited a water and experienced a quite tangible sense of déjà vu. Little by little, as the day unfolds, I realise that I am living a Crabtree scene; a willow tree, a bridge, a bankside I first visited thirty years back beside a bedside lamp, warm under quilts, when a winter's night raged outside.

Very recently, in a fishing hut on a Border river, well hidden by broken cane furniture and the accumulated gloom and debris of years, a carved, wooden salmon was seen. Perhaps a stray beam of sunlight chinked through the rafters to catch its eye or perhaps, with a crash, it fell to the floor from its rusted nail and rotted rope. However, attention was drawn to it and the piece went off to be cleaned and polished. The caudal fin was chipped and a pectoral was broken clear off but the carving was highly skilful, the fish that was its original model had been a large one and, when the carving went to sale, an enormous sum was paid for it.

Carvings of fish, generally Atlantic salmon, entered the art world from the late

Salmon in ceramics – a new angling art form by Neil Dalrymple, who, after success in Canada, returned to Britain in 1985 and has set up a studio in North Wales

A fine Hardy's carved and painted cock salmon – it weighed 36lb and came from the Don in 1920 – an autumn run fish

Victorian period until World War II. The very best examples of the genre were finely worked and beautifully and realistically painted. They were copied from actual fish with remarkable accuracy and art really did mirror life itself. Malloch and Perth offered a service. So, inevitably, did Hardy Brothers and Farlowe's. Research by Simon and Edwina Brett suggests that the greatest of the creations came from the studio of John Russell (1819–93), his daughter Isabella (1864–1950) and her husband John Tully (1862–1913).

One of the prime patrons of this art form was the Duke of Richmond and Gordon who fished the Spey each autumn with his guests. Fish, leviathans, that were caught and weighed over 40lb were immortalised in wood and swam eternally on the walls of the smoking room of the duke's Scotland seat. Not eternally, of course, nothing is, and now the shoal is dispersed and gone but what a sight it must once have presented. How great was the beauty, how important that history and how inspiring were the memories that glinted off those submarine bodies in the lamplight. Imagine their captors sitting there beneath them, proven anglers, perhaps even great ones, looking through brandy glasses and cigar smoke at the fights of their lives. In the silences the triumphs must have flooded back and how tragic for collectors, artists and fishermen that the room is no more, that the fish are gone and that the anglers are long since dead.

CHAPTER 11

THE GREAT WRITERS

*T*here is a closed season for trout but not for books.
With these in hand we can fortify ourselves throughout the winter months
with new ideas, new theories and new hopes to put to the test when spring
comes around again.

Colonel J. Lane *Fly Fisherman's Pie*

PHOTO:
Scrope's beautiful frontispiece

*F*or many years now angling literature has attracted the compilers of anthologies, understandably considering the breadth and depth of literature available to them. In a relatively short chapter such as this it is not possible to touch upon all masterpieces of angling literature, and indeed such an exercise would be futile in the light of the last and most excellent of the anthologies available. *The Magic Wheel* by Swift and Profumo exemplifies an art in itself. The amount of research the two men have indulged in is massive. Simple précis of their work would here be futile.

Until very recently I was a teacher of sixth-form pupils and it was suggested to me that I should approach the chapter in this way: that I should prepare a list of my top ten books for some of the boys who are angling fanatics. At least this concentrates my efforts and makes me think intensely about the books that I feel are the most important to today's reader. In every way this is a streamlining approach and one that I do believe has merit. Of course there will be argument about my choices. I hope in fact that this is the case for the task before me is obviously a subjective one and controversy must naturally arise. Indeed, my dream would be that perhaps sometime in the future, in bars or on riverbanks, anglers may gather together and discuss the top ten that follows.

About my number one book there is no doubt whatsoever. This must be *The Fisherman's Bedside Book* by B.B., first published in 1945 and, as it says, '. . . produced in complete conformity with the authorised economy standards' that were demanded during the war years. I have had my own particular copy for virtually thirty years now and I have never been long parted from it. Whenever I have been troubled before sleep this is the book to which I have turned for comfort and a passage into the world of water that I love so well. Though every story is well known to me, I still find new delights in certain pictures, in a new sentence, in a new thought that has never struck me before.

Indeed B.B. has assembled some of the most magical writers that have ever appeared in angling print: Patrick Chalmers, Negley Farson, Francis Francis, Plunket Greene, Lord Grey, Haldane, Halford, Hills, Jefferies, St John, Ransome, Sheringham, Skues, Thoreau, Walton and many others stud the near six hundred pages of this volume. Every freshwater fish is covered in exciting and atmospheric detail. If I want some action then I can turn to the battles with mammoth barbel or salmon and if I feel more in need of gentleness then I can turn to the description of tench lakes, carp lakes or sleepy meres in July evenings.

B.B.'s book has also been responsible for one of the driving inspirations in my own angling life; the search for a ferox in Scotland. I was only a handful of years old when I read the descriptions of quests and battles for these huge cannibal brown trout of the vast Scottish lochs and the stories so fired me that I determined that when I was old enough I would follow in the footsteps of the Victorian masters. For the last ten years or so, this is exactly what I have been doing with every spare week and every spare pound that I possess. For this alone I must thank B.B. and ever hold his remarkable bedside book in affection. Nor is it possible to complete this hymn of praise without mention of B.B.'s remarkable woodcuts. Now, towards the end of the twentieth century, we live in an age where size of fish seems to mean everything. This was not so for B.B. and the

FISHERMAN'S CHOICE
GENERAL EDITOR COLIN WILLOCK

A CARP WATER
(WOOD POOL)
AND HOW TO FISH IT
BY
"BB"

Decoratio
D. J. Watkins-Pi

The Wood Pool

'A good book is the best of friends, the same today and forever.'

pages of his bedside book are decorated not with men grinning over huge fish but timeless pictures of anglers by riverbanks, of lakes with the moorhens tripping over the lilies, of bridges where the trout rise eternally under the parapets or of dashing moorland streams where one can forever envisage a salmon hanging behind the beautifully portrayed rocks. In short B.B. and the writers that he assembled have created another world, an eternal world, a world that cannot be defiled, a world of proper values and a world that is accessible to anyone with the time and the inclination to enter it.

For much the same reasons my number two book must be *Going Fishing* by Negley Farson. The very subtitle is inspirational – 'Travel and Adventures in Two Hemispheres'. This book too was published in the war years, obviously a time when men thought seriously about their lives and their true pleasures. To a world threatened by Fascism, angling and the love of beauty and nature must have seemed wondrous things. Indeed that spirit portrayed in *Going Fishing* possibly even saved the sanity of some. Hugh Falkus has written an introduction to one of the later editions of Farson's book which illustrates exactly this point.

I first read Going Fishing *in 1943 when, as a prisoner of war, I was serving a term of solitary confinement following an escape attempt and a friendly guard smuggled the book into my cell. For a couple of months it was my only literature, so I can claim to have read it*

pretty thoroughly! But Negley Farson proved more than a solace; he was a revelation. Of all the fishing books I have read, his was the best.
     It still is.

The book has such scope. Farson talks about fishing in Russia, America, Scotland, the south-west of England, Ireland, Chile, France, Norway and Yugoslavia. In each country Farson as a wandering fisherman is able to get to the very spirit of the people, the landscape and the fish themselves. Whatever he sees he is capable of describing with enchantment. I have never picked the book up without being transported to different countries in different times. Again, like B.B.'s book, the illustration seems to fit the words almost perfectly. S. F. Tunnicliffe has captured the essential spirit of Farson with every single drawing. Drawings can be magical in a way photographs very rarely can. Indeed, although every word of *Going Fishing* must be true, the spirit and the tone is more like a novel than some factual fishing book. Like a novel, it is a book to be picked up and read and considered until it is fully understood. Like many of the great novels it is a story of a man happy in a landscape and fishing is almost incidental to that pleasure.

My third choice is one of some debate. I feel it is about time to bring in something of the meat of angling, the instructive, one of the 'how to do it' masterpieces. There have been remarkable books in this respect that reflect deep knowledge of all fish species by a single person. John Bickerdyke had a tremendous effect on angling with his two books around the turn of the century, *Angling for Coarse Fish* and *The Book of the 'All Round Angler'*. Indeed both these books are well worth reading even today and that excellent modern angler Jim Gibbinson recently told me that Bickerdyke was his own inspiration and that Bickerdyke's books were his own bibles. Of much the same period and with equal influence is Cholmondeley Pennell, the author of *Angling Naturalist*, *The Book of the Pike* and *Fishing Gossip:* even today that modern pike master, Barrie Rickards, says that Pennell's book is well worth reading for its pike lore. William Bailey and J. W. Martin both wrote all-encompassing books that had a great effect on the development of Victorian fishing. Coming into the twentieth century Eric Marshall-Hardy wrote enormous works on coarse fish and coarse fishing that still have validity. In fact Marshall-Hardy's discussion on roach–rudd hybrids is definitive. Many of the methods used by Marshall-Hardy would find favour with today's experts too. However, for third place and in this category, the accolade must go to *Fresh Water Fishing* by Hugh Falkus and Fred Buller. The reviews say it all. 'One of the great fishing books of all times,' Peter Lapsley. 'If in the future some writer attempts a similar book, and it will need great talent to do so, he will find himself drawing greatly on the polished wisdom of this work', *The Field*. The book is indeed masterful. Every freshwater fish, every method, every bait, every item of clothing, every safety measure, everything possible is included in the pages of this book. As one would expect with Falkus and Buller the work is meticulously researched and beautifully written. The illustrations are apt, well chosen and well captioned. Since the book came out in 1975 I have read it at least three times and dipped into it three hundred times more. Rarely has there been anything with which I have disagreed or even quibbled over, and the amount I have learnt is astronomical.

My number four book is again an instructive one: *Still Water Angling* by Richard Walker. Some, I have no doubt, would put this book, by far the best of Walker's products, higher than number four. I admit totally that the book had massive influence from the 1950s until the present day and in it Walker introduced a whole new approach to angling, not merely in still waters alone. It is quite true that *Still Water Angling* has influenced most of the top anglers today in one way or another, and it is hard to think of any other book that has had such an immediate and powerful impact on the way that angling has progressed. Indeed, having said all that, I feel guilt at only putting the book at number four. I do this because in many ways the knowledge in it has been superseded in technical terms. *Still Water Angling* is in date now, but only just, and the next ten or fifteen years will see its relevance even further diminished. Furthermore, Walker was a good writer and a clear writer but not a writer of genius in the way of Farson or B.B. *Still Water Angling* and other books, notably *Drop Me a Line*, are all written with charm and precision but they are not dusted with that magic that Farson had in his fingertips.

I still read *Still Water Angling*, and I always will, but the periods between readings will I know grow longer. In fifty years *Still Water Angling* will be a dusty testimony to the mid-twentieth century whereas Farson will be as alive as the moment the ink hit the paper. Walker was a technical genius but as techniques move on his influence is bound to recede. That is not to say the angling world will not always need the Walker of commonsense and of generous and clear-sighted debate. Indeed as angling moves on toward the twenty-first century so many aspects are worrying and so many debates seem to have no level head to conduct them. If only Walker had laid down some moral ten commandments by which men could judge angling . . . That would have been the book to have taken Walker inevitably to the top of this list.

The battle for number five spot is intense. After Falkus and Buller and Walker again I feel need of some transport away from the hurlyburly of the modern fishing scene. The clutch of books able to effect this is large: *Fly Fishing* by Lord Grey of Falloden, *A Summer on the Test* by John Waller Hills, *At the Tail of the Weir* by Patrick Chalmers, *Path By the Water* by A. R. B. Haldane and Plunket Greene's masterpiece *Where the Bright Waters Meet* are all books that have become hallowed over the years. A book that comes close from the modern era is *Days and Nights of Game Fishing* by W. B. Currie, first published in 1984. It is a comprehensive and sensitive book that describes game fishing in the most aware and openminded fashion. In this book he makes angling appear as it should really be: a journey into nature where fishing and humanity are both discovered. Despite this my number five book must be *The River Never Sleeps* by Haig Brown.

Haig Brown was born in Dorset and as a boy knew Thomas Hardy. He came from a fishing family that had rods on the Frome. His background was, then, that of an angler and naturelover and both these he combined to take him as a young man to British Columbia. There he roughed it on Vancouver Island in the logging camps, on the commercial fishing boats and as a trapper. By the 1930s he was emerging as a writer of genius and *The River Never Sleeps* capped his work. The scope of the book is enormous. He describes his early love of dace and an intriguing adventure after a pike. From old England he takes us to the New World and his adventures after the steelhead are epic. What a fish the steelhead sounds. 'And when the shock of his take jars through to your forearms and you lift the rod to its bend, you know that in a moment the strength of his leaping body will shatter the water to brilliance, however dark the day'. Moreover Haig Brown has been able to express as well if not better than any other writer the essential beauty of rivers. 'A river is water in its loveliest form; rivers have life and sound and movement and infinity of variation, rivers are veins of the earth through which the life blood returns to the heart.' On the 'true' angler, he says:

> *The angler is usually a good conservationist, little concerned with killing more fish than he can use. His sport is not in any way dependent upon the death of his quarry; it is entirely in the hooking, the playing and netting of the fish, and the blow of the club that ends a fish's life is no part of it at all; rather it is a necessary but rather unpleasant preparation for supper or a slightly less defensible precaution against the doubts of his friends.*

I came close to seeing a tie for sixth place. Both Francis Francis and Hugh Tempest Sheringham dominated the nineteenth-century angling writing world. Both men were angling editors of *The Field* and both talked constant commonsense on the angling debates of the period. Francis Francis produced one truly outstanding book, *A Book on Angling*, and its message was one of thoroughness and commonsense. The vote for number six, however, must go to Sheringham, if only because of the scope of his writing. *Fishing, its Cause, Treatment and Cure* was a fun celebration of the sport. *Elements of Angling*, *An Open Creel* and *Coarse Fishing*, were all a perfect mix of fact, commentary and description. But the number six book must be Sheringham's *An Open Creel*. The book simply rejoices in angling. It has been an inspiration to readers for decades. Read it, if you have not done so already.

The number seven place I also want to give to a work of fun and gaiety and again there are three contenders. In the 1980s Christopher Yates produced *Casting At The Sun* and immediately it became discussed as a future classic. It is rare that a modern work has such impact. Today the emphasis appears to be on successes and not on the type of things that Chris discussed: beauty, brotherhood, joyful expeditions, exciting times, and the wondrous appreciation of boyhood carried on into adult life. Chris has said that his entire life is a holiday and this is how angling is portrayed in *Casting at the Sun*. Chris reminded an entire generation that fishing was for fun and once the fun stops so should the fishing. Just as Chris is a charming companion, so this is a charming book that delights anyone with a sense of humour and a sense of the majesty of nature.

Two men from the pre-war world challenge Chris closely for number seven spot. Arthur Ransome's book *Rod and Line* is a collection of the articles he wrote for the *Manchester Guardian* during the 1930s. They were brought to the TV screen by Michael Hordern and this proved that wisdom in angling is eternal and that the words Ransome wrote half a century before still had merit and interest in a much changed world. However, my vote for the number seven book goes to a little known work called *The Philandering Angler* by Arthur Applin. This book is simply ridiculous. It was written in the 1930s by an actor of extravagant genius. The work describes Applin's adventures around Europe with a fishing rod, one suspects with an open-top sports car and with an eye cocked for any attractive maiden that he might meet on the way. He does fish, but this is almost incidental to the lively flow of life that transports him through these merry days of fishing. Fishing today for many is such a serious and deadly business that these anglers should read Yates and Ransome and Applin. Some laughter and some more generosity on the riverbanks today would go far from amiss.

At eighth place we do have a tie. Always impressive in angling literature is a book that looks with microscopic detail at the waterside. F. M. Halford did not start this trend but was a master of it. Halford wrote copiously but possibly his book *Dry Fly Fishing in Theory and Practice*, published in 1889, is his most important. The book is full of the fascination that Halford experienced as he learnt more and more about the dry fly fishing on his river, his laboratory, the Test. This excitement leads to a freshness and an enthusiasm that bubbles over. Moreover what Halford wrote a century ago is still valid today and has never been outdated. Hills himself said 'There have not been many changes since he wrote . . . The method of fishing is unchanged . . . Halford's directions are as good and as useful as on the day that they were written.' Though these words of praise date from 1921 they are still relevant in the 1990s. Halford has been accused of being dogmatic and a blind purist but this he never was. Halford was a sportsman of the truest kind and in 1891 in *The Field* wrote an article under his pen name of Detached Badger which said '. . . the bottom fishers are as true sportsmen as the most severe purists in fly fishing.' It is sentiments like these that abound in dry fly fishing in theory and practice. Halford was not starchy, blinkered and conceited but a man merely thrilled with the new developments that he was forging. The dry fly fisherman of today should still owe great gratitude to this book.

A favourite Watkins Pitchford illustration from *The Philandering Angler*

Two other anglers blessed with similar perception and vision push Halford close in this category. G. E. M. Skues was the master of nymph fishing and was the one-time disciple of Halford. His books *The Way of a Trout* and *Nymph Fishing for Chalk Stream Trout* both show that type of attention to detail that the original master possessed to an extraordinary degree. That fierce debate broke out between the disciples of Halford and Skues is not necessarily the fault of either man – though Skues himself could be vitriolic in later years when discussing his former teacher. In 1913 Halford published his last book, *The Dry Fly Man's Handbook*, which was of course purchased by Skues. In the margin, apparently, Skues pencilled comments of serious criticism. 'Rubbish', he sometimes said. Or 'Impossible'. Or 'Must have had three hands'. For this little fact alone perhaps Halford was the greater of the two men.

The modern day parallel to Skues and Halford must be John Goddard. He is now arguably Britain's foremost angler–entomologist. He has written many books including *Trout Fly Recognition*, *Trout Flies of Still Water* and, with Brian Clarke, *The Trout and The Fly in 1980*, and all have become standard works on fly recognition, fly dressing and fly fishing. My own favourite book of his is *The Waterside Guide* that was published in 1988 with telling line illustrations by Charles Jardine and photographs by the author himself. This, in many ways, is a book condensed from his past masterpieces but how wonderfully small and compact and precise it is. It is a book that over the past year I have slipped into my Barbour jacket pocket to take with me to the riverbank on numerous occasions.

However, even Goddard is edged fractionally outside of this joint eighth place by his colleague and longtime friend Brian Clarke. In 1975 Clarke wrote *The Pursuit of Still Water Trout*. This book was reviewed by *Trout and Salmon*:

Brian Clarke has ploughed a lone and deeply satisfying furrow in a desire to understand the sport of fly fishing. He has set out to remove the guesswork by showing how everything anglers observe at the waterside, the behaviour of fish, the nature of the water they swim in and the creatures they eat, can be analysed and be made to work for us in our pursuit of trout.

The case exactly! Like Halford, Skues and Goddard, Clarke has looked at the environment of the trout and analysed it in a way that we can all understand. Stillwater trout fishing had started its boom in the 1960s but the lift-off began ten years later and Clarke became the mentor for a whole new type of angler. The book combines in-depth detail with an ease of telling and infectious excitement. Clarke describes his own journey from bungling amateur to expert and he seems to have the ability to take the reader with him on this journey along the rainbow.

Space now is very tight coming to tenth place. I am very aware that not yet included is one of the acknowledged game books. For salmon and sea trout especially there have been many classics over the years. Victorian England saw the publication of Scrope's *Days and Nights of Salmon Fishing in the River Tweed*. Scrope was the all-round Victorian sportsman and not only was he a skilled salmon fisher but a mighty shot and deerstalker too. He was very well read, a fine painter and possessed a deep knowledge of natural history. In London he was talked about as a man of 'superior accomplishments'. The book reflects all these gifts and also possesses a spark of imagination and flair that still burns brightly today. Scrope describes fishing by fair methods, but also night and spear fishing from boats. For this he was criticised by some but the overall picture of the salmon fishing world on the Borders in mid-nineteenth-century Britain could not be better painted.

A. H. Chaytor, Jock Scott, Balfour Kinnear and Anthony Crossley all gave salmon fishing a remarkably informative and inspirational literature by the mid-twentieth century. In 1947–59 Richard Waddington wrote three books on salmon fishing which took the sport still further along the way to the modern day. Waddington was a fly fisherman only and never used a spinning rod. He was one of the first to introduce a scientific explanation for the behaviour of salmon, and his books developed the view that the oxygen content of water was important in the success or failure of salmon angling. He also believed that salmon preyed largely on runs of small eels and he designed a range of treble-hooked salmon flies known as the Waddington flies. Equally inventive was Reg Righyni when, in 1965, he published his thoughtful book on salmon taking times. He and Terry Thomas and Bernard Venables had obviously considered the importance of oxygen to salmon activity and this book is a fine example of the fisherman thinking in a deeply analytical way about a profound angling problem.

Through the 1970s and 1980s the books have continued to come and Arthur Oglesby and Major Ashley Cooper have both been giants in the field of salmon fishing. The best books of either man could happily qualify for this number ten spot. The book that does clinch it, however, is Hugh Falkus' work, *Sea Trout*. The revised 1975 edition has simply become a bible to the sea trout angler. It is vast in its scope, is beautifully written and lavishly illustrated. Never can a book have had such profound effect on one single species. It has gone to many editions and sold round the world, and has made sea trout the fashionable species that it never really was before Falkus took it and elevated it to the position it now enjoys.

To compile a top ten in this way has been a nightmare and all manner of giants have been left out and not even discussed. There is, for example, no mention of Walton or Cotton or Colonel Venables. Nor is there mention of the great writers of the history of angling, for example T. Donald Overfield who produced the thrilling portrait of Skues. Nor the magical survey of *Redmire Pool* by Kevin Clifford and Len Arbery. There is no mention of Courtney Williams or C. F. Walker who produced fly-tying bibles. Where are the modern carp classics by men such as Hilton, Hutchinson or Sharman? Nor, as was recently pointed out to me, has there been any mention of the naturalist angler. Reelscreamer is an old friend of mine, he teaches English and he fishes and the two skills have engendered in him a love and understanding of naturalist angling writing. He has generously added this final piece to make my own selections seem more complete.

FISHERS OF MEN

Some writers appeal only to the specialist angler, others take the general reader, the poet, the aesthete or the environmentalist by the hand and lead them all through hedges and copses, metaphor and allusion, across meadow and rill towards pool and riffle. They feed the fancy until it flows from chalk-springs as surely as Test or Wylye, or nurture the imagination so that it can stroll beside moorland water or glen-fed river. These writers are fishers of men.

When I was a child in the fifties streams still ran pure, fly fishing in Wiltshire was the preserve of the retired major who lived in the millhouse across the road and allowed me to dabble with my Sealey Octofloat in the pool by his lawn, cars overheated on Porlock and I met, and fell under the spell of, Henry Williamson on Croyde Beach. He brought me a plate of wild strawberries from the dunes and spoke to my father about Tarka. We had gone there by steam train but probably represented the growing invasion and crowding of North Devon which Williamson grew to resent in proportion to his disappointment at not being recognised by the literary establishment. His *Chronicle of Ancient Sunlight*, a major sequence of novels, was never to bring him the OM or CH for which he longed, and it seemed that he would always be remembered for 'little Tarka' or Salar together with his stories about Georgeham, which had so alienated the villagers. His heavy drinking, loneliness and a misconceived popular conception of him as a Nazi-sympathiser were not apparent to me, clad in my knitted woollen swimming-trunks embroidered with a sailing ship, as I gobbled down the fruit and was aware of his baggy, khaki shorts and thin, suntanned and sinewy legs, which were the result of his long Exmoor walks and river wanderings.

I still cherish the postcard that he wrote on 1 January 1954, with its brownish twopenny stamp of George VI and a franking beyond deciphering. The sepia photograph of Morte Bay and Baggy Point has an inscription hovering in the air: 'You were down here between the two promontories'. Everyone accepts that he had a marvellous way with children, and it may be that his relationships with them were more fulfilled and uncomplicated than those with adults. The text of the card is worth printing in full:

> *Thank you for your appreciation of little Tarka. There is a similar book, called* Salar the Salmon, *but more for bigger boys. There are also some stories,* The Old Stag *etc, written years ago. Meanwhile I am writing about the 1st battle of Ypres 1914. A change – far from little Tarka: though things seem to be catching up down here, now!*
>
> *All good wishes. H.W.*

Dame Julian Bernars and Izaak Walton remain touchstones of the literary anglers read by many who have never dangled a worm or cast a fly. In our own day the poet laureate, Ted Hughes, has been at the forefront of cleaning up the Torridge and his poem 'Pike' has captured the fear and apprehension of that special, charged loneliness of casting into the dark when the mist settles and imagined monsters cruise around a bait, maybe ready to strike as the hackles rise at the call of the owl or an evening gust rearranges the hovering mist over the ancient pond. At that time every nerve is alert, and ghostly steps walk over bridges as the glowing bite-indicator twitches and then is still.

OPPOSITE
'Fly fishermen are generally well camouflaged . . . indeed a senior member of the Flyfishers' had the reputation of being practically indistinguishable from a tree' (Conrad Voss Bark). *Dermot Wilson nets an Avon trout* (Dermot Wilson)

A pond I fished, fifty yards across,
Whose lilies and muscular tench
Had outlasted every visible stone
Of the monastery that planted them –

Stilled legendary depth:
It was as deep as England. It held
Pike too immense to stir, so immense and old
That past nightfall I dared not cast

But silently cast and fished
With the hair frozen on my head
For what might move, for what eye might move . . .

                    Ted Hughes, 'Pike'

Of all sports, angling has produced the greatest literature. More books may have been written about cricket, technical manuals excluded, but fishing by its solitary nature has evinced all that is most thoughtful and personal. Even the most dedicated trophy or specimen hunter has those moments of stillness and fear as the evening light fades and the river noises grow ever more unpredictable and uncanny. H. W., however, did not dwell on romantic notions of being alone with the elements, was not seduced by nymphs and dryads nor caressed into seductive notions of the literary angler. He looked beneath the surface film, was not carried along in the tense thrill of surface tension but looked through the glass darkly into the natural history of his great fisherman, Tarka, and the otter's occasional quarry, Salar.

We live in a 'green' age, and it has become more and more obvious that if man has reached the top of the food chain then to protect the environment and safeguard the continuance of species he must know what he is doing. Through our intervention, there are no longer any wolves on Exmoor, to cull the weaklings amongst the deer. Otters have all but vanished, and the slower and weaker fish may well be the first ones caught as our baits probe the deeper pools and the slacks beyond. There are few fishermen, now, who are not conservationists and keen naturalists. If there are no dabchicks nor kingfishers, anglers are the first to notice and make this known. Farm slurry seems to be the cause of oxygen starvation, as Ted Hughes identified on the Torridge, and water extraction worries the keepers and anglers of the great sporting rivers.

We must hope that the indiscriminate killing of wild fish is now a thing of the past. Catching for the pot has a sound basis in man's hunting and sporting instincts and will only offend the most rabid and urban activists. Whilst H. W.'s most popular books amongst non-academics, *Tarka* and *Salar*, guarantee his continuing popularity amongst young and old his occasional writing and particularly his *A Clear Water Stream* must surely make him required reading amongst those philosopher anglers who trace their descent from Walton and who now find themselves involved in environmental debate.

OPPOSITE
R. V. Righyni grayling fishing on the River Nidd, Yorkshire (Arthur Oglesby)

In Richard Jefferies' *A London Trout* it is now easy to see a harbinger of present environmental concerns: the account starts with 'sword-flags rusting at their edges'. As the doomed and fatal tale continues, the stream is gradually exploited by creeping civilisation (perhaps urbanisation is a better term) and inexorable silence gradually descends. Jefferies concentrates, in 1879, on the view from a bridge where he watches a trout still hovering over a sandy bottom 'at the tail of the arch'. We have all lingered on such a bridge, arches neatly constructed in stone or brick and reassuringly denominated as medieval. For these summers Jefferies had the simple satisfaction of seeing the trout 'day after day', which even survived the joint efforts of a keen-sighted navvy and questing angler. In the fourth season 'the brook was dammed up on the sunny side of the bridge, and the water let off by a side-hatch, [so] that some accursed main or pipe or other horror might be laid across the bed of the stream somewhere far down.'

With the diminished flow of water the pool below the bridge became shallow, and men with all sorts of spears and traps invaded it one, ironically glorious, Sunday but they did not land the beautiful, wild and aged trout. Jeffries asks, 'Is it possible that he could have escaped? He was a wonderful fish, wary and quick.' He hopes that the trout has escaped downstream to deeper pools and clear water. Nonetheless, and distressingly enough for us a century later, he ends his story:

> I never failed to glance over the parapet into the shadowy water. Somehow it seemed to look colder, darker, less pleasant than it used to do. The spot was empty, and the shrill winds whistled through the poplars.

As a youth, I once followed the otterhounds up the River Bourne above Salisbury. The river, then, still had feeders which transected water meadows, even though I now realise that they were silting up and the golden, tigered, finger-long and surface-slashing pickerels were soon to vanish, as were red-bellied and hackled sticklebacks (which seldom survived in the aquarium for all their devilry) and lapwings, which always seemed to call and dummy near their nest in the doomed, lush water meadows of a boy who luxuriated in kingcups, frogspawn, and crayfish that backed into the jar.

Of course, we found no Tarkas even if the huntsmen wore green and carried ash sticks. I had no inkling of death, knew nothing of supposed depredations on trout stocks and only knew the snickering laughter of otters which reached me, as I lay in my bed of innocence, from across the water meadows. In *Tarka the Otter* the controlled instincts of man in the veteran hound, Deadlock, finally kill off the untrammelled joy of the protagonist in the last hunt. We are left with the knowledge of Tarka's offspring and of the elemental and often cruel nature of his life. Williamson presents a battle as glorious and heroic as that of Hal and Hotspur, but with the death of both combatants. Deadlock has been trained and exploited yet loved by man, and Tarka, though the moral victor with his three bubbles as moving as Bedivere's triple struggle to consign Excalibur to the waters, proves the doomed, tragic hero.

Ted Hughes in his poem 'An Otter' captures this same mystery and nobility. He speaks of the animal bringing '. . . the legend of himself/From before wars or burials . . . Like a king in hiding . . .' His otter can 'outfish fish' and the great fishing writer can out-angle the angler and catch any reader.

Henry Williamson's abiding strength is that whilst giving names to animals he never sentimentalised their lives by anthropomorphic wizardry. He was a naturalist and observer. In his own attempts to find human happiness he never used nature as an emotional crutch: rather he saw in it instinctive loyalties and inexorable cruelty and unfairness when assessed by conventional standards. Life is unfair, but there are moments of glorious instinct and fulfilment.

In *Salar the Salmon* and *Tarka the Otter*, H. W. may have given infinite inspiration to artists and countrylovers, and the economy and memorable richness of his prose may still make us all see a heron as 'Old Nog' or recognise a mended kelt as it is washed down and along an Exmoor stream. Williamson recalls for us the kingfisher's flash of halcyon blue, the uncontrollably nodding, brown-and-white courtesy of the dipper, the escape from a seal and all the other petty miracles which bring Salar to Tarka, salmon to the stream, and the resigned excitement of losing a grilse to the red power of the spate as the wild fish turns across the current and presents its silver flank to the force of Barle or Lynn.

Fortune may bring us the salmon of our dreams whilst application and a knowledge of ichtheology may land a ferox in the fastnesses of the Highlands, but H. W.'s account of *A Clear Water Stream* may well be the text that sustains us as we feast off roasted chestnuts and crusted port, staring into the hissing logs.

Some anglers are technicians and scientists, others are dreamers of dreams who nod more than they cast and dream more often than they catch. H. W. was a London lad from a middle class home, who early on discovered the excitements and rewards of the countryside. After a formative and traumatic experience of the trenches, which was never to leave him and which was to inform his great novel sequence, he found himself settled in a cottage in a village in North Devon with a young wife and family, and with the control and keepering of a stream running from Exmoor and populated by trout and invaded by salmon. 'An advertisement in the local paper said that two miles of fishing were to be let with the place. A trout stream!'

H.W.'s water flowed through a deer park, was varied and included a three-arched bridge. Even as one reads H.W.'s account one can see, before he speaks, the water dividing and meeting in the pool and one can predict the slim, torpedo-shaped fish which he will see when he looks over the parapet.

'There lay, sleepily, several trout, their hues varying with the colours beneath them: dark brown of back where they rested upon water-moss growing on rock-layers; brown over beds of gravel; and one, which had its stance by a little glacis of sand, was light golden yellow ... While I stood there I experienced a feeling that the day was fixed immortally, for ever, in blue space. For a moment I was back in the summer of boyhood.

Most trout anglers dream of their own stretch of water, whether single or double-bank. Depending on dreams or memories the river is moorland- or chalk stream-fed and runs within earshot of the perfect home where a rod can be left made up by the door and the evening rise can be addressed after a gentle stroll past ancient barns where owls call in the dusk. In this piscatorial arcadia there is no pressure to fish to the limit, the latter-day Walton can linger and watch and never cast to his own fish which hang beautifully below the clear pools. This dream underpins much of the imaginative energy of the true angler: whilst grateful for an invitation to some remote and fecund stream he dreams of an underfished water, replete with wild fish, not the plump and gormless products of the stockists.

Early in his oversight of a trout stream H.W. found himself meeting an experienced angler and his assistant, who had a suspiciously successful fly called the Poacher. They had caught many fish in a morning, all the size of small herrings, and were very confident in their presence on H.W.'s stream. They felt that they had fished within their rights and questioned the definition of bank fishing rights. Reading H.W.'s account in the 1980s, one catches one's breath at the following:

> He went on to say that if I looked in the fish book at The Fisherman's Arms, I would see an entry made by a visitor that he had already taken out of Devon streams one thousand, two hundred and forty-nine fish that season.

H.W. makes mistakes over the introduction of ranunculus into a moorland-fed stream, stocks his river unsuitably, occasionally fishes his own river and presents an irresistible image of the relaxed gentleman angler of our childhoods. The water is relatively free of pressure, bottles of pale ale can be cooled in a stock tethered below a pool, split-cane rods and brass reels parallel a lost world of tweeds, leather boots and silk fly lines.

In H.W.'s world, which is not so far away, steam trains still shuffle warmly over the viaducts, the fishing hotels of Exmoor are as remote as Loch Garry is today, fishing is still courtesy of the lord of the manor, and only the author seems to realise the pressure on the streams and rivers which had always seemed remote and exclusive.

A Clear Water Stream is diminished by summary and report. It does not have the narrative drive of Tarka or Salar, but for even the most inexperienced game angler or the most endowed business executive it tells of the excitement and rewards of knowing a river. Every cast, perfect in itself and the result of skill or luck, may land a fish. H.W.'s account, when truly read, is that of a man alone with dipper and heron and otter. It may be no longer possible to reproduce his experience, but it is rapidly becoming overwhelmingly clear that anglers who have a sense of self-esteem and a love of the environment in which they pursue their applied skills are having to be more intelligent, well informed, and self-sacrificing. No longer can a huge butcher's bill be appropriate and a weighty deep-freeze quota be defensible.

Fishers of men seem to laud the challenge of the catching of the truly wild fish. The great fishermen go forth in the misty morn and the bat-haunted twilight to try their skill against the willow-shrouded shallow of moorland stream or the clear gravel-caressed lie of the chalk stream. All have doubts about their rods, the weight of their lines, the strength of their leaders and the appropriateness of their flies. Their doubt is universal. Each angler hopes that his choice is right and yearns for some fatherly local expert who can give him or her the key to success.

If catching a fish were easy then the 'finny race' would be left alone. If a salmon or wild trout were to turn athwart and succumb to the net at the first touch then we would not pursue them. It is their tragedy that, like their hunter, they fight against their entrapment with a vigour and courage that command the respect of the hunter.

To read Jeffries, Hughes and Williamson is to extend our humanity. To study them is to increase our stature as selfless naturalists.

CHAPTER 12
THE GREAT TACKLEMAKERS

*T*he pleasures of fishing are chiefly to be found in rivers, lakes and tackle shops and, of the three, the last is the least affected by the weather. The sight of rods in a window brings a fisherman to a full stop as surely as a sight of a footbridge.

Arthur Ransome *Rod and Line*

PHOTO:
A shot of the rod room at the Hardy's factory, where such innovations as Lockfast joints, winch fittings, bridge rings and a tapered central spine of steel wire were incorporated. Such was the fame of the tackle makers that when George V was reminded that it was Hardy's birthday he sent his best wishes to Hardy Bros rather than Thomas!

*T*his is NOT a chapter concerning that most recent of vogues, tackle collecting. The only tackle that can be justifiably discussed here is a tackle that has always done the best job for the angler himself, though, obviously, this is often the most highly valued and collectable fishing tackle today. It is, of course, not hard to understand the appeal of handling old fishing tackle that represents such a tangible link with the past. Nothing helps demonstrate better the progression that angling has made over the decades.

The items are frequently beautiful to the eyes of the fisherman and there is a warmth about them, a memory of the devotion they once attracted, have absorbed and can now pass on to their collector or admirer. The old brass reels and the close-whipped split-cane rods are relics to be revered, and collectors like Fred Buller, Graham Taylor, Jess Miller, Jamie Maxtone Graham and David Beazley have added much to our knowledge by their researches and publications. Because of men like these, there is now a scholarship surrounding these antique works of art and engineering skill. The pity of the present situation is that now old fishing tackle has been discovered in this way, prices have risen, putting the nicest items out of reach of the average angler. And it is the angler above all who appreciates the richly woven old creel, a smooth geared reel or a beautifully proportioned rod, and not a man who is simply looking for another avenue in which to channel his wealth.

An extraordinary amount of fishing tackle has been created in the past hundred and fifty years alone and chunks of it must still exist, undiscovered, in dusty old attics. After all, in his recent book *Fishing Tackle – a Collectors' Guide* Graham Turner lists over two hundred and fifty tacklemakers in London alone who operated during the Victorian and Edwardian eras. Certainly, the choice of tackle has always been great and it seems that anglers have always been avid amassers of it, ever since the late fifteenth century at the least. Berners, Walton, Cotton, Barker and Venables and all the earliest writers make it plain that anglers have always loved innovative techniques and tackle and been inveterate collectors of it. Tackle has always been revered by the angler. It has been hoarded in sheds, rooms, cupboards, attics and now garages. Christmas, birthdays, anniversaries and any excuse for a present have meant the very latest rod, the very best reel or whatever the angler has always felt he must have to bring him closer to his heart's desire.

This obsession with tackle is hardly surprising for, in the earliest of his days by the bankside, tackle has always been at least as important as the fish itself, simply because the tackle is there and tangible, and the fish so rarely are that they seem more imaginary than real. Also, the tackle of the novice has always been impossible to handle smoothly. The combination of the beginner's lack of skill and of cheaper gear always results in an endless succession of bad casts, knots, tangles and tears. The possibility of good tackle seems in these early days to present a frustration-free future at the water when the job of catching fish can begin in earnest. Good tackle, the best tackle, has therefore always been coveted by the beginner and acquired piece by piece as his career develops.

Every generation of freshwater fishermen has witnessed new developments, added improvements and a state of the art constantly moving onwards. Hickory, greenheart,

'The choice of rod has some affinity with a marriage. One hopes it will last for some time.'
Conrad Voss Bark

bamboo cane, split-cane, glass, carbon and now boron rods have enthralled anglers for decade on decade and so it is with reels, lines, hooks, flies, spinners and floats . . . Floats especially so, for they are the first focal point of attention for nearly all of us. It seems that in those first seasons we all stare at an ever-hostile water when there is never a chance of a fish. We have all had our favourite float, that lucky object, traditionally red, that once saw fit to dip beneath the surface to the unseen force of a fabled fish. Even as our own particular ladder is climbed and our tackle becomes sophisticated, that old, chipped float remains safe, retired and dignified, loved and revered, for evermore.

Most good anglers begin as children with clumsy rods, nasty, rasping reels, inadequate clothing, and uncomfortable, striped collapsible seats and with ever-bending rod rest. Mature anglers today can easily remember the fishing tackle that was so longed-for in the 1950s. The developing angler wanted first one of the new Intrepid fixed spool reels. The Standard was a clumsy, clunking affair but the Supreme was something quite different. This was silently geared with a sensitive clutch and was the objective of all young men in the fifties. K. P. Morritt made these reels down in the South West and he became a millionaire out of their construction. He deserved to be so, for he rescued the careers of many young men who might otherwise have turned to other sports. From the Intrepids the progression was to the Ambidex, then perhaps to a Felton Crosswind and then, almost certainly, to a Mitchell 300. Mitchell 300s, even today so long after their introduction, are the flagship of reels. There is probably no harder wearing, more robust, more adaptable reel in the world today.

It was around this time also that Richard Walker began to revolutionise the tackle scene. His split-cane Mark IV Carp rod and its sister rod, the Avon, both made by B. James and Sons, were the rods that every man wanted. These rods from twenty and thirty years ago still hang in tacklerooms as beloved objects. It is hard to understand just how greatly these rods shaped the angling world. Before the Mark IV Carp rod there was no weapon marketed to deal with big fish in a satisfactory fashion. Walker saw that need and created 10oz of split cane capable of landing 30, 40 and even 50lb fish. Walker also realised that the tackle industry was lacking in other aspects. In his book *Drop Me a Line* with Maurice Ingham, all manner of tackle innovations are discussed. Walker designed landing nets capable of holding the fish that the Mark IV Carp rod might well get to the bank. He began to look at the possibility of an electric bite alarm that would serve the angler who had long vigils at the waterside. He looked at lead weights, at floats, at every item of the angler's tackle bag that had remained comparatively static for so long. With his B. James-built, Walker-designed rods, his pair of Mitchell 300s, a man could now fish for carp and pike right down to roach and bream with tackle of a previously unknown efficiency.

This was all tremendously stimulating and the fishing journals of the 1960s and 1970s were full of the excitement of new, developing tackle techniques. At the beginning of the seventies, as all anglers of over thirty years of age remember, the trend was for home-built glass blank rods. It was then not 'done' to be seen on the bankside with rods bought straight from the shop. Every man had to have his own home-built affair, built to his own specifications, whipped with the silks of his own choice. It was a phase when anglers became deeply in touch with their tackle and many today remember it with affection. By the later seventies the trend had moved to the custom-built rods and now smaller firms proliferate, preparing beautifully made weapons, each one tailor-designed for a particular task on a particular water after a particular species. Graham Phillips' and Terry Eustace's are just two of the smaller concerns that provide these top quality rods for the committed angler of the modern age.

So it has always been. At every twist and turn in angling's history over the past hundred and fifty years there have been items of tackle that the good angler has always aspired to own. There have always been the equivalents of the Mark IV Carp rod, the Mitchell 300 reel, or the Intrepid Elite and many examples exist today in collections all over the country. Reels have always figured large in the collections of anglers and there are outstanding examples of reels that have been masterful in their design. In 1896 the Coxon Aerial reel was marketed by Allcock & Co. The unusual feature of this reel was the use of spokes which connected the hub to the rim of the flanges. This made for a very light reel and allowed the non-nylon lines of the day to dry out very quickly.

The inventor of the reel was almost certainly Henry Coxon, the well known fishing writer of the time who took the design of the reel from the model of the bicycle wheel. He discussed the concept of this reel in his book *A Modern Treatise On Practical Coarse Fishing* and from then on, through the Edwardian period, his name was revered both in the angling magazines and by such giants as the Trent Otter who all gave him the credit for this marvellous invention. The Aerial reel went on from 1896 well into the twentieth

'Old men owned these long roach poles. Their hands were gentle, their touch masterful, their skills with rod, float and bait sublime.' Parsons

century. In the mid-1920s the name Coxon was dropped but the reel went from strength to strength and is still seen in frequent use on riverbanks today. The Aerial range provided one of the best centre pin trotting reels imaginable. Its light and smooth action is unsurpassed and provides perfect control over the float in a current. The Coxon Aerial, the Match Aerial, the Aerial Popular are all examples of this reel invented almost a century ago that has thrilled coarse anglers on rivers countrywide.

In certain ways the Aerial reel took over from the other majestic coarse fishing reel of the nineteenth century, the Nottingham reel. The Nottingham reel was developed in the 1850s, probably by Joseph Turner, Samuel Lowkes and William Brailsford. It was publicised most notably by William Bailey, the Nottingham tackledealer, fisherman and writer. In 1857, in *The Angler's Instructor* Bailey wrote,

> *. . . you cannot have a reel too light or that runs too free. The best is a four-inch common wood reel, varnished to keep the rain from swelling the wood – the only brass about it being the hoop for fastening it to the rod. Brass inside and out adds to its weight and lessens its utility. To cast a long line you must have a free and easy running reel.*

The Nottingham reel that Bailey publicised came in different sizes and he used a 4in reel for pike, a 3½in reel for trotting for barbel and sometimes went down to a 3in reel

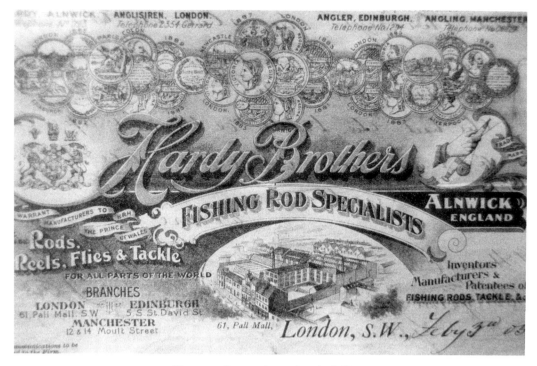

The most famous letter-head of all . . .

for smaller fish like chub and roach. Like the later Coxon Aerial, the Nottingham reel was the definitive centre pin for coarse anglers of the earlier and mid-Victorian period.

It is hard to overestimate the importance of this period in angling history. Conditions seemed suddenly ripe for a great surge in the development of angling tackle. The first full-length split-cane rod had appeared and lines and reels had been found. Victorian industry and engineering were reaching new peaks of production, efficiency and invention and growing prosperity meant more money to spend on leisure activities. It was into this favourable situation that the Hardy brothers stepped. In 1872 they decided to expand their cutlery business to include shooting and fishing equipment. By the turn of the century their firm had become the most progressive company in its field and almost certainly the most famous fishing tacklemaker in the world. The item that effected this rocket to fame more than any other was created in 1891 when the brothers introduced their first patented fly reel. It was a brass, frameless, centre pin reel with a simple wire line guide. Importantly, its drum ran on ball bearings which reduced wear and friction. The reel was also fitted out with a ratchet and pull check mechanism on which the breaking tension could be adjusted. The Hardy catalogues made a great deal of these advances and, with the confidence typical of the Victorians, they named the reel model the Perfect. It became without doubt the most famous fly reel in the world.

The Hardy company did not restrict itself to reels alone but built the whole range of fishing tackle from accessories to the most important rods of the day. Hardy's marketing was also way ahead of its time. The firm worked closely with the most famous anglers of the period to create rods that bore the true stamp of authenticity. Bickerdyke,

Pennell, Senior, Sheringham, Martin and many others were consulted about rod design. So too was Sir Edward Grey who had the Perfection rod named after him and who wrote a glowing testimonial of the rod in fly fishing.

I bought my first split-cane rod, a powerful two-piece ten foot six rod, off Messrs Hardy in 1884. The button joint to that rod is still as sound as ever after landing many fish of all weights up to ten pounds, and though I have worn out one or two tops, not one has ever broken suddenly in the act of fishing and they have stood faithfully against most fearful shocks caused by weeds or bushes in the act of casting. This toughness of split cane in my opinion settles the question decisively in its favour . . . Split cane is most staunch of all materials; like an old and faithful servant, it is incapable of treachery or sudden change, and when it fails it does so gradually. My own original split-cane rod has become a trusted companion, used to all winds and weathers, to burns, chalk streams and rivers of many kinds.

A better testimonial by a more respected statesman could hardly be imagined for the Hardy firm.

Salmon rods were equally covered, and in 1914 the Wye rod was brought out. This was unusual in being shorter than the norm. The Wye rod was made between 10ft 6in and 13ft 6in out of split bamboo. As usual, Hardy's recruited an expert to give his opinion on the rod. In this case, the commentator was the Wye expert Robert Pashley.

Dear Sirs, I have killed over two hundred salmon on your Wye rod. On looking through my diary, I find I killed a hundred and nine fish on it last season alone, weighing from five to thirty two pounds, and also a thirty one pounder the season before. It is a two-jointed rod with two tops, both of which are in good order, and with fair usage may yet account for another century apiece. Robert Pashley from Ross.

The success of the Wye salmon rods continued until 1978. In 1926 Hardy's recruited the salmon sensation of the time – A. H. E. Wood – who gave his name to a range of single-handed rods. As the catalogue said:

. . . the twelve foot rod was designed with the assistance of Mr Wood for his particular and successful style of salmon fly fishing. During the last two seasons we have made many experiments to improve the balance of these rods. (Mr Wood has again been good enough to assist us). One of the chief objects was to make a twelve foot rod feel lighter in the hand and not be so tiring to the wrist, and yet retain all the power necessary for long casting and handling of a heavy fish.

The Hardy catalogues are now sought-after collectors' items and particularly fine and rare examples can fetch £100 or more at sales. They are delightful reading, say a lot about the tackle of the time and also about the firm's love of self-image. The catalogues are full of testimonials from all the lords of the land, all of them full of praise for what were obviously considered the Rolls Royce rods of the nineteenth and twentieth centuries. Certainly Hardy rods not only dominated in this country but also all over the

A part of the Hardy museum at Alnwick . . . when is angling going to achieve its national museum centre? Which country home will open such rooms to the public and attract even more people through the turnstiles?

empire. Photographs were regularly included of great fish from India and Australia, strange exotic fish that had bowed to the power of the cane built in the northern borders of this country. Hardy's itself was quite definite about the excellence of its own rods:

> *We are frequently asked how is it Hardy's rods are so much better than others? The reason is very simple. In the first place, fifteen sixteenths of all the rods offered are either factory made or imported and there is not that careful detail given to construction which is so necessary.*

Hardy's by contrast consulted with the Indian forestry department to find the precise area which would give the very best canes, had them prepared to its very particular instructions and then had them shipped to its technically advanced factory where they were made by skilled craftsmen into some of the best rods of their day.

Nor did Hardy's neglect the coarse fisherman. 1894 saw the building of the Special Chub and Barbel rod and the Guinea roach perch and bream weapon – both built out of greenheart and bamboo and coming in three pieces. In 1913, F. W. K. Wallis designed a bamboo and split-bamboo three-piece perfect Nottingham rod for the firm, which continued in production until 1931. In 1914, the Perfection roach rod was built. Again this was out of split bamboo and had a remarkable run, being built 1914–66. Indeed this was one of the author's first serious rods as a boy in the 1950s. The Special pike rod was built out of bamboo and greenheart and was a two-piece affair that also ran from 1919–51.

The turn of the century saw a major invention break onto the angling market, the thread line or fixed spool reel. Credit is generally given to Alfred Holden Illingworth, who patented his reel in 1905. Undoubtedly the fixed spool has been one of the greatest boons to coarse anglers and salmon spinners in the last century but it was an invention that led to much controversy. Certainly Illingworth himself loved fly fishing for trout and did not invent the thread line reel to displace this particular love. He would invariably fly fish until low summer water made spinning by far the more practical method. In 1907 the Light Casting Reel company began commercial production of Illingworth's reels and advertised what became known as the Illingworth Number 1. Illingworth himself never made any money whatsoever from the invention and passed all the commercial rights to the company itself. Illingworth was a natural inventor and an engineer by trade, and took the idea of the thread line reel from the bobbin used in the silk weaver's shuttle. In 1910 the Illingworth Number 2 reel was developed and in 1913 this was superseded by the Number 3. Fixed spool reel production continued

Left to right, top to bottom: an Illingworth 'Mark I' Threadline Reel; a Featherstone & Hart 4in Salmon Fly Reel; a Hardy's Fortuna Big Game Reel; a Farspure Casting Reel; a Hardy 4in Walnut Starback Reel; a Hardy Zane Grey Big Game Multiplier Reel; Hardy's – the Barton 3¼in Dry Fly Reel

through the 1920s and 1930s and many different models appeared on the market, frequently less effective and less well designed than Illingworth's earlier creations.

Rods and reels are only part of it. Of course over the hundreds of years of the tackle industry massive developments have been made in every item of the angler's tackle box. Whether rods and reels are more important than line and hooks is of course debatable – the true answer is that each piece of angling tackle is complementary and it all fits together like a great jigsaw puzzle. Angling has seen so many great inventors that it is impossible to mention all of them and even today, when it might be considered that angling tackle makers reach peaks of perfection unknown in any previous period, inventions still continue and tackle companies still search constantly for new ideas to revolutionise the trade. To some, this obsession with fishing tackle is not a good thing. It can be seen as a type of blind, misleading anglers and taking them away from the truth of angling skill. The core of a good angler is the understanding of the fish and the waters and not necessarily the man who worships his tackle. Of course a good angler knows exactly how to use tackle but from this baseline he goes on to develop his skills as a naturalist above all. Yet, tackle in the hands of an expert is a wonderful thing. Think how happy the rod and reel designers would have been to have seen their creations in the hands of such casting experts as Jack Martin or Lionel Sweet or F. W. K. Wallis or Hugh Falkus or Arthur Oglesby. Men like these can make tackle sing and can make the work of the tacklemakers seem greatly justified and rewarding.

A Hardy's '2/0 Casapedia' Salmon Multiplying
Fly Reel – stamped by appointment to
HRH The Prince of Wales

CHAPTER 13
THE MEDIA MEN

*M*ost anglers get their information by word of mouth and by copying other anglers on the bankside and most of it is wrong. The only stop-gap to a slide into total inefficiency is provided by the tackle shops where long-suffering dealers constantly correct the misconceptions . . . there are signs that things are improving, that anglers are realising that the most accurate way to learn is to copy from a magazine or book then test it themselves, improving as experience dictates.

Barrie Rickards *Angling – The Fundamental Principles* (1986)

———————————————————————

PHOTO:
R. B. Marston: 'True to his convictions, true to his friends, and true to himself, he fought his way through many campaigns so often undertaken for the preservation of fish.' A. Nelson Bromley

*T*here are sports where those who cover them can be justifiably regarded as hacks, as men who make a living out of reporting something with which they have no real identity. This can rarely be said of angling; angling is the poor relation in the media and most definitely there has never been the money in angling reportage to attract charlatans. Paper and magazine men, TV and radio men even, have almost invariably been anglers who have believed in communication for love not for money.

This is important, for the public image of angling has never been more crucial than now. From the 1980s angling has been under pressure from all manner of anti-blood sport and environmental groups, and public relations are essential if angling is to continue unchecked and liberated into the twenty-first century. The second priority is of course to disseminate knowledge. It is vital to teach angling skills to the newcomer and to the young, and in this alone the angling press has fulfilled a vital function over the generations.

The better magazines have also provided a steady and wise commentary on events. Their leader writers have generally portrayed a sensible down-to-earth view of angling, and controversies, generally good for the sport, have raged in the angling pages of magazines for generations.

The media are important for providing an up-date of news. News becomes history. It is essential that the major catches are reported accurately so that myth does not become taken as fact. The press can also act as a pressure group on water authorities and governments. Without the angling media, watchdogs on the water fronts would be few indeed. The angling press has provided and always will provide a mouthpiece for the aquatic environment.

Also the pages of the magazines and newspapers are in many ways a switchboard for ideas and views that bring together all types of anglers and opinions. The letters pages of these journals provide a vital barometer of angling's mental health. Furthermore, the media provide a marketplace for angling tackle. In the press the industry explains and advertises. Without the press anglers would not know what was on offer and would not be able to read the market reports on new pieces of tackle. Without these essential items, the development of angling and the techniques used would remain comparatively static and immobile.

The angling media, whether concerned with the spoken or written word, have also provided over the years an inspirational element. The articles, photographs and illustrations all motivate anglers to improve on their past results. And the last major purpose of the media is to bring pure pleasure. Angling is of course a sport that can be enjoyed at the fireside almost as much as at the waterside, and the angling media over the years have provided an attraction on dark winter nights or to anglers too ill or too old to be able to wield the rod any more.

The tragedy has always been that not all anglers have sought access to the media. The circulations of newspapers and magazines have always fallen woefully short of the number of anglers actually participating in the sport. Those who will not read must find that their development is stunted. Even worse, they are not aware of the most up-to-

The Fishing Gazette – 'the authority on piscatorial subjects'

date environmental issues or the most humane ways of treating their catch. A tragedy of the sport is that there remains a large, ill-informed body of anglers who are still outside the mainstream of current thinking.

The lift-off in the angling newspaper business took place in the later nineteenth century. This was helped by late Victorian prosperity and most especially by the growth of a railway network. Now there was comparative ease of communication and newspapers and magazines could be ferried quickly from one end of the country to the other. The public became more used to reading. One should not underestimate the impact of W. H. Smith bookstores at railway stations over the last century. The number of fishing magazines and newspapers sold over their counters in the past hundred years must be colossal.

The Field, *The Gentleman's Magazine* and the *Fishing Gazette* were all examples of magazines that portrayed fishing in a highly intelligent light. Francis Francis and Hugh Tempest Sheringham were both angling editors of *The Field* whilst the *Fishing Gazette* was bought and edited by R. B. Marston. All these three men had tremendous ability as editors and huge commitment to the sport itself. They were also fortunate in the quality of the contributors who flourished in the last years of the nineteenth century and the first ones of the twentieth. John Bickerdyke and Cholmondeley Pennell and Frank Buckland are only three examples of a whole school of angling writers of great skill in the sport and in literature.

Marston was typical of the great editors. He was born in 1853 and in 1878 bought the *Fishing Gazette* which he edited until his death. The gazette was, right until its final demise, regarded as *the* voice of angling. Marston made it as intelligent and concerned as he himself was. Marston fought for the passing of the Mundella act that gave protection to the fisheries of this country. He fought for the limitation of tar on roadways that, during heavy rains, could pollute fisheries. In 1880 he won the silver medal and diploma at the Berlin International Fisheries Exhibition for his services to fishing literature and the environment. He worked for the recognition of Izaak Walton and it was his influence that brought about the memorial window at Winchester Cathedral. He was the chairman of the Thames Angling Preservation Society and there he linked up with such men as Francis and Buckland in promoting the capital's river, one of the most testing barometers of fish health in this country. He was a founder member of the Fly Fishers' Club and was president in 1897 and again in 1910.

His skills were not confined to fly fishing. He caught pike of up to 26lb and was a frequent companion of that great piker Alfred Jardine. He was a trout man and caught them to 8lb and also a lover, like Halford himself, of grayling which he caught to 2lb 10oz. There is no more fitting tribute to Marston than what is called 'the Marston trout', a memorial named after him in New York state in recognition of the good that he did in linking British and American anglers. This tiny profile has given an indication of the

OPPOSITE
'The wild rush of a 20lb salmon thrills through the frame as nothing else in the nature of sport does.' Francis Francis

Jack Thorndyke, former editor of *Angling Times* and *Trout and Salmon*, looks inspired by a 12lb fish!

breadth of knowledge and commitment that men like Marston, Francis Francis and Hugh Sheringham found time both to amass and to give. They were highly gifted, highly respected men who had great impact on the sport, politics and the environment.

The 1950s, sadly, saw the end of the *Fishing Gazette*. Other excellent magazines like *Creel* and *The Anglers World* died in the 1960s. However, the picture was not all one of gloom. In this period the *Trout and Salmon* magazine was co-founded by the well known broadcaster Howard Marshall and edited by a line of men beginning with Ian Wood and progressing through Jack Thorndyke and Roy Eaton to Sandy Levington, all of whom have set a standard of excellence. Just as important was the foundation of *Angling Magazine*. Brian Harris was its editor in the 1970s when the magazine was in its heyday. His production standards were high and covered all three branches of the sport: game, coarse and sea. Harris was fortunate in being able to assemble some of the most gifted angling writers: Jim Gibbinson, Ian Gillespie, Dave Collyer, Dave Stewart, Clive Gammon, Dick Orton, John Darling and Digger Derrington were all regulars. Walker contributed frequently and Harris also encouraged new writers like Hutchinson and Yates to contribute to the magazine. All in all it was a magazine that talked sense, was well written and illustrated and was a standard-bearer for the sport.

Ken Sutton, Bernard Venables, Jack Thorndyke, Fred J. Taylor and Richard Walker toast Fred Buller (hidden by Walker's arm) the Top Angler of the Year

During the 1970s two new coarse fishing magazines came into print. David Hall produced *Coarse Fisherman* which was a platform for some of the most exciting coarse fishing anglers to emerge in recent times. Brian Moreland, Kevin Clifford, Rod Hutchinson, Graham Marsden, John Wilson and the author himself were all contributors to a magazine that was brash but important. A year later *Coarse Angler* was founded and its co-editors were Colin Graham and Colin Dyson. Both men were respected in the media business. Colin Dyson, upon the death of Colin Graham, has continued to run the magazine which is a constant beacon of sense and intelligence in a world not always renowned for either.

Fishing has seen a succession of papers come and go. The *Angling Times*, however, remains and has a great history. In 1953 it was founded with great excitement and Howard Marshall the broadcaster was a director. Colin Willock, of TV wildlife fame, was its first editor. Bernard Venables was an executive editor and Jack Thorndyke was features editor, later to take over as editor in 1956. Peter Tombleson wrote the Match Angle column and helped organise the whole paper. Ken Sutton, now of ACA fame, was its first circulation manager. Dick Walker was the first big-name contributor who wrote for it until the mid-1980s. Incidentally the Marston line of newspaper men was continued through Dick. Pat Marston, the daughter of the great R. B. Marston became Mrs Richard Walker. What an angling spirit flowed through from the nineteenth century into the twentieth and on into the *Angling Times*!

It must not be considered however that Walker was always an easy man to get on with, as Jack Thorndyke, the editor of the *Angling Times* makes clear.

I have the interesting if unrelenting job of editing an angling newspaper and hardly a day passes without my thoughts of what to publish and what to leave out being disturbed by the impatient ringing of the telephone. A voice, so unlike its owner, greets me with the ungentlemanly 'Wotcher cock! It's Richard'. I have just time to return the greeting with 'What, you again?' when the one-sided conversation gets under way, something like this:

'That was a lot of codswallop you published about the fellow who caught a 2 pound roach from the so-and-so river. There aren't any roach in there. I should know, I fished it for years.'

When I tried to assure him it was a genuine catch I am, as always, rudely prevented from continuing by the voice, now in a different dialect, exclaiming 'Did you see the fish yourself?'

I have not had the opportunity of replying when I am told 'Of course you didn't, you just took the chap's word.' When I endeavour to strengthen my case for using the story by confirming that the capture was witnessed by two other anglers who saw it weighed, I achieve precisely nothing, for Richard is now giving me chapter and verse on why he knows the fish must have been a chub.

I have said little, but am too exhausted to continue the discussion. It is just as well, for by this time Richard has switched the conversation to some '. . . clot who doesn't know what he's writing about.'

The prolonged and almost daily telephone discussion on such subjects as what we should do with pike, why we should not nationalise waters, and the load of nonsense I allowed to be published about the balance of nature, frequently ends with the voice of Richard, suddenly changing from the dialect of a Liverpudlian to that of a former university scholar, telling me that I'm not such a bad chap after all. Politely, appealingly, he asks 'And now, I wonder if you could do something for me?'

In the national newspapers of this country angling has often been poorly represented. Despite being a great participator sport, angling has often been way behind even the minority sports in coverage. Still, what has been done in the national papers has often been done very well. Maurice Wiggin in the past and Conrad Voss Bark and Brian Clarke in the present are two examples of excellent reporters on the game fishing scene. Stan Piecha has run an equally excellent match fishing column in *The Sun* over many years. But Arthur Ransome is the model if only for the scope of his writing. Through his years as angling writer for the *Manchester Guardian*, Ransome covered game fishing, coarse fishing, tackle developments, literature in angling and the environment as a whole. His writing was not in any way restricted by the branch of the sport or by class. His tales, still in publication, remain inspirational.

The radio is not really a medium suited to angling. However, local radio over the past few years has provided an excellent news service. In East Anglia, for example, Radio Norfolk employs Tom Boulton, the matchman and tackle dealer, who gives vital, up-to-date information on matches, on big-fish waters and the angling scene in general. It is a lively, well presented programme enjoyed by thousands. A wider programme, however, is presented by Martin James, the Radio Lancashire presenter. Martin is a natural on the radio with his rich northern accent but he has also extended the scope of his programme to include the largest environmental problems of the day. He also **reviews all the new books and he travels to meet the anglers in question. In all, Radio**

Lancashire is lucky in having this man to give his programme its professional caring direction.

Angling has been brought onto the TV screen and some shocking mistakes have been made. There is an embarrassing tendency to wheel in celebrities. These are almost inevitably men who know little or nothing about angling, but having what is known as 'star status', are expected to draw a wider audience. True anglers see this only as a massive insult. Fortunately, however, there have been programmes in the past that have not condescended to anglers and have portrayed angling in a reasonable fashion.

There have been some adventurous if exciting near misses and the prime example of this was the BBC series *The Fishing Race*. Eminent anglers, mostly drawn from the ranks of *Angling Magazine*, **were split into teams for 48 hours and asked to pursue**

LEFT: Martin James at his studio: an angler, a campaigner for water purity, multiple sclerosis and children in need

John Wilson – the writer, angler, tackle dealer and television presenter – with a very fine barbel

as many fish species as possible. A point was given for each species and a second point given for the biggest fish of that species. Generally the programme worked well and showed skilful anglers in a humorous and entertaining light. However, raids upon local zoos for piranhas and on neighbourhood ponds for tame carp hardly portrayed anglers as environmentalists, caring for wildlife!

John Wilson's series *Go Fishing*, made by Anglia TV, is an excellent attempt. John has charisma and is an exceptional angler. The programme is entertaining, informative and shows anglers as capable of appreciating the environment. John's programmes came at a valuable time in the 1980s when angling was under attack from many different quarters. The programme achieved very high ratings nationwide and there can be little doubt that its success has blunted many of these attacks on our sport.

One of the two best programmes ever to appear on television was Jack Hargreaves' series *Out of Town*. Jack Hargreaves had very much the feel of the country in him. He was the son of a Yorkshire farming family and began training as a vet in London before lack of funds forced him away. Whatever the programme was about, Jack had the sense to use the experts of the moment. One of the greatest showed his partnership with Owen Wentworth on the River Stour for roach fishing. It was a film that presented fishing at its best. Owen was a perfect teacher and roach were caught without the programme ever flagging. Richard Walker was employed to catch some barbel, which he did with his customary efficiency and flair. In series after series Jack Hargreaves went round the country talking to local experts and catching fish that many anglers could only dream about. His programme was watched by countrylovers everywhere and fishing again benefitted through its showing.

The second of the two great angling series featured Michael Hordern. Here audiences saw an excellent fisherman and a fine actor involved in a dramatisation of some of the great Ransome articles. The combination was unbeatable. Nobody who watched the programmes could forget them. Hordern managed to portray the absolute essence of angling. A gentle elderly man on a riverbank, looking out over sunsets and flashing waters, a man who knew how important fishing was to the life of wisdom.

The man who must personally have done more for angling in the media than any other must be Terry Thomas. Sadly this remarkable man died in 1989 in his late sixties. He was a skilful angler, and as able with a fly rod as he was after pike, roach or barbel. It was this ability that led him into the tackle world, where he became a consultant in later days for the Gladding and for the Shakespeare companies. It was, however, as a media man that he will be best remembered. For years he wrote for *Trout and Salmon* and contributed his reflections on the past masters, on angling giants that he had known and fished with through the twentieth century. He presented many radio programmes and TV series where he appeared as a benign and expert angler. He had the ability to get the best out of men who appeared with him and must be remembered as *the* great public relations man of angling. It is doubtful whether Terry Thomas will ever be fully replaced.

CONCLUSION

*J*ust a few of the great anglers of history have been discussed, but the future will demand that more follow them. J. W. Hills made it plain that angling is a continuing process with never any final conclusion in sight. 'Angling is an endless quest in which no one ever attains perfection and we stumble towards it not by conquests but by defeats. Our triumphs are for the most part poor things compared with what we have not attained.' Over and over, the great anglers have echoed this sentiment. Within ten minutes, for example, of meeting Dermot Wilson, he said, 'The more that I fish, the less that I feel I know.' Buller, Walker, Falkus and many others have repeatedly affirmed this belief that angling is a continuing and unfolding process and we will never be in a position to know all the answers hidden yet, from us.

Whether we need any more advances in the development of fishing tackle I do not know. If the mechanics of deception progress very much further then perhaps the element of skill will be seconded entirely. Should tackle developments make fish too easy to catch, is there then any point in the catching of them? Obviously we can expect continued superficial developments but anything major must be analysed carefully. Would we in fact want an invisible line, for example, or would that simply stack the odds so heavily in our favour that we could no longer be described as sportsmen? Our tackle now pretty well provides us with about all the advantages that we should surely require, and to demand many more begins to smack of greed. Into the next century I rather hope for different paths to be followed.

In the knowledge of fish and their behaviour we still have a long way to advance. There are grey areas, for example, in the life history of salmon and eels, and no one knows when and why the burbot disappeared from this country. We do not understand the effect of a falling barometer on fish, nor the full extent of their powers of taste, smell, sight and understanding. Since the advance of carp fishing we are just beginning to appreciate the extent of some fishes' learning processes. How far this goes is still to some extent guesswork. Many fish diseases, the perch disease in particular, remain a mystery and frequently the side-effects of stocking waters are ill-understood. Much more research is needed into these and many other problems and many more Bucklands and Wheelers will be needed as our waters face increasing pressures in the years to come.

What future there is for angling is hard to decide. With most, if not all, of the governments of the world devoted to the philosophy that a sufficiency of material possessions and synthetic entertainments will guarantee human happiness, the outlook is bleak . . . Where politicians are concerned, conservation is something about which they are prepared to lie and mouth platitudes, but is not yet a cause they wish to espouse with sincerity. They talk gravely about the importance of conservation while they permit rivers and streams to be destroyed by abstraction, pollution and indiscriminate dredging.

Richard Walker (1975)

The twenty-first century will demand greater effort in the conservation of our waters and the defence of our sport. Technology and population growth will together increase the demands on our already hard-pressed environment. Abstraction and pollution will remain constant threats. So will acid rain, the menace of forestry, barrage schemes, overnetting, damaging drainage schemes and a hundred new attacks as yet undreamed of. Equally, there will be continued and sustained attacks by those who do not fish and do not appreciate that anglers are the guardians of the aquatic environment. The future must provide the sport with the likes of David Clarke and Allen Edwards, men with the courage and determination to fight off the people and the developments that would destroy those things we love.

As much as anything else, angling needs just and fair philosophies to carry it along the path upon which Walton set it. Success by all and any means is a sad trend in many branches of the sport today. Sven Berlin spoke for the future of us all in *Jonah's Dream*. 'A young fisherman has the making of a man of vision who might learn to tie his own fly, fight his fish and then release it into the great stream of life for another migration. Until the time comes when the catching of fish is not the purpose of fishing.' Salmon, trout and sea trout must sometime in the future be taken and put back, not caught and taken out as a matter of course. Big coarse fish must come to be seen as a blessing and a privilege. The unity of purpose that is above self, a brotherhood of feeling and hope for the fish and their waters must one day embrace all anglers if truly great things are to be achieved and if the great anglers of the past are to be followed honestly and effectively by their disciples in the future. There is a heavy responsibility on all of us whether we teach the young to fish, write about fishing, or simply hold the rod all the precious moments of our life.

ACKNOWLEDGEMENTS

I have received the most generous help, in writing this book, from anglers almost too numerous to name. Some, however, cannot go unmentioned. I would like to thank Hugh Falkus in Cumbria, Dermot Wilson in Wiltshire, Fred Buller in Buckinghamshire and Arthur and Grace Oglesby in Yorkshire for their generosity, time and for the supply of photographs. Robin Armstrong, whom I contacted as a subject for the book and who became a dear friend as well as provider of paintings and photographs, deserves special thanks. I would also like to make special mention of Chris 'Reelscreamer' Rowe who contributed so handsomely to the chapter on literature. Colin Dyson, Barrie Rickards, Tim Paisley, Kevin Clifford, Bob Church, Tony Pawson and Bernard Venables were all constant sources of advice and came up with the most excellent photographs.

Many of the excellent photographs were supplied by the following people, who also advised me. Hardy Brothers, Bill Bachman, Paul Elliott, Chris Turnbull, Mrs Blanche Allen, Jim Gibbinson, Bob Gledhill, F. J. Taylor, Bonhams, Peter Stone, Roy Shaw, Bruno Broughton, Mrs Ann Voss Bark, Chris Ball, Chris Yates, Alan Rawden, Alan Wilson, Neville Fickling, John MacDonald, John Sidley, Martin James, Martyn Page, Roy Eaton, Mrs Florence Miller, Jim and Shirley Deterding, John Wilson, Neil Dalrymple and all at *Coarse Fisherman* and *Angling Times* magazines.

The ACA and Allen Edwards deserve mention for their help and hard work, as do John Rollings and the ladies at the Norwich Alfred Marks Agency for their care in typing the often chaotic manuscript.

I would also dearly like to thank David Clarke and especially Michael and Audrey Robins for opening their angling libraries to me so frequently and often at such short notice. Finally, thanks to Jack Heddon, Fred Crouch, Mike Mee and Sir David Nickson for their valued written contributions.

INDEX

Howman, Jean, 166
Hudson, Charlie, 39
Hughes, Ted, 59, 209-12
Hughes-Parry, J., 65
Humphries, John, 143
Hunt, Miss Alex, 103-5
Hutchinson, Rod, 13, 88-91, *90*
Hutt, Reg, 115

Illingworth, Alfred Holden, 147, 221, *221*, 222
Ingham, Maurice, 26, 86, *86*
Inwood, Cyril, 30, 48, *64*
Ivens, T. C. (Tom), 61-3

Jackson, John, 66
    Simon, 139
Jacques, David, 81
James & Sons, B., 216
James, Martin, *124*, 230, *230*
Jardine, Alfred, 102, 112
    Charles, 204
Jeffries, Richard, 198, 210-12
Johnson-Smith, Sir Geoffrey, 143
Jones, Jack, 149

Keale, Bill, 30
Kefford, Dick, 86
Keith, A. C. 155
King, Tricia, *71*
Kingsley, Charles, 155
Kite, Oliver, 58
Knight, A. Roland, *185*, 190-1

Lane, Billy, 30, *169*, 172, *175*
    Col J., 197
Lapsley, Peter, 200
Law, Bill, 155-6
Leadbetter, Brian, 181
Leary, Dan, *173*
Levington, S., 228
Little, Crawford, 73
Litton, Dave, 116
Lowkes, Samuel, 217
Lunn, William James, 80, 149-51, *150*

MacDonald, John, 111
    Ritchie, 88-91
Maddocks, Kevin, 91, 116
Maitland, James, 148
Makins, Billy, 180
Manns, Laurie, 116
Mansfield, K., 112
Marks, Ivan, 179-80, *179*
Marlow, Roy, 180

Marryat, G. S., 49, 55, 67
Marsden, Graham, 100
Marshall, Howard, 58, 228
Marshall Hardy, Eric, 200
Marston, R. B., 67, 223-8
Martin, J. W., (The Trent Otter), 35-40, 102, 112, 118-20, 133, 200
    Jack, *18-19*
Mason, Roy, 143
Maxtone Grahame, Jamie, 214
McClane, Al, 61
Mead, Peter, 30
Mee, Mike, 65-8
Middleton, Lenny, 91
Miles, Tony, 100, 134
Miller, Mrs Florence, *163*
    Jess, 214
    R. M., 112
Moreland, Brian, 229
Morgan, Moc, 48
Moore, J. C., 11
Morritt, K. P., 193, 215
Mummery, Mr, 85
Munroe, Sir Hector, 143

National Association of Specialist Anglers (NASA), 145
National Federation of Anglers, 143
Nicholson, Alastair, 100
Nickson, Sir David, 141
Norman, John, 86
North, Roger, 147

Ogborne, Chris, 65, 181
Ogden Smith, Mary, 80
Oglesby, Arthur, 13, *72*, 73-4, *74*, 81
    Grace, 160, 205
Onslow, Cranley, 143
Orme, Andy, 118
Orton, Dick, 140
Overfield, T. Donald, 205

Page, Martyn, 116, *127*
Paget, Sir Julian, 166
Paisley, Tim, 26, 88-91, *174*, 175
Parker, Capt. L. A. 11, 120, 125, *126*, 128, 133-4
Pashley, Robert, 75-7, 219
Pawson, John, 120, *121*, 181-2
    Tony, 120, *121*, 181-2
Perch Fishers, The, 114
Piecha, Stan, 230
Phillips, Ernest, 169

'Farewell! then, dear brothers of the angle. And when you go forth to take your pleasure, may your sport be ample and your hearts light!' Scrope